AF073028

POOR
BICKERTON

The excellent Lord Verulam has noted it, as one of the great deficiencies of biographical history, that it is, for the most part, confined to the actions of kings, princes, and great personages, who are necessarily few; while the memory of less conspicuous, though good men, has been no better preserved, than by vague reports, and barren elogies.

> Sir John Hawkins, 'The Life of Mr Isaac Walton',
> *The Complete Angler* (1760 edition)

Derangement assumes a thousand different shapes, as various as the shades of human character.

> Leonard Shelford, *A Practical Treatise of the Law Concerning Lunatics* (1847)

And thought shall turn, poor Bickerton, to thee!

> James Shergold Boone, *The Oxford Spy* (1818–19)

POOR BICKERTON

A JOURNEY TO THE DARK HEART OF GEORGIAN ENGLAND

STEPHEN HADDELSEY

In memory of my father,
Michael Noel Haddelsey,
who taught me to conjure a Roman forum
from a pile of rubble.

First published 2024

The History Press
97 St George's Place, Cheltenham,
Gloucestershire, GL50 3QB
www.thehistorypress.co.uk

© Stephen Haddelsey, 2024

The right of Stephen Haddelsey to be identified as the Author
of this work has been asserted in accordance with the
Copyright, Designs and Patents Act 1988.

All rights reserved. No part of this book may be reprinted
or reproduced or utilised in any form or by any electronic,
mechanical or other means, now known or hereafter invented,
including photocopying and recording, or in any information
storage or retrieval system, without the permission in writing
from the Publishers.

British Library Cataloguing in Publication Data.
A catalogue record for this book is available from the British Library.

ISBN 978 1 80399 425 3

Typesetting and origination by The History Press
Printed and bound in Great Britain by TJ Books Limited, Padstow, Cornwall.

Trees for Life

Contents

Foreword by Professor Jerry White   7
Acknowledgements   9
Family Tree   11
Introduction   15

1   A Death in Westminster   21
2   Origins   35
3   An Incident at St James's Palace   47
4   Bow Street   63
5   The House of Correction   73
6   Lunatic?   95
7   Middle Temple to Hertford College   115
8   Place-Seeker   151
9   Debtor   161
10   Death and Resurrection   183

Notes   207
Bibliography   227
Index   235

Foreword

Attempting to rescue the lives of obscure individuals from the indifference of posterity is one of the most difficult tasks historians can set themselves. Until recently it usually took some small trigger of notoriety to bring a name to our attention in documents and newspapers, though now the infinite resources available to family historians has meant that we can all claim ancestors to be sought out in the public records and made an object of study. Both those factors are inspirations in the case of Stephen Haddelsey's intriguing study of John Bickerton.

'Poor Bickerton' had been an object of some wonder at various times in his long life, and the tragic circumstances of his death were sufficient to endow him with more than a brief footnote in the periodicals of the 1830s; and Bickerton happens to be reputedly connected to the historian's own family, so Haddelsey was familiar with a copy of Bickerton's portrait as an heirloom. But having inspiration for a project is one thing, bringing it to a triumphant conclusion as Stephen Haddelsey has done here is quite another.

John Bickerton was an exceptional eccentric. Born into yeoman prosperity in deeply rural Shropshire in 1755, he ended his days starved and neglected on the bare floor of one of London's many slum rooms, some seventy-eight years later. How he travelled from one place to the other, with an interrupted university education in both Oxford and Cambridge, a spell attached to organised religion sufficient for him to describe himself as 'the Reverend' and a loose attachment to the law that made him known as 'Counsellor', is the stuff of Bickerton's life story. It is as weird as any history of Don Quixote and with some of the same characteristics.

Delusional paranoia drove Bickerton to reinvent himself in a new guise at different periods of his life. Throughout, he was marked for attention by his oddity and his inability – or unwillingness – to conform to 'normal' expectations of behaviour. His life in Oxford – that enduring agglomeration of wayward misfits – found him among people even more odd than he. Yet, as Haddelsey brilliantly shows, oddity and nonconformity were all around him, even if frequently buried under surface respectability, from the governor of the gaol, where he was kept for a time in preventive detention, to the coroner who sat on his inquest.

As this indicates, *Poor Bickerton* tells far more than the story of one unconformable character. It is an adroit, intelligent and painstaking social history of the world in which John Bickerton lived and died. Haddelsey follows every lead to delve deeply into the many institutions and individuals impacting on Bickerton's troubled history. He takes us into the hidden corners of London and Oxford, into the precarious uncertainties of the criminal justice system, into prisons for both miscreants and debtors, into Inns of Court and Oxford colleges, into the contemporary understanding of madness and the good and bad among private madhouses, and into the slums of early nineteenth-century London and the semi-derelict plague house of Tothill Fields, where Bickerton breathed his last. It is all done with rare scholarship and a true feeling for past realities. In all, *Poor Bickerton* offers us a luxurious tapestry from which everyone interested in English social history in the late Georgian period can learn something new and surprising.

Jerry White
Emeritus Professor of Modern London History
Birkbeck, University of London

Acknowledgements

All historians owe an enormous debt to the archivists and librarians who preserve and make available the documents in their care. I am no exception, and I would like to offer my sincere thanks to the following individuals and organisations who have responded so helpfully to my enquiries regarding the life and career of John Bickerton and the world that he inhabited: Amber Druce, Curator of Social History, Blaise Museum, and Bristol Museum and Art Gallery; Katy Green, Archivist at Magdalene College, Cambridge; Victoria Hildreth, Assistant Archivist to the Honourable Society of the Middle Temple, London; Oliver House, Superintendent, Special Collections, the Bodleian Library; James Howarth, Librarian at St Edmund College, Oxford; Andrew Lott, Senior Information Officer, London Metropolitan Archives; Saffron Mackay, Library and Archives Assistant, Royal College of Surgeons; Janet Payne, Archivist at Apothecaries' Hall; Matthew Payne, Keeper of the Muniments, Westminster Abbey; Helen Sumping, Archivist of Brasenose College, Oxford; Karen Young, Alison Mussell and Nathaniel Stevenson of the Shropshire Archives; and the staff of The National Archives in Kew.

I would also like to express my particular gratitude to: Professor Jerry White for his generous help and support, and for kindly agreeing to write a foreword to this book; my brother Martin for his typically astute remarks on the draft text; my niece Anna for her endeavours in The National Archives, Kew; Oliver Richardson of the Wem Civic

Society; and Margaret Markland, who very kindly provided not only a transcription of the memorial inscriptions in the churchyard of St Peter's in Myddle, Shropshire, but also took the trouble to visit the churchyard in order to photograph the headstones.

Finally, I must thank my wife Caroline and my son George for their patience when listening to my accounts, not only of family history, but of the trials and tribulations associated with my quixotic quest for the minutest of details relating to the strange life of John Bickerton; as always, they have displayed Herculean resilience.

Stephen Haddelsey

Family Tree

PEDIGREE OF 'COUNSELLOR' JOHN BICKERTON

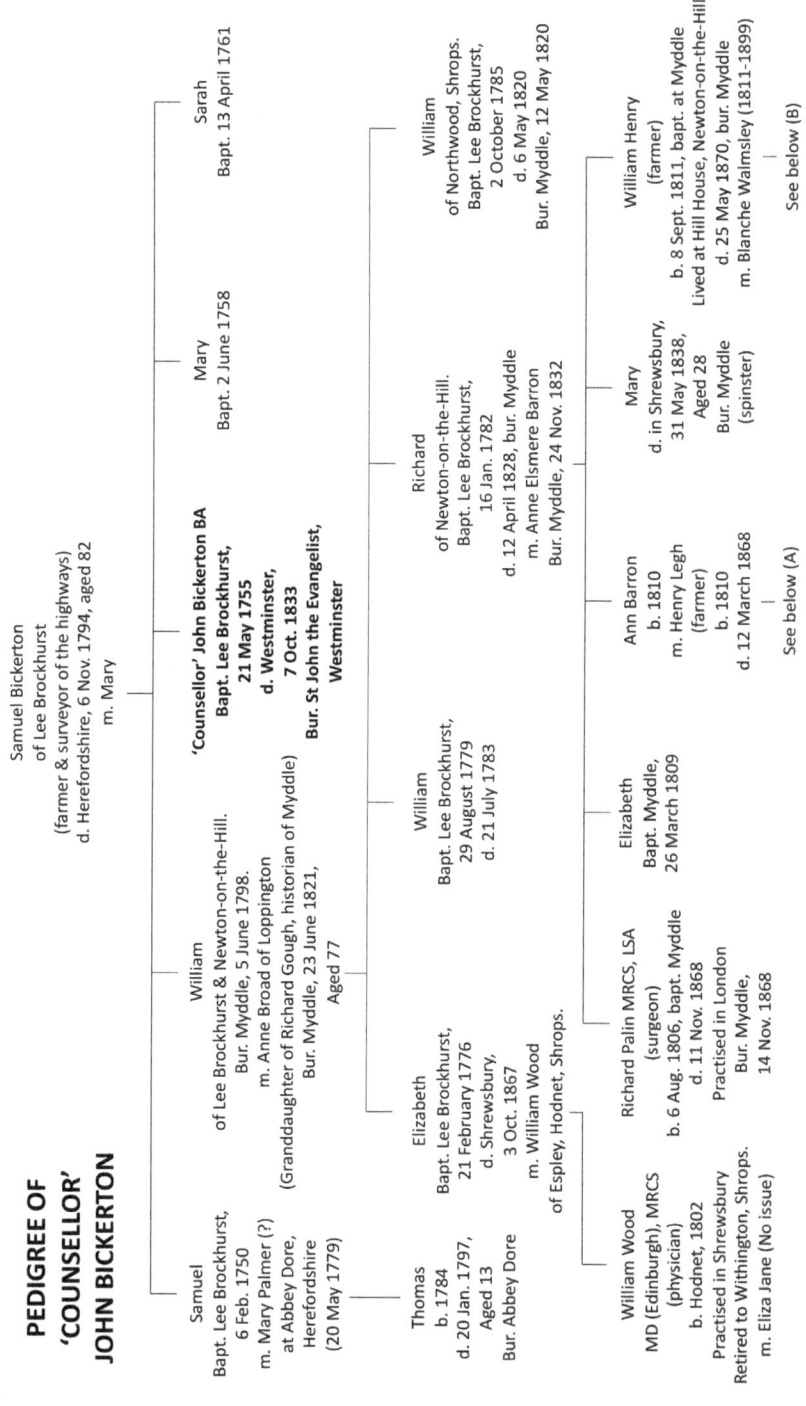

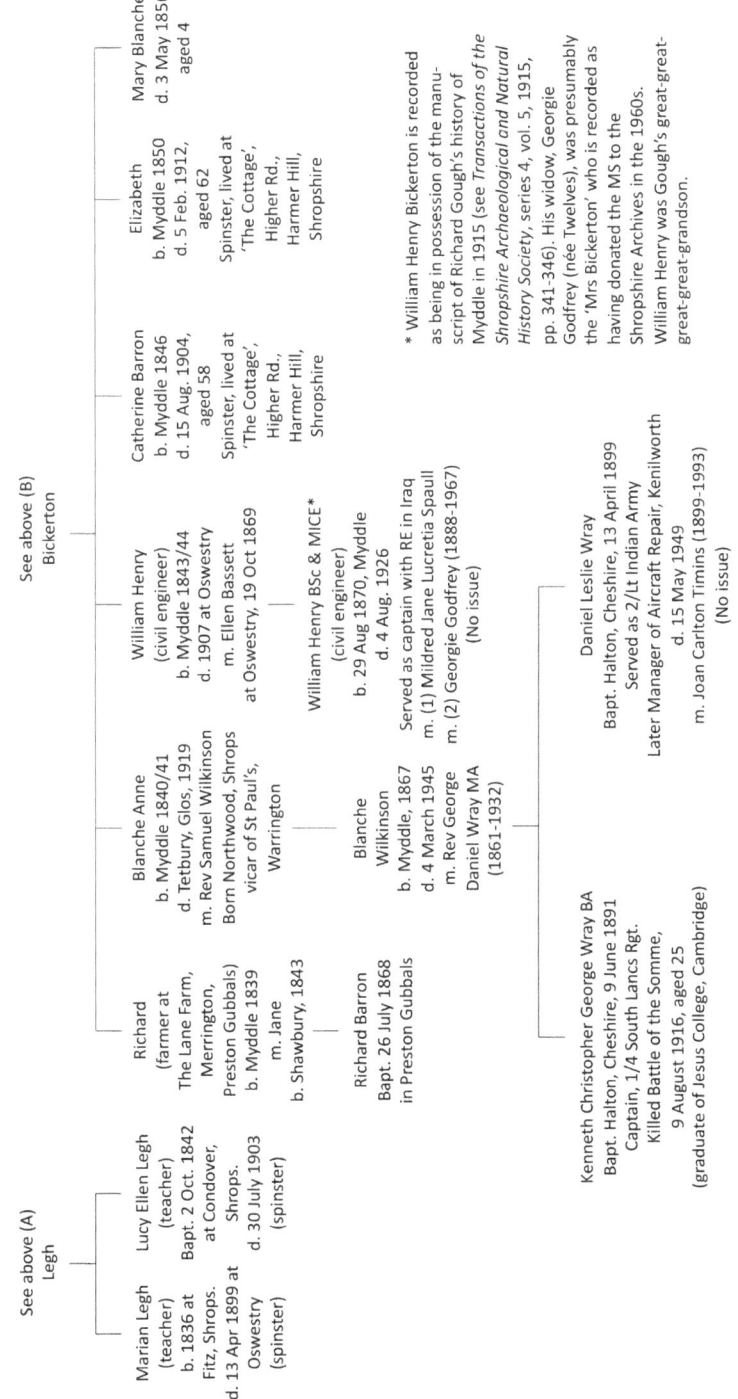

Introduction

Though almost entirely forgotten today, during his lifetime, and for several decades afterwards, John Bickerton, or 'Counsellor Bickerton', as many called him, was a known character of early nineteenth-century Oxford. He was written about in prose and verse during his lifetime, and his death resulted in a number of lengthy notices in *The Gentleman's Magazine* and elsewhere. The question is, why? What led memorialists, journalists, poets and artists to commemorate a man who, as far as we can tell, was neither exceptionally talented, influential nor vocal? A man, moreover, about whom, in real terms, they knew practically nothing.

Born to comparative affluence and well educated – he studied at Cambridge, Oxford and the Inns of Court in London – Bickerton ended his life in abject squalor, 'from the want of the common necessaries of life'.[1] There is, however, nothing of the parable in his story: no opportunity for a moralist to point the finger and tell his audience, 'learn from this man's mistakes, his flaws, or his hubris'. Instead, for many years, he led a quiet, apparently studious existence, well away from the public gaze.

But he was also subject to increasingly severe bouts of mental illness which, over time, made it difficult for him to provide for himself; his eccentricities grew ever more pronounced, so that he became at best a curiosity, and at worst, the butt of cruel or unthinking humorists. Reporting on Bickerton's demise, one angry journalist berated the Westminster authorities for their failure to help the ailing eccentric in his last days, but his was a voice crying in the wilderness, and the story of the old man's miserable end was not picked up as a *cause célèbre* by social reformers seeking to improve the provision of poor relief.

While some elements of his biography were correctly reported after his death, the facts were alloyed with pure fiction, and no one appears to have devoted much time to investigating the genuine circumstances of Bickerton's life and death. His contemporaries described him variously as 'poor', 'eccentric', 'singular' and 'unhappy' but none sought to explain his oddness, being satisfied that the oddness itself made him worthy of observation.

Is it Bickerton's oddity that makes him worthy still of consideration nearly two centuries after his death? In part, the honest answer must be 'yes'. The descriptions of his life, death and peculiarities catch our attention, just as the man himself caught the attention of those with whom he came into contact, no matter how fleetingly. But there is more to it than that. By tracing Bickerton's footsteps from rural Shropshire to the universities of Cambridge and Oxford, from Oxford to the Inns of Court, into Bow Street Magistrates' Court, through the portals of two prisons and, ultimately, to the squalid ruins of a derelict pest-house, it is possible to see something of late Georgian and Regency England, albeit through a glass darkly. For, while Bickerton's life may have been exceptional when taken in the round, facets of his experience, including the most demeaning, were common to many – as we shall see.

During Bickerton's own time, John Wight, a journalist who reported on hearings at Bow Street, thought it important for his readers to be:

> … made acquainted with the states and conditions of human nature, with which, from the sympathy due to the more unfortunate part of the species, he should not be entirely ignorant; it is by such means alone that the prosperous and more orderly portion of society can know what passes among the destitute and disorderly portion of it; that they can rightly appreciate the advantages they enjoy.[2]

In this context, we might almost think of Bickerton as we think of some of the minor characters in the novels of Charles Dickens: it is their very abnormality – their marked deviation from the accepted norms of behaviour – that makes them not only fascinating but also an essential part of our perception of the wider world they – and he – inhabited. Through the pursuit of such misfits, we gain access to parts of a world that might otherwise remain entirely invisible to us. At the same time, an examination of Bickerton's life and experiences might very well lead us to accept that some of Dickens' characters were not as remote from reality as we might once have thought.

Bickerton was born in 1755, during the reign of King George II; he would live through seventy-eight of the Georgian era's 123 years, witnessing the entire reigns of George III and George IV, and dying less than four years before the accession of Queen Victoria. In many respects, the age into which he was born was a violent one. The Bloody Code – the laws of England, Wales and Ireland that mandated the death penalty for crimes ranging from treason to the theft of property worth more than 12 pence – would reach its zenith during his lifetime, with no fewer than 220 offences made punishable by death by 1800 – more than a fourfold increase since 1689. Branding, flogging and pillorying remained on the statute books until well into the nineteenth century, while imprisonment for debt was commonplace, with some 10,000 individuals imprisoned every year, often for very small sums. As far as the treatment of the insane was concerned – and Bickerton was certainly considered mad by many of his contemporaries – conditions were all too often degrading and wilfully cruel, with the unfortunate inmates of Bethlem Hospital displayed to paying spectators as late as the 1780s.

As the following pages will show, Bickerton had the misfortune to experience first-hand some of Georgian England's worst horrors, and yet the period through which he lived was also one of positive change. By the late eighteenth century, the more brutal forms of corporal punishment were viewed with increasing abhorrence, and the Bloody Code itself came to an end in 1823 when the passing of the Judgment of Death Act made the death penalty discretionary instead of mandatory for most crimes.

Both of the prisons in which Bickerton was incarcerated were new structures, designed according to the recommendations of social reformers like the Calvinist John Howard – after whom the Howard League for Penal Reform was named – and built to replace the dark, dank and disease-ridden medieval gaols that the Georgians had inherited. The appalling treatment of the insane, too, had become a matter of public scandal, with many demanding that asylums should be regularly inspected – demands that ultimately resulted in the creation of the Lunacy Commission in 1828.

Another piece of Georgian legislation, the Anatomy Act of 1832, brought an end to a further source of outrage in Georgian society – the illegal trade of the body-snatchers, or resurrection men. Ironically, while the timing of the Act removed the risk of Bickerton's body being 'snatched', its clauses actually increased the risk of his being anatomised after death – snatching and anatomisation both falling to the lot of his friend, Demetriades, the Greek.

Of course, none of these innovations constituted a panacea. New prison buildings, even those built to the latest design, did not necessarily beget a revision in the attitudes of those who ran the institutions, as Bickerton would discover when he was placed in the 'care' of Thomas Aris, Governor of Coldbath Fields House of Correction. Victorian asylums for the insane, meanwhile, would themselves become bywords for neglect; while that last great throw of the dice of Georgian reformers, the Poor Law Amendment Act of 1834, would become infamous for its inhumanity – thanks in no small part to the writings of Charles Dickens.

On balance, then, it is probably true that Bickerton experienced very few of the benefits of Georgian innovation, whether social, penal, medical or judicial: a reality brought home most poignantly, perhaps, by the fact that he died in the near-derelict remains of a seventeenth-century plague hospital in Westminster – a ruin that not only survived the swelling tide of Georgian urbanisation but would outlive the Georgian age altogether.

I first became aware of Bickerton through Burt's sensitive portrait of 1818, a copy of which hung in the drawing room of my paternal grandfather, Noel Henry Fitzwilliam Haddelsey. His grandmother, Alice Emily, was a Bickerton by birth and the portrait had passed through the family for generations. The exact relationship between John Bickerton and my family remains unclear – though Alice Emily's elder brother, Joseph Jones Bickerton, Liberal councillor and Town Clerk of Oxford, certainly claimed him as a relative.

The surviving facts of his life I have gathered from a multitude of sources, both published and unpublished. Though it seems highly improbable that we will ever really 'know' Bickerton, I hope that this book will at least endow him with greater substance and serve to dispel some of the myths surrounding his troubled existence. With Bickerton as their guide, readers might also discover at least something of a Georgian and Regency England altogether grittier than that to be found in the novels of his contemporary, Jane Austen.

1

A Death in Westminster

At eight o'clock on the evening of Tuesday, 8 October 1833, Mr Thomas Higgs, Coroner to the Duchy of Lancaster and Deputy Coroner for Westminster, called for an end to the hemming and hawing, the chatter and the laughter inseparable from any public gathering, so that he might open, with due ceremony, an inquest into the death of John Bickerton of the Five Chimneys, Tothill Fields, Westminster.

Having enforced silence, Higgs turned his attention to the prospective jurors herded in by the parish Beadle: his task, to choose at least twelve – and no more than twenty-three – all male, certainly, preferably local freeholders, 'good and honest' and not foreigners, convicts or outlaws. Otherwise, their only definite similarity was their inability, or unwillingness, to bribe the Beadle and thereby dodge the summons to serve – a practice so common among the moneyed classes that most coroners' juries were made up almost exclusively of tradesmen and shopkeepers, with the gentry and professional classes made conspicuous by their absence.

After he had completed both his selection and the process of swearing-in, Higgs, his twelve jurymen and the usual ragtag crowd of idlers and newspapermen attendant upon any inquest then walked the short distance from the Crown and Sceptre, a public house located at the junction of Douglas Street and Chapter Street, to the dead man's residence.[1] Without the benefit of a public morgue (London's first would not be opened until 1856, in St Anne, Soho), until fairly recently most coroners had required that the body of the deceased should be moved to the site of the inquest – commonly, as in this case, a local inn, but also, on occasion, a barn, private residence or anywhere immediately available and sufficiently large for a public hearing – where it would lie throughout the proceedings. On this occasion, though, it had been left at the place of death, perhaps because the two buildings lay in such close proximity to one another, but more probably because the autumn of 1833 was proving unseasonably warm and neither Higgs nor his jury wished to have their nostrils assailed by the stench of putrefaction during their deliberations.

Fortunately, Higgs was not setting a precedent: while it had long been held that the presence of the corpse underpinned the authority of a coroner's inquest – indeed, Tudor legislation demanded that 'the body should lie before the jury during the whole of the inquiry'[2] – in practice, it was no longer considered mandatory to keep the body under the eyes (and noses) of the jury throughout the proceedings.[3] But, whatever the weather conditions and ambient temperature, an inspection of the body by the jury could not be avoided: without it, an inquest could – and almost certainly would – be declared invalid.

In crossing Chapter Street, the coroner and his entourage moved from one of the newer buildings in Tothill Fields to one of its oldest and most dilapidated.[4] In the medieval period, the fields – a marshy tract of land located between Millbank and Westminster Abbey – had been home to a number of noblemen, whose halls could be found scattered across an otherwise sparsely populated wasteland. The Elizabethan antiquarian John Stow notes that, in 1256, Sir John Maunsell, Chancellor to Henry III, invited the kings and queens of both England and Scotland, as well as their courts, to his house in Tothill Fields, but his guests proved so numerous 'that his house at Totehill [sic] could not receive them' and he was 'forced to set up tents and pavilions to receive his guests, whereof there was such a multitude that seven hundred messes of meat did not serve for the first dinner'.[5]

Jousts and trial by combat are known to have taken place here, with one of London's earliest chroniclers observing that in 1441, 'yere whas a fyt at the Totehill betwixte two thefes a peller [thieves appellant] and a defendaunt. And the pellar had the ffelde and victory of the defendaunt within thre strokys'.[6] Duels, too, were fought here throughout the seventeenth century, with the last recorded occurring on 9 May 1711 when Sir Cholmley Dering and Colonel Richard Thornhill faced each other with swords and pistols after Dering had physically assaulted the colonel during a violent quarrel. 'They fought at sword and pistol this morning in Tuttle Fields,' Jonathan Swift told Stella, 'their pistols so near, that the muzzles touched. Thornhill discharged first, and Dering having received the shot, discharged his pistol as he was falling, so it went into the Air.'[7] Dering died some hours later after admitting his guilt in the affair and forgiving his adversary.

Even as late as 1757, Tothill Fields was still being chosen as the ground for the determination of civil suits by force of arms, with two gentlemen, William Kent and Richard Allen, both 'furnished with competent armour', expected to fight in order to settle a land dispute. Kent, it appears, decided that discretion was the better part of valour and, when 'solemnly called', he did not grace the field with his presence, thereby surrendering his claim.[8]

Tothill Fields was also a spot where, traditionally, convicted necromancers were forced to watch the destruction of their instruments and talismans. In the reign of Richard I (1189–99), for instance, Ralph of Wigtoft, clerk or chaplain to Geoffrey, Archbishop of York, 'had provided a girdle and ring, cunningly intoxicated, wherewith he meant to have destroyed Simon [the Dean of York] and others; but his messenger was intercepted, and his girdle and ring burned at this place before the people'.[9] Perhaps claiming benefit of clergy, and no doubt reminding the court that his master was half-brother to the king,* the unscrupulous Wigtoft appears to have suffered no punishment for dabbling in witchcraft, going on instead to involve himself in various other nefarious

---

* Geoffrey (1152–1212) was the illegitimate son of King Henry II and therefore half-brother to Richard I and King John, and uncle to Henry III. He served as Chancellor to Henry II as well as being Archbishop of York. Simon of Apulia (died 1223) was created Dean of York in 1194 after a lengthy election dispute resulting from Geoffrey's desire to appoint instead his brother, Peter. A further argument erupted when Simon refused to resign his position as Chancellor of the Cathedral. Perhaps Ralph of Wigtoft's attempt to assassinate Simon was a consequence of these disputes. It is unknown whether he acted with the sanction of his master, though it is worth remembering that Geoffrey's father, Henry II, had himself dealt in summary fashion with another turbulent priest, Thomas Becket, Archbishop of Canterbury.

acts and dying peacefully in his bed in Rome around 1196 – though not before confessing to the Pope 'that he had acquired many false letters in the Roman court, both about the business of his master, the Archbishop of York, and about his own business'.[10]

On another occasion, in Edward III's reign (1327–77), a culprit caught 'practising with a dead man's head' was 'brought to the bar at the King's Bench, where, after abjuration of his art, his trinkets were taken from him, carried to Tothill, and burned before his face'.[11] Whether the head was counted among the incinerated trinkets is not stated. The records of the Royal College of Physicians confirm that, in the reign of Queen Mary, the 'unwholesome and sophisticated remedies' of quacks were still being burned in the open market at Westminster and this could have been at either Tothill or outside Westminster Hall.[12]

In the seventeenth century, the chronicler James Heath tells us that, following the destruction of the Royalist army at the Battle of Worcester on 3 September 1651, thousands of Scottish prisoners were 'driven like a herd of swine through Westminster to Tuthill Fields',[13] where they were held prior to being sent to New England as bondservants.[14] Subjected to harsh treatment and riddled with disease, many did not survive long enough to be transported, and the parish records of St Margaret's, Westminster, include reference to a payment of 'thirty shillings for sixty-seven loads of soil laid on the graves of Tothill Fields, wherein the Scotch prisoners are buried'.[15]

The Scottish prisoners of war would not be the last to be interred here because the emptiness and comparative remoteness of Tothill Fields made it an ideal spot for another essential activity: the housing of plague victims. Severe outbreaks of plague in 1603, 1625 and 1636 had finally convinced the Westminster authorities that the city required its own dedicated pest houses rather than temporary hospitals, and some sources suggest that the pest house in Tothill Fields may have been erected as early as 1638, though others give 1644 and even 1665 as the years of construction.

The seventeenth-century physician and botanist Nicholas Culpeper comments that parsley, which 'rejoices in barren, sandy, moist places [...] may be found plentifully about Hampstead Heath, Hyde Park, and in Tothill-fields',[16] and it might even be the case that the abundance of this herb, which was well known for its ability to eliminate or at least mask bad odours, was one of the reasons for the choice of Tothill Fields. What all accounts agree on is that the pest house at Tothill was a substantial building (or collection of buildings), and not one of the ephemeral 'pest sheds' relied upon elsewhere.

The fact of its being so well constructed appears to support a suggestion in the *Mirror of Literature* for 1823, that it was not purpose-built, but that 'several houses, which stood apart from the rest, were appropriated as pesthouses'.[17] The surviving images, the last of which date to the 1840s, show the building to have been a large gabled structure made of stone, with two storeys and multiple chimneys of great size. Indeed, it is so substantial that it seems quite possible that the ruin in which Bickerton died might have begun its life as the home of one of the noblemen mentioned by Stow.

To add to the grimness of the location, those who died in the pest house could expect to be buried there, with Samuel Pepys recording on 18 July 1665 that he felt 'much troubled this day to hear at Westminster how the officers do bury the dead in the open Tuttle-fields, pretending want of room elsewhere'.[18] Daniel Defoe tells us that only 159 plague victims were buried at Tothill Fields;[19] nonetheless, the fear of 'pernicious exhalations' and the fact that the burial ground was unconsecrated only served to darken the area's reputation still further.

Towards the end of the eighteenth century, the buildings had been converted for use as almshouses for 'twelve aged married couples'.[20] If, as was commonly the case, the almshouses bore the name of the benefactor who had dedicated them to charitable use, that name has long been lost to time, and the buildings had become known commonly as the 'Seven Chimneys', the 'Five Houses' or a conflation of the two, the 'Five Chimneys'. Soon afterwards, they appear to have changed use again, being divided into a number of private dwellings – though one contemporary thought it 'somewhat remarkable that houses built for such a purpose as refuge from pestilence should have been allowed to remain to our time; since it might have been expected that popular prejudice would long since have condemned the buildings as unfit for habitation'.[21]

In 1823, an observer described what remained of the pest house as 'an antique looking row of red brick dwellings [...] inhabited by poor people'.[22] A more romantically inclined writer for *The Builder* magazine of 1832 remarked, 'With the moss and lichens growing on the roofs and walls, and their generally old-fashioned quaintness, a very small stretch of the imagination removed the buildings which had surrounded them even then and brought them once more into the open ground'.[23]

In fact, to those not in search of the picturesque, the Five Chimneys were less houses than hovels. A reporter who accompanied Thomas Higgs found not quaintness but abject squalor, noting that the building in which Bickerton's body still lay 'had neither windows nor doors, and part of the walls nothing more than loose bricks piled together'.[24]

Once inside, the coroner and jurors found little enough to inspect. Bickerton remained where he had died, on the dusty, rubble-strewn floor of a room otherwise utterly devoid of interest and with no furnishings of any kind. Besides the naked corpse – that of an emaciated elderly man, his 'bones nearly protruding through the skin'[25] – the only objects in the dark, low-ceilinged chamber consisted of a shabby wig and gown such as a barrister might once have worn in court. After a cursory examination, the whole party beat a hasty retreat, some expressing 'their astonishment that any individual could live in such a miserable hovel',[26] and all glad to return to the comforts of the Crown and Sceptre, which, in comparison with the Five Chimneys, seemed little short of palatial. Now, having viewed the body and the place of death, the jury could at last turn their minds to the events surrounding Bickerton's demise.

It transpired that two days before, during the early evening of Sunday, 6 October, Police Constable Burke of 'B' Division of the newly established Metropolitan Police Service had been patrolling his beat on the Vauxhall Bridge Road when a party of gentlemen approached him to ask that he 'remove a crowd of boys and women who were disturbing the dying moments of an old man in an empty house'.[27] Burke accompanied the party to the Five Chimneys and, with their aid and that of some residents, at last succeeded in dispersing a raucous group of idlers who had gathered outside Bickerton's squalid rooms. On entering, the constable had discovered the old man alive, but in all other respects just as the jury had seen him, lying naked on the earthen floor, 'He was to all appearance in a dying state, and not a person to assist him in his last moments. Nourishment was immediately procured, as the poor creature appeared to be quite helpless and imbecile, and nearly starved to death.'[28]

Bickerton's next-door neighbour, a young ivory-turner named Charles Rice, had entered the room with Burke and, kneeling next to the sick man, had asked him how he was:

> He replied that he was as bad as he could be to be alive. He had not strength to put his own clothes over him he was so exhausted. Witness seeing him in such a wretched helpless state, went out and got him some tea. He said, 'I am too far gone for that or anything else.' By persuasion he took about two sips of the tea, but immediately threw it off his stomach, remarking, 'Now you see I cannot drink that or anything else'.[29]

Concerned neighbours – all of them very poor – brought alternative food and drink, which the old man refused to taste, and a Mr M'Carthy sent for a surgeon and provided a straw mattress so that he might at least lie in more comfort. Rice, meanwhile, 'in the kindest manner', offered to sit with him all night.

According to Rice's testimony, the only event of note that occurred during the hours of his vigil was when Bickerton 'gave him a packet of papers which he desired him to send to a Mrs Wood, at Wens [sic], in Shropshire, after he was dead'.[30] This Mrs Wood, whom Bickerton declared was to be 'the sole successoress of all that he was possessed of',[31] was his niece, Elizabeth – the daughter of his brother, William – who had married William Wood at Hodnet, near Wem, on 11 July 1798.

The following morning, when Inspector Bannister of 'B' Division visited the Five Chimneys, he admitted to being 'quite astonished' at what he found. Bickerton, he thought, 'appeared to be dying in a state of mental imbecility [...] He frequently called out for Wise [Rice], who volunteered to attend upon him, to get him change for a ten-pound note, and seemed as if in a state of unconsciousness'.[32] Shocked at the old man's plight, Bannister gave instructions that 'every care should be taken of him' and immediately hurried away to encourage the parish authorities to assume responsibility for the invalid.

Under the terms of the Poor Relief Act of 1601, administration of relief to the poor fell to two overseers in each parish, those selected being usually churchwardens or local landowners, who worked under the supervision of a magistrate. Unpaid and often appointed against their will, it is not surprising that many overseers proved far from conscientious in the performance of their duties and Bannister's request for urgent assistance fell on deaf ears.

On reaching the home of the first overseer, he was informed that 'the case was not in his district'.[33] He then proceeded to St Margaret's parish workhouse on Dean Street, just half a mile or so from his station house in Queen's Square. Here he found that the overseer was out. Frustrated, Bannister 'left word that as soon as any overseer arrived to inform him at the station-house close by, as he wished to speak to him'.[34] But these instructions were either forgotten or ignored, and no one attended him. Despite these rebuffs, Bannister refused to give up and he applied, next, to one of the three stipendiary magistrates attached to his station house.

At last, in the 43-year-old David Gregorie, a barrister at Lincoln's Inn who had been appointed as a Westminster magistrate in 1825, he found someone both willing and able to take action. The son of Charles Gregorie, who had made his fortune as a ship's captain with the East India Company, and the grandson of the Whig historian Catherine Macaulay, David Gregorie was a handsome and wealthy man – wealthy, or reckless enough, indeed, to indulge in the fashionable pastime of high-stakes gambling and to lose £300 in a single night's play at piquet against one of the best players in England.[35] Fortunately, he also had the reputation for being conscientious in the performance of his duties as a magistrate. On hearing Bannister's statement, Gregorie 'gave immediate directions to Woodberry, one of the officers of the establishment, to go instantly to the parochial authorities, and inform them of the wretched state of the dying man, and, added the Magistrate, "If they will not remove him to some place of comfort, we must"'. But it was too late.

When a reporter for the *Morning Post* arrived at the Five Chimneys that afternoon to enquire whether Bickerton had been removed to the workhouse, Charles Rice told him, 'There is no occasion now, Sir; the poor creature died about an hour ago, there on that blanket on the floor'.[36] He went on to say that, about half an hour after Bickerton took his last breath, a cot had arrived from the overseers to convey him to the workhouse infirmary.

If this delay had lasted only from the time of Bannister's first visit to the workhouse that morning, it might have been forgivable. However, it later transpired that the old man's plight had been notified to the authorities some days previously, and they had done nothing:

> He has been laying in the same dreadful state of imbecility for some days, without a friend or acquaintance to come near him, without any covering, on the bare boards, and had it not been for the interference of some casual passengers, who informed the police of the circumstance, the whole affair would have been hushed up, and the unfortunate deceased would have been sent to the dissecting-room.[37]

Having learned all the circumstances of Bickerton's death, Coroner Higgs now called the surgeon who had responded to Mr M'Carthy's urgent summons of Sunday evening: the 28-year-old Dr John Hastings of 39 Vauxhall Bridge Road.

Senior Physician to the Blenheim Street Free Dispensary and Infirmary and a member of the Royal Medical Society of Edinburgh, the Parisian Medical Society, the Microscopical Society and the Ethnological Society,[38] Hastings would later be described by one contemporary as possessing 'consummate tact, and a pleasing, genial manner' but only 'moderate ability and little acquirements'.[39] At the time of the inquest, he stood on the threshold of a medical career that, after some initial success, would eventually become mired in accusations of incompetence and quackery, the accusations resulting from his later decision to specialise in, and to publish on, the subject of consumption – a topic about which, in the opinion of his obituarist, he displayed 'much ignorance'.[40] According to the same critic, his medical writings as a whole would meet with 'the hostility of the entire medical press', and his advocacy of 'the excreta of reptiles' as a failsafe remedy for tuberculosis would lead to his being lambasted both mercilessly and publicly.[41] When he decided to sue a mocking critic in *The Lancet*, Hastings was further humiliated by the Lord Chief Justice, Sir Alexander Cockburn, who declared, 'it was not to be wondered at that the matter was treated rather sarcastically when the public were told that phthisis could be cured by the dung of snakes'.[42]

But Hastings' notoriety lay in the future. In October 1833, he appeared before the inquest as a respectable physician with a growing practice. He told Higgs and the jury that he had known Bickerton for some time and was sufficiently knowledgeable about his health to confirm that 'For the last five years he had been subject to a disease of the kidneys'.[43] He went on to state that, at the time of his visit, he had found his patient:

> ... in a state of great exhaustion; he was in the arms of death. He was just able to say 'Let me die quietly' [...] he had seen him beg a crust of bread of a Lady that she was going to throw to a dog. He thought it a piece of extravagance to wear shirts; he would pick up bones or anything in the streets. The deceased was an excellent scholar. Witness was of opinion that if he had been better fed and taken care of he might have lived ten years longer.[44]

In the absence of a post-mortem report, we must assume that the doctor relied on his previous knowledge of the dead man in order to make such an extraordinarily bold statement regarding the life expectancy of a 78-year-old suffering from kidney disease.

Whatever the value of Hastings' predictions, there was little or no chance of establishing the precise cause of Bickerton's death as post-mortems remained exceptionally rare. In 1842, for instance, one of Westminster's coroners held over 300 inquests, but summoned a physician to give evidence on only eighteen occasions and ordered just four post-mortems. As one modern commentator has remarked, 'Coroners often simply guessed at the causes of death at many of their inquests. If there were no witnesses, no obvious signs of violence, and no obvious suspects, if the victims were poor, unknown, unimportant, why bother with an extensive and expensive investigation?'[45] Nonetheless, Hastings' opinion must have made uncomfortable reading for the workhouse overseers who, by implication at least, had already been accused of neglect and indifference.

The last witness, Daniel Friend of 4 Bleeding Hart Yard, Hatton Garden, was able to add a little more regarding Bickerton's background, character and habits. According to his evidence, the old man had been 'complete master' of five or six languages, including Hebrew. He had previously kept a school among the dilapidated Elizabethan townhouses on Wych Street, off the Strand, and approximately six years prior to his death he had purchased the freehold of the Five Chimneys for £380; he also owned one or two houses on nearby Edward Street.

Friend also stated that, some time ago, Bickerton had seized upon a Mr Dance, a broker, who had inhabited one of these properties, claiming arrears in rent. Dance had then countersued, with the result that Bickerton had been thrown into Whitecross Street Debtors' Prison in Islington – a prison with a particularly bad reputation since its inmates occupied common wards rather than individual rooms, meaning that 'the well-disposed debtor when so inclined, had no means of protecting himself from association with the depraved'.[46] Friend had last seen Bickerton the previous Friday:

> He was then knocking up some old tin saucepans, and picking the wire out to sell for old iron. He went out with the wire, and brought home a salt herring and a pound of potatoes. He also brought a bottle, containing some vitriol and water, which he took for his complaint.[*] He always complained of being ill-used by Mr Dance.[47]

Having heard testimony from all the available witnesses, the jury now asked that they be permitted to examine the documents given by Bickerton to Charles Rice. These papers, which a fastidious reporter from *The Times* described as being in a 'dirty state',[48] consisted of an agreement between Bickerton and a Mr Nightingale for the sale of the Five Chimneys for the sum of £400, and a small bundle of letters, one each from the Duke of Portland and the Earl of Liverpool, and a third, addressed by one William James to David Gregorie, the magistrate. All proved highly interesting.

The one from the Duke of Portland, dated 28 May 1808, confirmed the availability of an unspecified position for Bickerton in Oxford – thereby appearing to prove that Bickerton did, indeed, possess some scholarly attainments. The second, from Robert Banks Jenkinson, the

---

[*] Bickerton may have been using cupric sulphate, or blue vitriol, as an emetic.

2nd Earl of Liverpool, apologised for a tardy reply to Bickerton's correspondence before going on to invite him to an audience at his London home, Fife House, on 29 or 31 August 1818. What made these letters extraordinary was that, at the time they set pen to paper, both writers had been serving as prime minister. What, the jurors might ask, could these men, at the pinnacle of their fame and power, have to do with the miserly – and potentially insane – resident of the Five Chimneys?

However, in the context of recent events, it was the third letter that proved of greatest significance. In it, William James – a man of unknown rank and profession – recommended that David Gregorie, the magistrate, investigate Bickerton's claims against Mr Dance who, he asserted, had 'got possession of all his writings relative to his property, of the value of seven or eight hundred pounds, and that Mr Bickerton was in a state of starvation'.[49] This correspondence revealed that, while Gregorie had immediately swung into action when approached by Inspector Bannister on Monday, 7 October, the case had been brought to his attention long before and, seemingly, he had done nothing: a further damning indictment of the failings in the administration of poor relief in the Borough of Westminster. Moreover, it suggested that Bickerton's penury might have resulted from a fraudulent act on the part of Dance; if so, a proper investigation on the part of Gregorie could have resulted in an alleviation of the dead man's predicament.

At this point in the evening, proceedings were interrupted when Inspector Bannister asked to approach the bench. Having been granted permission, he informed the coroner that 'there was a very respectable Gentleman below who claimed kindred with the deceased, and wished to bury him in a respectable manner, but he did not appear willing to give evidence'.[50] Upon the jury's request for an opportunity to examine this interested party, his objections were overruled by the coroner who ordered him to appear before the inquest.

The 'very respectable Gentleman' proved to be Richard Palin Bickerton of 4 Adelaide Street, the Strand, a Licentiate of the Society of Apothecaries, a Member of the Royal College of Surgeons and surgeon to the St John's Wood and Portland Town Provident Dispensary.[51] Having taken the stand, Dr Bickerton proceeded to tell the inquest that the dead man was:

… his nearest relative. He had not seen him for many years, nor should he have known of his death had he not read a paragraph in the papers of that day.

Juror – What relation are you to the deceased?

Witness – He was brother to my grandfather, and I claim his property.

Juror – It is stated in the papers that he is supposed to have a brother very wealthy in the City – is that so?

Witness – That is not the case; if he has any brothers they must be in Herefordshire.

Juror – What was his father?

Witness – He was a farmer. The deceased studied at Oxford, and was brought up for the Church.[52]

According to a report published in the *Examiner*, the doctor then stated that 'he was willing to be at the expense of the funeral, on condition that he was reimbursed, if he failed of establishing his relationship'.[53] The coroner responded tersely, observing that he 'could say nothing on that subject'.

With no further witnesses to call and no more evidence to examine, the moment had come for the jury to assimilate the information presented to them, to deliberate and, with Higgs' guidance, to reach a verdict in this curious case.

2

Origins

The fact that John Bickerton's death and the subsequent inquest featured so prominently in the newspapers of the day is probably due, in no small part, to Thomas Higgs' delight in having his inquests reported. At the time of his suicide by poison in January 1857,* *The Observer* noted that the coroner was 'exceedingly partial to reporters for the press, and formerly his office in the Cloisters, Westminster Abbey, was open to them for information as to where his inquests were to be held, and, should business take him away, in order to accommodate them he posted his list in the window'.[1] This desire for publicity could, though, produce its frustrations, and the same source tells us that when one of his inquests was misreported, the eccentric Higgs handed a hammer to a journalist, saying, 'Sir, take this, and you will do me a great favour by knocking out my brains, for the papers […] containing the report of my inquest yesterday have brought me into ridicule with the Queen and the public generally'.[2]

Higgs seems to have carried a hammer almost as a matter of routine because, on another occasion, he showed to a reporter 'a small preparation about the size of a pea, and having a hammer in the other hand, he seriously assured the party that, if he were to strike it but one blow, it

---

* Described as 'an inveterate opium-eater', Higgs was found to have committed suicide by swallowing essential oil of almonds while the balance of his mind was disturbed. He was, perhaps, the only man ever to write his suicide note on a blank coroner's inquest report form. See *Daily News*, 12 January 1857.

would have the effect of hurling the cloisters and Westminster Abbey high into the air'.[3] Of course, one can only wonder why the coroner chose to carry such a deadly substance about his person.

Higgs' partiality for newspapermen does not, however, fully explain the public interest in Bickerton's death. Even before he expired on the floor of the Five Chimneys, rumours regarding his background were rife, and they grew apace once he breathed his last. Perhaps the most comprehensive summary of these stories is to be found in the *Morning Post* of 8 October 1833:

> He is said to be most respectably connected, and that he had a brother living in Oxford in affluent circumstances, and that another brother lives in London. It appears, however, that he had received a most liberal education, and that he took his degrees [*sic*] at Oxford. The rumours abroad in the neighbourhood are various. From one person we heard that he was the brother of a Gentleman of rank and title, and that he had left the world, as a recluse, through unjust treatment. There are also rumours of his immense riches, which we believe only to be derived from his singular and eccentric life working on the fertile imaginations of old women, ever fond of the marvellous.

Most of the other newspapers seem to have relied for their material on this, the first published account of Bickerton's demise, though *The Times*, not content with slavish duplication, provided some additional colour, claiming that he had held the entirely fictitious position of 'Usher of the Black Rod' at Oxford, and that he was thought, by some, to have poisoned himself[4] – this last suggestion was probably based on the fact that a bottle had been found close to Bickerton's corpse, though at the inquest, Dr Hastings had described its contents as 'quite harmless'.[5]

Given Bickerton's strange behaviour and the manner of his death, it is not surprising that certain of the claims published in the newspapers – such as those regarding his fabulous wealth and his kinship to the aristocracy – had emanated from 'fertile imaginations'. But the old man had lived at the Five Chimneys for some five or six years, and he had spoken to a number of his neighbours during this period. This being the case, it is to be expected that some portion of his real history should come to light at the inquest. For instance, though some cynical observers may have thought that Richard Palin Bickerton's claim to kinship was more likely to be based on the hope of financial gain from the convenient death of an unrelated namesake than on any genuine blood tie, the surgeon was indeed the grandson of Bickerton's brother William, William and John being the second and third sons of an affluent yeoman farmer, Samuel Bickerton, and his wife Mary, of Lee Brockhurst in Shropshire, some 12 miles north-north-east of Shrewsbury.

Though his origins are obscure, Samuel Bickerton seems to have been an able and ambitious man who, benefiting from a period of relative prosperity for British agriculture, succeeded in engineering a rapid rise in his family's fortunes. With export bounties and the increased demand resulting from population growth helping to force a rise in the price of grain, land values and rents also increased, bringing substantially improved returns to anyone like Samuel who farmed his own land or rented a portion of it to his neighbours. His appointment in 1766 to the administratively demanding post of Surveyor of the Highways for the parish of Lee Brockhurst[6] indicates that he was both literate and numerate and, making the most of the prevailing conditions, he gradually accumulated property in and around the hamlets of Lee Brockhurst, Harmer Hill and Newton-on-the-Hill.

Nor was Samuel's a case of 'boom and bust'; on his death in Herefordshire in 1794, his Shropshire properties passed to his son, William, and thereafter, to his descendants, including Richard Palin Bickerton and his brother, William Henry, who would later be described as 'principal landowners' in Newton-on-the-Hill and elsewhere.[7] While his Shropshire estate passed to William, it appears probable that Samuel left some portion of his wealth – either in land or other investments – to his other children, and that this patrimony enabled John to purchase the Five Chimneys and the properties on Edward Street.

John had been born on 26 April 1755 and baptised in the tiny parish church of St Peter's, Lee Brockhurst, on 21 May. By his own account, he had enjoyed 'the privilege of a virtuous parentage [...] and education at Boarding and Grammar Schools',[8] and the latter institution was probably

Wem Grammar School* just 4 miles north-west of Lee Brockhurst, though it is impossible to be certain because the school registers for the eighteenth century have not survived.

Founded in 1650 by Sir Thomas Adams, a native of Wem who had amassed a fortune as a draper and became Lord Mayor of London, in Bickerton's day, the grammar school was housed in a handsome two-storey brick building, with stone quoins and a bell turret in the centre of its slate roof. Samuel Garbet, historian of Wem and second master of the school from 1712, tells us in addition that the first and second school occupied the ground floor, which was panelled and lit by twelve windows, while the first floor contained the third school and the library, 'in the former of which, plays were used to be acted by the scholars'.[9] Garbet thought the library well stocked – but its books were unlikely to have been of particular interest to the young Bickerton who was, by his own admission, much more concerned with 'going to football playings, and other sports, which I had eagerly followed'.[10]

Throughout the first century of its existence, the school had been managed by a series of able and energetic headmasters, and by the middle of the eighteenth century, its scholars were being taught mathematics, geography, astronomy and Hebrew in addition to the classics, and the standard of education was such that boys were being removed from the larger Shrewsbury School to be sent to Wem instead.[11]

Bickerton, however, had the misfortune to become a pupil after the end of this golden age. Under the headmastership of John Spedding, who was appointed in 1755 and remained in post until 1804 – despite attempts to dismiss him for being 'grossly negligent in his calling'[12] – the school's fortunes and the quality of its teaching declined significantly, with a resulting reduction in pupil numbers.[13]

Despite these failings, as far as the Bickertons were concerned, Wem Grammar School possessed one key advantage over its competitors: it accepted boys from Nonconformist backgrounds. The family regularly attended services at the small purpose-built Presbyterian Chapel on Noble Street in Wem, where William Hazlitt's father would serve as minister from 1788 until 1813, and it is quite possible that Bickerton and

---

*   Now Thomas Adams School.

the young Hazlitt worshipped together, at least occasionally, though the substantial difference in their ages – Hazlitt was Bickerton's junior by twenty-three years – makes it seem improbable that they were more intimately acquainted. Besides, at this point in his life, Bickerton's attitude towards his parents' religion was largely one of indifference:

> Nothing could be more irksome [...] than learning religious things, religious exercises, and also religious company was to me; they were so wearisome to me, that I hated them [...] though I had heard the Bible read, and read it myself, and heard it explained [...] yet I knew nothing more about law or gospel [...] than if I had been brought up among heathens.[14]

However, this attitude would change dramatically over the coming years.

In his evidence to the coroner's inquest, Richard Palin Bickerton asserted that his great-uncle had been 'brought up for the Church',[15] and it is clear that over time, Bickerton's opinions regarding religion underwent a significant revision – a result in part, no doubt, of his parents' pious urgings, but also a product of the influence of the preachers whose sermons he attended with increasing willingness and even enthusiasm. The catalyst for this change appears to have been a sermon given by the Reverend Richard de Courcy, curate of St Mary the Virgin in Shawbury. Though one critic would later describe de Courcy as 'never knowing when, or where to stop' and his preaching as 'rash and bewilder'd',[16] the Irishman proved very popular with the Presbyterians and Bickerton would later describe him not only as 'that dear and honoured servant of the Lord' but as the man who encouraged 'the first awakenings of my mind'.[17]

Despite these awakenings, the transformation was neither swift nor painless and for some time Bickerton seems to have led a dual existence, willingly attending church on Sundays, but during the week seeking 'nothing but carnal pleasure to please or give me joy'.[18] Inevitably, he felt confused, with neither side of his life proving satisfactory:

> Let me be in the pursuit of what pleasures I may, they appeared trivial, and rather vain, and went contrary to my mind [...] so it was, that

> all pleasures which I now had, were so imbittered to me, that instead of satisfying they gave me grief; neither did my religion satisfy, and by reflecting I grew worse and worse: then I thought I would seek more pleasures [...] I went to dancings; but this did not do: I tired my body, and increased the trouble of my mind. This, after a while, was also imbittered to me, the same as others, though the music rather pleased, so that induced me to buy a German flute. Thus I went on for a time, eagerly seeking happiness and pleasure, but still became more miserable.[19]

A natural inclination towards physical activity and the desire to tire his body could also involve him in pursuits altogether more dangerous than 'dancings'. In particular, he recalled that at about this time:

> My Father had a very excellent mare, that cost him twenty guineas [...] which I was advised to have entered to run for the plate. This mare I kept too well, and was too bold in riding her, so she ran away with me, and threw me several times very dangerously [...] so bold and resolute was I, that I was determined to ride her, wild as she was.[20]

It was only when he joined services led by students from the Countess of Huntingdon's Trevecca College for the training of Methodist ministers that his bewilderment seemed to clear somewhat, though he still found that 'as soon as ever I heard of dancing or horse-race, away to them I was drawn; and if card-playing was where I was, I must play'.[21]

To some degree, Bickerton's writings from this period read much like those of other 'redeemed sinners' keen to share the details of their own salvation. But he seems, too, to have been embarrassed by his growing faith, admitting to being 'afraid [...] of being seen to be religious'.[22] Sometimes, he would participate willingly in and even lead public prayer meetings, at others, he 'hesitated about going'.

Despite the ebb and flow of his faith, he considered taking the first step towards joining the ministry by becoming a student of the Methodist Academy at Abergavenny – a course that was very much encouraged by his father, though his tutor, evidently aware of the uncertainty of his vocation, told him 'that unless I were very religious, and had great gifts for preaching, he would not advise me by any means to enter into it'.[23] For a while he shelved the idea, but when his father invited students from Trevecca to preach in the family home, their passion and conviction swayed him to such a degree that he entered the college to begin his own training for the ministry. But, within six months, 'a deadness of soul, a leanness of mind, and barrenness of heart came on, and though I was assisted in prayer and preaching […] yet my zeal for religion was much abated […] and religious services becoming rather irksome to me, I found an unwillingness to engage in them'.[24]

Imputing his 'spiritual deadness' to too much academic study and not enough divinity, Bickerton requested, and was granted, permission to leave the college temporarily and to embark on a preaching tour of Somerset. According to his own account, he enjoyed marked success as he journeyed from town to town and attracted large audiences – but still he felt doubtful. 'I was afraid I should grow tired with it,' he recalled, 'and the people would leave off coming to hear.'[25]

He appears to have become more attracted to the forms of the Established Church and less enamoured of the Calvinism championed by the Countess of Huntingdon. In order to better understand the practices rejected by both the countess and his own immediate family, he sought out the Reverend William Miles of Kidderminster – a man 'who was spoken very highly of' at the time, but who would subsequently be relieved of his post as Master of Kidderminster Grammar School because of his increasing eccentricity and 'strange views on religion'.[26] With Miles, Bickerton discussed the possibility of ordination in the Church of England and was advised that he must fill the gaps in his education before he could have any hope of reaching either Oxford or Cambridge as a first step towards ordination. He dutifully 'applied chiefly to the Latin and Greek at first, and after to Algebra; and so disposed was I for it, and finding so much internal satisfaction from it, that I applied to it with the greatest pleasure'.[27]

During their conversations, Bickerton and Miles must have discussed the significant compromises he would be required to make to matriculate at either of the English universities. At the time of the Glorious Revolution of 1688, it had been laid down in law that only those dissenting ministers of religion who were willing to subscribe to the

Thirty-Nine Articles of Anglican belief affirming the Trinity and the Divinity of Jesus would be permitted to practise their ministry. Oxford and Cambridge followed suit, requiring that all young men attest to the Articles before being allowed to matriculate.

In the opinion of many, these requirements pushed Nonconformists who wished to receive a university education into hypocrisy and casual mendacity, forcing them to accept Articles in which they had no belief merely in order to take a degree. Bickerton, though, had moved sufficiently far from his father's faith to accept the need for attestation. 'I examined the doctrines and services of the church,' he declared, 'and, so far as I could discern, those things which were the cause of *dissenting*, went rather far, but appeared to me to be externals, and non *essentials*'.[28]

It seems probable, though, that Samuel did not agree with his son's liberal interpretation of the requirements for matriculation. According to Bickerton, his father 'liked, and was very desirous, for me to go to Dr Davis'[29] at the Methodist Academy, but the teaching there would have been entirely in agreement with the old man's beliefs; that at Oxford and Cambridge most certainly would not. This may well be the reason why Bickerton did not enrol at Magdalene College Cambridge until 20 May 1786, at the unusually advanced age of 31.[30] This interpretation of events is further supported by the fact that he was admitted to the college as a '*sizar*', meaning that he financed his studies, at least in part, by undertaking a variety of more or less menial tasks such as waiting at table in the college's sixteenth-century dining hall or even acting as servant to one of the more affluent undergraduates.

In reality, from a Nonconformist's point of view, there could be few colleges less objectionable than Magdalene under Dr Peter Peckard, who served as Master from 1781 to 1797. A highly intelligent and well-read man who had served as a chaplain with the Grenadier Guards, on assuming his post, Peckard had declared, 'We must derive our importance, not from opulence, but virtue',[31] and over the course of his mastership, Magdalene College would obtain a well-deserved reputation for academic excellence.

In terms of religion, Peckard has been described as 'an exponent of rational Broad Church benevolent Christianity';[32] he was a vocal critic of the requirement for clergymen to subscribe to the Thirty-Nine Articles and he would establish Magdalene as 'the general resort of young men seriously impressed with a sense of religion',[33] throwing open its doors to those of an Evangelical background.

Historians of Magdalene have remarked that its Evangelicals formed an unusually tight-knit brotherhood, and Charles Jerram, one of their number and a close contemporary of Bickerton's, thought his pious undergraduate days the happiest of his life, reminding him 'of that happy state when the first Christians had all things in common, parted their goods as each of them had need, and continued daily with one accord eating their bread with gladness and singleness of heart and praising God'.[34] As well as its godliness, under Peckard, the college became remarkable, too, both for its unusually high academic standards and for its temperance – tea drinking becoming so popular that the Cam was 'absolutely rendered unnavigable' by the accumulations of tea leaves thrown from the undergraduates' windows into the river.[35]

Despite the apparent suitability of Magdalene College, Bickerton left the university without a degree, with the length of his stay and the reasons for his departure shrouded in mystery. But his studies did not come to an end; instead, he moved to Oxford, matriculating at St Edmund Hall on 6 July 1793. The most probable explanation for this move is a change of heart on Samuel's part, perhaps because at the age of 81 he had come to recognise that the ordination of one of his sons would help to cement the family's hard-won gentrification – a prize worth having, even if it meant relaxing his own Presbyterian principles.

As a sizar, John had been able to study at the University of Cambridge, but he was marked out as a poor man expected to perform menial duties to pay his way. With the financial support of his father, he could turn his back on that humiliating existence and, by changing universities, put physical distance between himself and the people and places that might remind him of it. In contrast with his lowly status at Magdalene College, when he graduated from St Edmund Hall in 1799, John was classed as a 'compounder', meaning that he had been obliged to pay enlarged fees for graduation, the excess charge being payable by all candidates who possessed an annual income in excess of £5. If his income fell within the range of £5 to £300, the candidate would be entered as a 'petty compounder' and would be charged more than 10*s* 8*d*; if possessed of an income in excess of £300, he would be entered as a 'grand compounder' and would be obliged to pay £30 instead of £7 for his Bachelor's degree.[36] In return, on the day of his graduation, a grand compounder would be entitled to wear the scarlet Convocation habit and to enjoy his own procession from his college to the Convocation House, accompanied by the vice chancellor, the proctors and any members of his college who chose to join the cavalcade. Following the graduation ceremony, he would return the same way while the bells of St Mary pealed in celebration. In earlier times, a grand compounder would have been preceded by a trumpeter.[37]

As far as Bickerton's academic attainments are concerned, a later acquaintance would assert that 'he had very little knowledge of the Greek and Latin languages, was totally ignorant of Hebrew, and knew no modern language whatever, except his own',[38] but these claims seem highly questionable. Although Bickerton acknowledged that he struggled, at least initially, with Latin grammar, which he found 'so exceeding hard that I almost despaired of ever knowing it',[39] he had 'a great liking to, and desire for learning of another kind, and went through decimals, and near all kinds of mensurations, superficial and solid'[40] – an enthusiasm that is likely to have endeared him to his Magdalene tutor, William Farrish, who, as well as being perhaps the most conscientious and gifted Cambridge teacher of his day, was an outstanding mathematician.[41]

Under the watchful eye of its conscientious vice principal, Isaac Crouch, St Edmund Hall had become a place of genuine learning; in fact, with 'a novel character for erudition no less than seriousness',[42] it stood at the forefront of the battle against the academic somnolence that had prevailed at Oxford for most of the eighteenth century. Described as 'a man quiet, undemonstrative, solid, widely learned, absolutely thorough',[43] the vice principal lectured on a wide range of subjects, including mathematics, Latin, Greek, Hebrew, French, Church history and natural philosophy. He also insisted that every student study the entirety of the New Testament in Greek and invited all junior members of the hall to dine with him once each term and to attend private sessions with him two or three times a term. It therefore seems incredible that he should have jeopardised the college's precious and fiercely guarded reputation for academic excellence by admitting any student incapable of performing to his expectations or that he should have been oblivious to such shortcomings, given that between 1790 and 1799 annual matriculations averaged just five students per academic year.[44]

Finally, we know that Bickerton's boyish enthusiasm for learning did not fade with time; if anything, it increased. As well as studying Latin, he 'had a mind to read history, to learn logic, to learn to write short hand, to learn to sing by notes, and to study the globes'.[45] In fact, when training for the ministry in his late teenage years, he had found himself at odds with one of his tutors because of his insistence on pursuing what the Reverend Mr Phillips considered too wide a curriculum. 'My preceptor did not seem willing for me to apply to so many things at one time,' Bickerton recalled, 'but there being some of my fellow-students who knew the Hebrew and French, I used to be enticing them, as much as I could, to teach me.'[46]

And yet, whatever Bickerton's enthusiasm for learning, Crouch clearly had his reservations regarding him. According to *The Gentleman's Magazine*, it was the vice principal who 'well knowing the state of his mind, declined furnishing him with the papers necessary for his entering into holy orders', thereby dashing any hopes Bickerton might have entertained regarding a career in the Established Church.[47] Of course, *The Gentleman's Magazine* cannot always be relied upon: it calls Bickerton the son of a Flintshire rather than a Shropshire farmer and, contrary to its assertion that he 'never took a degree', we know that he graduated as a Bachelor of Arts in 1799.

Although we have no independent source to corroborate the magazine's claim that Vice Principal Crouch blocked his ordination, Bickerton's own writings confirm the uncertainty of his calling to the priesthood, and it seems likely that a man of Crouch's intelligence would have picked up on his pupil's ambivalence. It is equally possible that the vice principal's concerns centred not on the strength of Bickerton's calling but on the state of his mind. Certainly, there is clear evidence that very soon after graduating he began to behave in a fashion that raised serious questions regarding his sanity. The scene in which these behaviours first came to public notice was no less a place than St James's Palace, under the eyes of the king himself.

3

An Incident at St James's Palace

The royal household of King George III was no stranger to intrusion by the eccentric, the erratic, the obsessive and even the dangerous. According to Walley Chamberlain Oulton, Irish playwright, theatre historian, man of letters and contemporary biographer of Queen Charlotte, the first significant breach of the royal privacy occurred on 23 June 1770, when 'a woman meanly dressed' made her way, seemingly without let or hindrance, up the backstairs of St James's Palace and succeeded in entering a room occupied by the queen and her Mistress of Robes, the Duchess of Ancaster. Here, she 'took a survey of the room with great composure' and was only with great difficulty ejected from the palace after the duchess summoned a page.[1] Her subsequent fate is unknown.

A year later, on 25 June 1771, the Bow Street Magistrate Sir John Fielding personally investigated a case of wanton damage of orange trees and other exotic plants in the Dowager Princess of Wales' garden at Kew. Known familiarly as the 'Blind Beak of Bow Street' and able, reputedly at least, to recognise some 3,000 criminals just by the sound of their voices, Fielding was a keen gardener and, despite his blindness, conducted a detailed survey of the vandalism. He discovered that, while the damage might have been wanton, it was definitely not haphazard, the bark of the trees having been stripped for about 12in near the middle of their trunks – a certain means by which to ensure that they died slowly through the interruption of the flow of sap. The individual responsible must have known precisely what he was doing, and suspicion naturally fell on a gardener recently dismissed from royal service.

The gardener escaped prosecution however and, instead, Fielding arrested a lunatic named Josiah Conyngham, the son of an Irish magistrate. Under questioning, Conyngham admitted to damaging the trees – but he admitted to other crimes and misdemeanours of which he was certainly guiltless. His knowledge of horticulture was also unproven, so his confession must be viewed with some scepticism; either way, no one doubted his lunacy and Fielding eventually placed him in a private asylum in Hoxton – almost certainly that of Sir Jonathan Miles, of which we will learn more later.[2]

Again, at St James's Palace, as the king dismounted from a sedan chair on 2 January 1778, 'a woman suddenly rushed before the chair' and the king only narrowly escaped her clutches.[3] When he asked who she was and what she wanted, 'she gave an impudent reply, and said her name was Queen Beck'. Upon further questioning, the woman admitted to being Rebecca O'Hara, said that she was Irish by birth but had been resident in England for five years, and that she lived 'near a public house in Red Lion-square'. Walley Oulton concludes his account of O'Hara's adventure with the statement, 'It having been afterwards proved that she was a lunatic, proper care was taken of her'. What this meant in practice was commitment initially to the Tothill Bridewell and afterwards, to the Bethlem Hospital for the insane, or 'Bedlam' as it came to be known, in Moorfields.

While the king prided himself on his popularity and accessibility, Queen Charlotte had become understandably anxious about the apparent ease with which anyone, even the patently crazy, could approach not only members of the royal family, but the king himself. After the O'Hara incident, she gave 'strict orders to her domestics to prevent as much as possible the ingress of any stranger',[4] and the additional vigilance appears to have paid off, for a time at least, because the next incident did not take place for another eight years.

Whether this hiatus resulted in a degree of complacency we don't know, but when they did occur, the events of 2 August 1786 would prove by far the most dangerous yet experienced, with the king's life threatened for the first time. His assailant was Margaret Nicholson, a 35-year-old seamstress described as being 'below the middle size, and of a very swarthy complexion',[5] originally from County Durham but then living in Wigmore Street, Westminster. According to *The Times*, the king arrived at St James's Palace between midday and one o'clock and, on his alighting at the palace gate, Nicholson, 'under pretence of presenting a petition to his Majesty, attempted to stab him with a knife; the first thrust missed, and on her making a second attempt, the knife was wrenched from her by one of the King's footmen'.[6]

On closer scrutiny, Nicholson's failed attack bore the hallmarks not of a determined assassination attempt, but the act of someone operating under the impulses of mental derangement. Her weapon of choice proved to be an ivory-handled dessert knife, usually known for their rounded blades, rather than a finely honed stiletto and, upon examination by the Crown lawyers, her answers were thought to be 'extremely incoherent, and her manner strongly expressive of a disordered mind'.[7]

Nicholson, who gave her evidence 'without any indication of fear', denied any intention to harm the king, her wish merely being to 'terrify his Majesty, by shewing the knife',[8] and by doing so publicise her own claim to the throne. A search of her rented rooms revealed a number of letters addressed to Lord Mansfield, Lord Chief Justice of the King's Bench, Lord Loughborough, Chief Justice of the Common Pleas, and Major General James Bramham, Chief Royal Engineer, in all of which Nicholson reasserted the same bizarre claim.

Asked whether she should be considered insane, Dr John Monro, physician at Bethlem Hospital and scion of a long line of distinguished 'mad doctors', 'said it was impossible for him to determine whether she was lunatic or not, unless she was under his inspection, and the direction of his people for some days'.[9] In the event, Nicholson would never leave his care, remaining a permanent inmate of the hospital for forty-two years, until her death in 1828.

The king had sustained no injury in the attack. In fact, his behaviour – he remained 'calm and composed' throughout[10] – and his subsequent forbearance towards his assailant won him a great deal of admiration and his popularity soared. And yet, despite its outcome, the incident could not be considered anything but alarming. After all, wielding a knife, Nicholson had got to within touching distance of the king. Had she been better armed, stronger and more determined, he might very well have been seriously wounded or killed.

In marked contrast to those of Nicholson, the intentions of Thomas Stone were amorous rather than murderous. Described as a 'heavy-looking man, about 33 years of age',[11] Stone was arrested close to the royal residence at Kew on Thursday, 30 October 1787. When examined by the Bow Street Magistrates the same day, he confessed to having 'conceived an attachment' for Princess Charlotte, the Princess Royal, 'also that she had conceived the same for him'.[12] According to *The Times*, 'A great many papers, on the subject of love'[13] were found upon him, and he repeatedly accused 'those about him of having stolen his papers, which consisted of unmeaning rhapsodies and quotations, applied to the object of his passion'.[14] On other subjects, Stone spoke rationally and with great composure, and even stated 'that he would never have entered on the business, if he had imagined such a rout would have been made about it'.[15]

Inevitably, like O'Hara and Nicholson before him, Stone was detained pending further enquiries, and we catch a glimpse of him in Bethlem Hospital two months later. 'Some gentlemen who visited Bethlem on Monday,' observed *The Times* on 28 December:

> … surprised at the decent appearance of a man who came from a cell, as they were passing, enquired from their attendant who he was; and on being told that it was Stone, entered into a conversation which, during their stay, he supported in a steady rational manner. He said, the letters he had written were occasioned by a fever on the brain, and that the confusion he felt at the recollection of his conduct, was equal to the sense of the situation it had occasioned. He knew his friends did not wish his continuance in that place; he yet did not censure the power that kept him in it. In one instance he had acted wrong; and though he felt there was no danger [of] a repetition, those against whom his insanity had been directed might naturally look for a relapse.

A native of Shaftesbury and educated at the Grammar School there, where he obtained a reputation for conscientiousness and gravity, for the last twenty-two years Stone had been employed as a law writer in the office of a London attorney, where he worked industriously in order to support his widowed mother. 'By what means his intellects have since become deranged,' *The Times* reported, 'his old acquaintance there cannot imagine; but from the general tenor of his former conduct, the unhappy circumstance is much regretted by them.'[16] As for Stone himself, his one wish was to be released from the hospital where he now found himself incarcerated – even if that meant transfer to a private asylum. 'Are these, cried he, fit companions for a man not desperately mad? To be obliged to live in such a place is of itself sufficient to create distraction. Oh! I could scarce have committed an offence that deserved such a punishment.'[17] He would be neither the first nor the last inmate of Bedlam to make such an impassioned plea.

Stone was not alone in aspiring to a royal alliance. On Saturday, 31 May 1788 the king's third daughter, Princess Elizabeth, was disconcerted when 'a stranger of mean appearance' burst into her private rooms in St James's Palace.[18] Seriously alarmed, she immediately alerted her attendants, one of whom, a page named Millar, seized the intruder, who refused to explain either his presence or the means by which he had gained entry to the royal apartments. Astonishingly, instead of being arrested the stranger was allowed to depart unhindered, only to return a short time later, insisting 'in peremptory terms' that he might be introduced to the princess so that he might 'pour out the ardency of his passion, and at her feet press for an equal return'.[19] This time, a party of guards took him into custody and the following day he appeared at the Bow Street Magistrates' Court.

At the bar, Henry Spang's demeanour justified 'the suspicion before entertained of his being in a state of insanity', though it also denoted 'honesty and good behaviour, notwithstanding the unhappy predicament in which he stood'.[20] When questioned by the magistrates, Sir William Addington and Sir Sampson Wright, he told them that he was a London-born hairdresser, the son of the Danish sculptor Michael

Henry Spang,* and he worked for Archibald Warren, a peruke maker with premises in Paved Alley, Pall Mall. With 'the appearance of being collected', he then went on to explain that, over the course of the previous years, he had been in and out of various asylums and workhouses, including that of Bethnal Green, where he had 'remained a month or five weeks in a straitjacket, handcuffed'.[21] When asked whether he had any friends or relations, he replied, 'he had, the Dukes of York, Cumberland and Gloucester, and the King of Spain besides'.

Of course, the magistrates – to say nothing of the royal family – were anxious to know how Spang had obtained entrance to the palace, but he proved far from informative on this point, saying only that he had met no opposition of any form and that 'he went in boldly as he ought like a man'. His object, he told the magistrates, had been to see the Duke of Cumberland and 'no innuendo was capable of recalling [to] his ideas any trace of the Princess Elizabeth, though much was attempted that way'.[22] Initially, the magistrates intended to continue their examination in the evening, but having decided that Spang's insanity had been fully established, they instead ordered that he be 'provided for at the expense of the parish'.

The first three months of 1790 witnessed a further three incidents, two of them in the precincts of St James's Palace. On 21 January, as the king proceeded to the State Opening of Parliament, a half-pay army lieutenant named John Frith hurled a stone at his carriage and was immediately arrested. Frith, it turned out, believed that he had been the victim of a grave miscarriage of justice, having been forcibly retired from the army in 1787 on the grounds of insanity. He had petitioned his regimental officers, Parliament and the King, as commander-in-chief, but having received no redress had thrown the stone as a means by which to draw attention to the injustice under which he suffered. It had never been his intention, he declared, to injure the king.

---

* Michael Henry Spang (died 1762) moved to London from Denmark in the 1750s. He married an English woman in 1752 and the couple had four children over the next five years. He is perhaps best known for his work at Kedleston Hall, Derbyshire, which was commissioned by Robert Adam, though he also worked for the anatomist William Hunter, for whom he made a small bronze statuette of a flayed criminal, which Hunter holds in a portrait executed by Mason Chamberlain in 1769.

In order to deter other malcontents from taking similar action to publicise their grievances, the Privy Council decided to try Frith for high treason, but the plan backfired when he was brought to the Old Bailey on 17 April. Having first complained of his 'three months in disagreeable confinement', Frith told Lord Chief Justice Kenyon that 'you are violating the laws of this kingdom' and went on to assert that he possessed 'some powers like those which St. Paul had' and he was labouring under 'the power and effects of what they call witchcraft'.[23] Although some believed that Frith was not 'so deranged as he appears to be',[24] the jury entertained no such doubts; the foreman informed Kenyon that they were 'all of opinion that the prisoner is quite insane' and the Lord Chief Justice had no option but to abort the trial.

Less than a fortnight later, on 3 February, a Quaker named Edward Derrick, said to be 'very mean in his appearance', presented himself before one of the gorgeously attired royal marshalmen and announced that he wished to be presented to the king. When told that his request could not be granted, he next stated that he possessed 'important letters that he must deliver to the Queen'. According to Edgar Sheppard, the Victorian historian of the palace, 'The persistent refusal of the marshalman to admit the intruder seemed to irritate him to such an extent that he became insolent, and was consequently taken into custody.'[25] Once he became sufficiently calm, Derrick told his interrogators that he was a native of Caldecott in Cheshire and he had slept the previous Tuesday in the neighbourhood of Romford in Essex. His reasons for seeking interviews with the king and queen remain unclear and the Middlesex magistrates committed him to Tothill Bridewell, probably on a charge of vagrancy.

Finally, on 1 March, 'a decent looking man [...] took an opportunity to seize and take down the Royal Standard from the staff in the Court Yard at St James's'.[26] When questioned by Sir Sampson Wright at Bow Street, Thomas Cannon declared that, in throwing down the standard, 'he had gained his point, which he had long had in agitation' and that 'he might have had the crown, but that he despised [it]'.[27] At first glance, Cannon's actions appeared to be overtly political in motive and reminiscent of those of the young Viscount Mountmorres, who is reputed to have driven a hearse adorned with satirical placards into the courtyard of the palace during the disturbances following John Wilkes' expulsion from the House of Commons in February 1769.[28] However, on further questioning, Cannon began to display the symptoms of delusion and paranoia, refusing to give the reasons for his behaviour 'to anyone but his Majesty, the Prince of Wales, or Mr Pitt' and hinting that 'he should discover several unknown traitors in the kingdom on his next examination'. Certainly, *The Times* had no hesitation in describing him as 'apparently a maniac' and, confident that he had nothing of value to disclose, Wright committed him to Tothill Bridewell, pending his transfer to the guardianship of the authorities of his home parish on the Isle of Man.[29]

During his examination, Cannon had taken the opportunity to deride the poor security at the palace, commenting sarcastically that his success 'shewed what attentive officers and sentinels his Majesty had got'.[30] In fact, the measures designed to ensure the monarch's safety had been tightened immediately after Margaret Nicholson's attempt to stab him in 1786 – but they remained far from perfect, as was amply demonstrated on 15 May 1800. That evening, the king and members of his family attended Drury Lane Theatre to watch a revival of Colley Cibber's 1702 comedy *She Would and She Would Not*.

As the orchestra struck up 'God Save the King', the audience stood and the king bowed to acknowledge them from the royal box. At this moment, a man in his late twenties, badly scarred about the head and face, stood on his seat two rows back from the orchestra pit, took deliberate aim at the king with a pistol, and fired.

The assailant, James Hadfield, was an ex-soldier, his military experience evident in his decision to double-shot his smoothbore flintlock pistol, thereby doubling the killing power of his weapon, albeit with the loss of accuracy and range. Hadfield missed – but not by much. The king's third son, the Duke of Clarence, subsequently found one ball lodged in the cornice of the royal box, just 18in above the place where the king had been standing, while the second had struck close to the princesses' box, before falling into the orchestra pit. No one had been injured.

On this occasion, with so many witnesses in the theatre, there could be absolutely no doubt regarding either Hadfield's actions or his intentions. From the first, he admitted that he had meant to kill the king, though he also stated in the immediate aftermath of his attempt that, on the evening itself, he had 'altered his mind, and intended to shoot near the King, but not to kill him. He would have taken the slugs out of the pistol, but had no worm.'[31]

Just as it had done in the case of John Frith almost exactly a decade earlier, the government decided to proceed with a trial for high treason – and achieved precisely the same result. From the outset of the trial, which began on 27 June 1800, Attorney General Sir John Mitford made no bones about the fact that he expected Hadfield's defence counsel to seek his acquittal on the basis of insanity; indeed, he would not attempt to deny that the prisoner was insane. What he sought to do instead was to demonstrate that insanity was not in itself a sufficient defence for this or any crime. 'Lord Chief Justice Coke states, in his *Pleas of the Crown*,' he told the jury:

> … that a *non compos mentis* cannot commit High Treason, but it must be an absolute madness. Lord Chief Justice Hale, in commenting upon this passage observes, that the true way is to judge as in the case of an infant, whether there was the power of distinguishing between right and wrong […] it was not necessary to have a complete possession of reason, but a sufficient degree to comprehend the nature of the action, and to discriminate between the moral good and evil, to warrant the judgment of the law taking place.[32]

In other words, Mitford intended to prove that Hadfield had sufficient command of his faculties not only to carefully plan and execute an assassination, but that he knew his actions to be wrong, both legally and morally. Given that Hadfield had himself given a clear statement regarding his preparations for the attempt and had even asserted that 'He hoped the people would fall upon him, and kill him'[33] for his crime, Mitford's argument seemed a strong one.

In making his case for the defence, Thomas Erskine called a number of Hadfield's fellow veterans from the 15th Regiment of Light Dragoons. To a man, they described the prisoner as an excellent and loyal soldier who had fought valiantly for his king in a series of actions up to and including the Battle of Tourcoing on 18 May 1794, when he had been cut down by a body of French cavalrymen. In particular, a Captain Wilson asserted, 'If any man had been proposed to be selected from the regiment who was most distinguished for his bravery, loyalty, and zeal, Hadfield would have been one of the first candidates.'[34]

Erskine then called two medical witnesses, Henry Cline, a surgeon, and Doctor Creighton, a physician specialising in the treatment of the insane. Upon examining Hadfield, Cline stated that he had identified at least three sabre cuts that had penetrated his skull and injured the brain. Creighton, meanwhile, 'had not the least doubt but the Prisoner was insane' and went on to confirm that there were 'many instances of that kind of madness that had been occasioned by injuries done to the brain'.[35] Other witnesses, including friends, family and work colleagues, all testified to Hadfield's erratic and often violent behaviour in the years following his discharge from the army, his wife even telling the court that he had threatened to kill their infant son because 'God Almighty had told him to'.[36]

So overwhelming was the evidence that Hadfield's actions were the product of mental derangement, and that his madness resulted from the injuries he had sustained fighting gallantly for his King and Country that, having consulted both the Attorney General and the defence counsel, the Lord Chief Justice stopped the trial and instructed the jury to find Hadfield 'Not Guilty, being under the influence of Insanity at the time the Act was done'.[37]

With this inconvenient and ground-breaking verdict having been reached, the government must determine how it might ensure the continued confinement of a man proven to be dangerously, albeit intermittently, maniacal and who, moreover, had been legally acquitted. It responded to the challenge with extraordinary swiftness, and on 28 July 1800 – a month and a day after Hadfield's trial – the Criminal Lunatics Act received royal assent.

The dust had hardly settled after Hadfield's trial when another attempt was made on the king's life, this time in the newly fashionable resort of Weymouth in Dorset, where he and his daughters regularly bathed.[38] On the evening of 31 August 1800, as the king and his party watched a performance in the Weybridge Theatre, a 25-year-old man named Urban Metcalf leapt to his feet, hurled a penknife at the king with such force that it lodged in the stage door, and tried to climb into the royal box, from which position he was plucked by a Bow Street royal protection officer.

Although some considered Metcalf to be a dangerous revolutionary rather than a lunatic, on further enquiry it turned out that he, like Hadfield before him, had demonstrated the symptoms of insanity long before his antics in Weymouth and that he had spent time in both Hoxton and Plaistow asylums. However, in stark contrast to the Hadfield case, which received a great deal of press coverage, this attempt on the king's life became the subject of a news blackout orchestrated by a government anxious to prevent both panic and the possibility of other disaffected citizens seeking publicity in similar fashion. Metcalf did not stand trial, being sent instead to Bethlem. Though released in 1804, he would spend the next few years in and out of various asylums before being permanently committed as incurably insane to York Asylum in 1822.[39]

Although there were to be no further attempts on the king's life during the last twenty years of his reign – nine of which he spent in almost total seclusion at Windsor Castle because of his own insanity – minor disturbances continued with ever-increasing frequency. In his comprehensive survey of what he describes as 'troublesome subjects', Steve Poole has identified an extraordinary collection of suppliants, claimants and self-publicists who, on one pretext or another, sought entry to the royal residences, and nearly all of whom were described as 'mad', 'lunatic' or 'maniacal'.[40]

Some believed themselves to be bearers of great secrets, others sought to petition the king for favours, a few were the blessed recipients of divine revelation and a handful sought acknowledgement of their own royal blood. The vast majority were halted at the palace gates by guards becoming increasingly accustomed to such visitors; however, two managed to penetrate much further, being prevented only at the very last moment from bursting into the splendid surroundings of a royal levee. One of these men was John England, a drawing master recently released from an asylum, who was spotted striding confidently through the rooms of St James's. The second was John Bickerton.

Throughout much of King George's long reign, levees were held at St James's Palace twice a week, on Wednesdays and Fridays. Only men were permitted to attend, and they must wear court dress, which meant that attendance was restricted to the upper echelons of society. Anyone could meet the king, as long as they had first found someone entitled to make the required presentation: country gentlemen might be introduced by the Lord Lieutenant of their county, a clergyman by his bishop, a ship's officer 'glorified in blue and gold'[41] by an admiral, and an army officer by his colonel. Those regularly present included members of the royal family, government ministers, Members of Parliament (but only those who supported the current administration) and foreign ambassadors. Given that the opportunity to be included in the king's orbit – and to be reported as having been so included in the Court Circular – was highly prized, the levees could prove to be uncomfortably crowded affairs.

The event usually began at midday, when the king, dressed in what came to be known as the 'Windsor uniform' of blue coat with red lapels and cuffs and buff-coloured breeches and waistcoat, would enter the Privy Chamber where the gentlemen of highest rank would be gathered. All conversation immediately ceased on his appearance and then the royal footmen would throw open the doors to the Presence Chamber, where the rest of the guests waited.

The king would turn to the first man on his right, a bow would be given and returned and a few words exchanged, another bow would mark the conclusion of the interview and the king would move on. As John Brooke, George III's biographer, has observed, during these encounters every 'gesture, every expression of the King's face, was noted by the political quidnuncs and its implications eagerly discussed'.[42] After all, the length of time the king spent in conversation with a politician was a clear indicator of how far he was in favour and an unaccustomed silence or brevity might even indicate the imminent end of an administration.

Beyond the lists of attendees to be found in *The Times* and elsewhere, there are remarkably few detailed descriptions of the royal levees of the period, perhaps because very few writers were admitted to the royal presence. However, George Augustus Sala, novelist, journalist, travel writer and pornographer, left an account of his own experiences at a St James's levee some years later. 'The first sensation of the individual to be presented, on entering the palace,' he recalled:

> … is one of blank disappointment. The corridor into which you press with a splendidly apparelled throng before, behind, and around you, presents anything but a palatial aspect. It is, to say the least, somewhat narrow, somewhat dark, and decidedly gloomy […] Indeed, but for the presence of a couple of the Royal marshalmen in scarlet and gold coatees and black and gold shakos of flower-pot form, and who bear gilt *bâtons* of command in their hands, there is scarcely anything Royal about the vestibule of the palace, which, all things considered, is an edifice not up to any date save that of the most tasteless and dingiest period of the early Georgian era.[43]

More cheerfully, Sala noted that on cooler days a blazing fire warmed those waiting to ascend the grand staircase up to the State Apartments and, at a baize-covered table at the foot of the stairs, a courteous official handed each visitor two blank pasteboards on which he was asked to write his name as legibly as possible, 'then you cool your heels, or warm them, as the case may be, for another quarter of an hour: speculating as to the identities of the sparkling throng around you'.[44] Of course, these fifteen minutes of heel-cooling gave the palace officials time to corroborate the identity and entitlement to attend of each guest, correct dress not being sufficient to guarantee entry.

Lessons had been learned after previous intrusions and levee-goers now passed through what has been described as 'an enfilade of spaces and rooms which acted as a powerful filter, gradually removing all but the titled, the expected and the invited'.[45] On the afternoon of Wednesday, 14 September 1803, this net would serve its function well, ensnaring Bickerton in its meshes as he tried to make his way, uninvited and unauthorised, into the king's presence.

The king and queen, accompanied by the Princesses Augusta and Elizabeth, had arrived at the palace from Windsor early on the afternoon of the levee, with the queen and her party enjoying 'an elegant collation' in the grace-and-favour apartment of Lady Charlotte Finch, the retired Royal Governess, while the king attended to the official business of the day.[46] As usual, the levee was well attended, even to the point of overcrowding, with the Chancellor of the Exchequer, the Lord Chancellor, Secretaries of State, the Lord President of the Privy Council, the ambassadors of Russia, Bavaria, Spain, Denmark, Naples and the United States all present, as well as high-ranking army and navy officers led by Viscounts Howe and Hood, and a host of lesser mortals.

In the Presence Chamber, with its throne and canopy of crimson velvet and its satin curtains trimmed with gold lace, events took their usual course. Presentations were made in the accepted fashion and the king exchanged a few words with individuals including the fossil-collecting Sir John St Aubyn, the Rembrandt enthusiast Reginald Pole Carew and Sir John Moore, soon to win lasting, if posthumous, fame at the Battle of Corunna. None were aware of the disturbance taking place on the staircase leading to the royal apartments.

The first and most comprehensive record of Bickerton's attempt to enter the levee appeared the following day in the *St James's Chronicle*. According to its report, at about three o'clock, 'a man decently dressed in black, with a large sword by his side, entered St James's Palace, and was proceeding upstairs towards the Levee, when the Yeoman of the Guard inquired of him where he was going, he not being in a court dress'.[47] When Bickerton replied that he wished to see William Cavendish-Bentinck, 3rd Duke of Portland and Lord President of the Privy Council, the Yeoman naturally refused him admittance.

Bickerton persisted, however, stating, 'the Duke was to lay his claims to an estate which he was kept out of by Lord Cholmondeley'. He then claimed to be 'brother to Admiral Sir Richard Bickerton; and by virtue of the noble family to which he was allied he carried the sword by his side, which cut on both sides'. Finally, he produced what the *St James's Chronicle* described as an 'extraordinary paper', entitled:

Multum Desideratum; or, a few Hints concerning the Bickertons, who lived in Cheshire, after they came into England with William the Conqueror: And respecting the R. J. Bickerton, AM, CP, Queen's College, Oxford, of the same Family; together with a concise Address to Friends, &c. to inform them how they may be rich and happy in the present time and future; with a representation of the Three Broad Arrows, the Family's Coat of Arms, and of the aforesaid Person. Reprinted by the desire of, and to accommodate his Friends who live at a distance.

The Lord Cholmondeley to whom Bickerton referred was George James Cholmondeley, the Earl of Cholmondeley, a politician and landowner whose estates abutted the village of Bickerton in Cheshire, and a possible original for Thackeray's Sir Rawdon Crawley in *Vanity Fair*.[48] The second personage was Rear Admiral Sir Richard Hussey Bickerton, at that time Commander-in-Chief of the Mediterranean Fleet and soon to become Nelson's second in command. The admiral is perhaps the most notable individual ever to bear the name Bickerton, and John Bickerton would not be the last of his namesakes to claim him as a relative. The paper itself appears to have been an expanded version of Bickerton's autobiographical writings of 1777, which he had published under the somewhat shorter title of *A Concise Account of the Fall and Rise of the Family of the Bickertons, of Maiden Castle in Cheshire, to which is annexed, The Gracious Dealings of God in the Life and Conversion of the Rev. John Bickerton, of the Same Family, Written by Himself* and which had included a representation of the Bickerton coat of arms on its title page.

Of course, the grand staircase of St James's Palace was not the place, and a levee-day certainly not the time, to properly investigate any of Bickerton's claims. This was no doubt explained to him by the Yeomen of the Guard but, clearly in no mood to listen to reason, he refused outright to leave. With a risk of the situation getting out of hand, the Yeomen now called John Townsend and John Sayer, the Bow Street Runners on royal protection duty that afternoon. These officers quickly made it clear that they were not to be trifled with and the *Chronicle* concludes its report with the statement that they took Bickerton 'into custody, and forced the sword from him, and took him before Sir Rich. Ford, at his house in Sloane-street'.[49]

4

Bow Street

No account survives of Bickerton's initial questioning by Sir Richard Ford; however, it is likely to have been a brief affair designed merely to establish his identity and the basic facts of the case, as testified to by the arresting officers. Almost certainly, Bickerton would then have spent the night of 14 September in a squalid room of the Brown Bear public house, which served as a lock-up for the ill-equipped Bow Street Police Office, or magistrate's court. The following morning, ill-kempt and unshaven, he was taken across the road to the court itself, to be questioned once again by Ford.

At the time of his appearance Bow Street had long been the most famous of London's magistrates' courts. Located on the edge of Covent Garden, with its reputation for prostitution and petty crime as well as theatricals, it had first been established sixty-three years earlier, when Sir Thomas de Veil, in common with all magistrates of the period, heard cases in his private house, at number four. Here he granted warrants and summonses, made orders, took recognizances, instigated inquiries into the more serious offences perpetrated in his locality, and committed to trial at the Old Bailey those accused of such offences. Sir Thomas proved a conscientious magistrate and a courageous and active pursuer of wrongdoers, quelling riots through the use of the Riot Act of 1715, and successfully investigating a significant number of crimes within his jurisdiction of Middlesex and Westminster. Two years after his death in 1746, his mantle, and his house, passed to the satirical novelist and playwright Henry Fielding, and thence, in 1754, to Fielding's younger half-brother, blind Sir John. The Fielding brothers followed de Veil's lead, maintaining a high standard of probity and fairness, and rooting out corruption wherever they found it, though the novelist was unjustly accused by his critics of having pursued the post on the sole basis of its expected emoluments, official or otherwise. As magistrates the brothers are perhaps best remembered for their important contribution to the development of the first organised police force, subsequently known as the 'Bow Street Runners', two of whom, Sayer and Townsend, had arrested Bickerton on the staircase of St James's Palace.

The first Runners operated largely in secret, endeavouring to maintain their anonymity because of the unpopularity of their role as thief takers. There were also very few of them, with only eight 'principal officers' as late as 1828 – the year before Sir Robert Peel's Metropolitan Police Act came into force – and no more than twelve at any time. Initially, they relied almost exclusively on the financial rewards received for the arrests they made – rewards usually paid by the victims of criminality – and even after Sir John Fielding introduced a weekly wage of 11s 6d, the fees they earned from private commissions remained a substantial portion of their income; indeed, Sir John himself continued to advertise the services of his 'brave Fellows [...] who have long been engaged for such Purposes, and are always ready to set out to any Part of this Town or Kingdom, on a Quarter of an Hour's notice'.[1]

It was this reliance upon rewards rather than a salary that had made the Runners and their predecessors so unpopular, with many, like the notorious Jonathan Wild, operating on both sides of the law, actively encouraging criminality before betraying those they had inveigled. Gradually, though, the stigma attaching to the profession of thief taking began to dissipate and stories of the Runners' intelligence, ingenuity and courage gained for them wider recognition and social acceptance. Shortly before his death in 1754, Henry Fielding described his Runners as 'men of known and approved fidelity and intrepidity',[2] and, over time, their exploits would become, in the words of Anthony Babington, historian of Bow Street and himself a Bow Street magistrate, 'a favourite subject for discussion in the home, the tavern, and the coffee shop'.[3]

Although the principal function of the Runners was to pursue and arrest malefactors, with some becoming specialists in certain types of criminal activity, they also performed other duties in a preventative capacity, some as private commissions and others as paid special employments, being hired out by institutions such as banks, theatres and government departments, as well as by wealthy individuals. Such work could be highly remunerative, with Townsend and Sayer, for instance, receiving a guinea a day for attendance at the Bank of England when the dividends were being paid out because, as Townsend explained, 'Depredations used to be committed there dreadfully at dividend-times'.[4] For this work, each man could expect to receive 40 guineas per annum, in addition to his salary, which by 1816 amounted to another guinea per day. In other examples, John Vickery benefited from regular employment by the Post Office, where he oversaw security and led fraud investigations, while Bond and Donaldson undertook crowd control and crime prevention for the nearby theatres of Covent Garden and Drury Lane.

Without doubt, by far the most prestigious of the additional duties undertaken by the Bow Street Runners was that of royal protection, for which the king paid each officer £200 per annum. Townsend described this role as having commenced:

> I think in the year 1792, when Mr Dundas was secretary of state, and Mr Pitt was minister, that employment took place in consequence of the various depredations committed at court, and in consequence of the King and the Royal Family being frequently teased with lunatics: that was the original occasion of that appointment taking place.[5]

Giving his evidence to a Parliamentary Committee 'On the State of the Police in the Metropolis', thirty years after the events he described took place, Townsend might be forgiven for misremembering. In fact, the incident that had first given rise to a review of royal protection was Margaret Nicholson's 1786 attack on the king. Although there is no reason to doubt Townsend's assertion that without such additional sources of income it would be impossible for a Bow Street Runner to 'maintain the situation which it is fit he should hold',[6] it is also true that their additional employments could enable them to amass considerable fortunes, as is evidenced by the fact that Townsend is thought to have left around £20,000 at the time of his death in 1832, while Sayer's estate was valued at £30,000.*

Beyond the facts that he had once worked as a turnkey at the Tothill Fields House of Correction and that he had served as a Bow Street Runner since the time of the Gordon Riots in June 1780, very little is known of John Sayer.[7] John Townsend, on the other hand, would become by far the best known of the Bow Street Runners, his fame no doubt increased not only by the publicity his exploits attracted – he was, for instance, the arresting officer after James Hadfield's attempt on the life of the king – but also by his long life, affability and enthusiasm for sharing anecdotes of his various adventures. His contemporary, the fashionable fencing master and memoirist Henry Angelo, recalled how 'many of the sprigs of fashion used to crowd round (for he was a general favourite), with "How are you, Townsend? what's the go?" when with good humour he would indulge their fancy'.[8]

Born around 1754 at the Middlesex Infirmary and educated at the St Clement Danes charity school on Drury Lane, just a stone's throw from Sir John Fielding's office, Townsend had begun his adult life as a coal-heaver or costermonger, only joining the Runners when he was 28. By the time he arrested Bickerton, he had been an officer of the law for twenty-one years and on royal protection duty for eleven; moreover, with a mind remarkable for its 'originality and grotesqueness',[9] he had established himself as a favourite of the king, whom he described as missing him 'in a moment if I am not there'.[10]

An etching produced by Robert Dighton in 1804 shows the 50-year-old Townsend as a man of strong features and rotund belly, not unlike the king himself – a resemblance he perhaps sought to emphasise by wearing, in his later years, a white hat with a broad ribbon, 'similar to one worn some years since by the late King'.[11] During his long career, and armed only with his 7in ornate tipstaff, Townsend had apprehended suspected murderers, conspirators, thieves, counterfeiters and fraudsters

---

*   Today's equivalents would be roughly £1.75 million and £2.6 million respectively. (Source: the Bank of England's inflation calculator, using the Consumer Price Index inflation data from the Office for National Statistics.)

and, as recently as February 1803, during one confrontation he had been stabbed 'high up in the side, nearly under the left arm', and his life initially despaired of, 'the discharge of blood was so considerable'.[12]

These, then, were the men who intercepted Bickerton en route to the king's levee. The *St James's Chronicle* reported that the Bow Street officers had 'forced the sword from him', but that contest must surely have been both brief and one-sided.

The building in which Bickerton appeared before Sir Richard Ford was the fifth house to the north from the junction of Bow Street with Russell Street. Built in the early years of the eighteenth century, the Magistrates' Court still occupied the erstwhile home of de Veil and the Fieldings, though it had undergone substantial remodelling following its gutting during the Gordon Riots, when the enraged and intoxicated mob made a bonfire of its wainscoting, furniture and the criminal records built up over the previous three decades. The alterations had included the creation of a 'Publick Office' measuring 29ft 2in by 19ft 4in, linked to the house by a passageway, with an adjoining private office and outdoor area.[13]

The public office was probably the chamber in which Bickerton underwent his examination. Even in de Veil's day, the courtroom had shed any semblance of domesticity, with the magistrate seated on a dais at one end of the room, while his clerk worked at a desk in front at floor level. Rows of seats on either side of the room and a raised gallery accommodated spectators, and the accused stood not in a dock but at a bar facing the magistrate and clerk.

Thirty-five years later, in *Oliver Twist*, Charles Dickens would describe this courtroom while setting the scene for the examination of the Artful Dodger, brought up on a charge of 'pick-pocketing'. The novelist had seen the room when reporting for various newspapers and periodicals in the mid-1830s, and his description indicates further evolutions in the layout:

> A dirty frowsy room, at the upper end of which was a raised platform railed off from the rest, with a dock for the prisoners on the left hand against the wall, a box for the witnesses in the middle, and a desk for the magistrates on the right; the awful locality last named,

being screened off by a partition which concealed the bench from the common gaze, and left the vulgar to imagine (if they could) the full majesty of justice [...]

The room smelt close and unwholesome; the walls were dirt-discoloured; and the ceiling blackened. There was an old smoky bust over the mantel-shelf, and a dusty clock above the dock – the only thing present that seemed to go on as it ought; for depravity, or poverty, or an habitual acquaintance with both, had left a taint on all the animate matter, hardly less unpleasant than the thick greasy scum on every inanimate object that frowned upon it.[14]

No doubt Dickens used a degree of poetic licence, but he was also a meticulous and circumstantial reporter and there is no reason to question the substance of his description of the room in which Bickerton now found himself. There was, however, an important difference between the examination of the Artful Dodger and the examination of Bickerton: whereas the former is undertaken amidst the theatre of open court, the latter was completed privately, with none but Bickerton, Ford and the other officers of the court present.

Whatever the appearance and atmosphere of the courtroom, the powers now arrayed against the unfortunate Bickerton were considerable. Under British law, a magistrate could try cases on his own and without a jury; he could determine guilt or innocence in the most summary fashion and, after logging a conviction, punish the convicted by fining, whipping, placing in the stocks or committing him or her to a house of correction or a county gaol. Moreover, while Parliament had continually added to the number of offences that could be tried in this manner, it had failed to protect the rights of the accused by formulating strict procedures for the conduct of trials. Consequently, writes Anthony Babington, 'often what occurred was a travesty of justice from which the convicted person, be he a thief, vagrant, poacher or brawler, had little or no chance of appealing either against his conviction or against his sentence'.[15] Fortunately for Bickerton, the magistrate before whom he now stood was a man of much greater discernment, integrity and humanity than the notorious Allan Stewart Laing, the original of Mr Fang, the irascible, brow-beating magistrate in Dickens' novel.

Only one portrait of Bickerton's interviewer, Sir Richard Ford, is known to survive. Drawn in 1796 by Henry Bone, the talented enamel painter to George III and his two successors, it is a preparatory sketch for an enamel miniature, based on an original by Ford's sister-in-law, Elizabeth Booth. It shows Ford aged 38, five years after his resignation as Member of Parliament for Appleby in Westmorland, four years after his appointment as a magistrate and another four before he became chief magistrate at Bow Street and was knighted. Wearing a fashionable high-collared coat and frilled cravat, and with his hair swept back from his forehead and curling about his temples, the portrait reveals Ford at the height of his powers, with high-arched eyebrows and an intense, penetrating gaze.

George Hodder, a court reporter for the *Morning Herald*, described the duties of a Bow Street magistrate as being 'as various as those of a clown in a pantomime, and sometimes almost as entertaining',[16] but anyone less clown-like than Richard Ford it would be difficult to imagine. The question to which he must now seek an answer was what had led Bickerton to attempt to force his way into a levee at St James's Palace – a levee hosted by the king himself and attended by senior politicians, the nobility and foreign dignitaries? Were his intentions malevolent or harmless? And, if the latter, why had he felt it necessary to arm himself with a sword?

A few days later, Ford himself described the circumstances of the case and the outcome of Bickerton's examination in a letter to Thomas Stirling, the Deputy Clerk of the Peace at the Middlesex Sessions House, Clerkenwell:

> In regard to Mr Bickerton, he was taken up as he was going into the Anti Room [sic] at St James's on a levee day, his conduct & conversation denoted derangement & he had in his hand an old rusty sword. On his Exam'n he appeared deranged – talked of Claims he had from his ancestors on Estates in Cheshire, to recover which he wanted to see the king & the Duke of Portland – the sword, he said, he always carried because he was afraid a man who lodged in the house with him, wanted to murder him […] I wanted Bickerton to let me send to his relations, or to give me some good security for his future conduct, but he did neither.[17]

By the time he met Bickerton, Ford had been a magistrate for eleven years and chief magistrate for three; his experience was, therefore, wide and varied. To obtain some idea of the breadth of that experience, one might scour the pages of *The Times* and other London and provincial newspapers, all of which carry reports of the more high-profile and sensational cases heard at Bow Street, including murder, assault, highway robbery and the like. For the more whimsical courtroom dramas, meanwhile, the reader might consult George Hodder's altogether more frivolous *Sketches of Life and Character Taken at the Police Court, Bow Street* or John Wight's *Mornings at Bow Street*, in which he will find himself 'placed, without personal sacrifice, amidst the various and somewhat repulsive groups of a police office, and made acquainted with the states and conditions of human nature, with which, from the sympathy due to the more unfortunate part of the species, he should not be entirely ignorant'.[18]

Clearly, Ford quickly formed the opinion that Bickerton would be better classed with 'the more unfortunate part of the species' – those who had been deprived of their wits, like the 'short, dumpy, sunburnt, orange and purple-faced old man' who had been arrested when 'trudging through the Mall in St James's Park, with his breeches on a stick over his shoulder',[19] or 'General Sarsfield Lucan, Viscount Kilmallock, a peer of France, and a descendant of Charlemagne', who presented himself before the magistrates 'to solicit a few shillings'[20] – rather than with rapists, poisoners, ruffians, footpads and other ne'er-do-wells.

Ford also took the precaution of seeking the opinions of two men who knew his prisoner. The first was Charles Lush, an attorney, Chief Clerk to the Worship-Street Police Office, Shoreditch, and an occasional contributor to *The Gentleman's Magazine*. According to Ford, Bickerton lived near Lush, who resided at Charles's Square, Pitfield Street, Hoxton, 'I wrote to that gentleman, and learnt that he bore generally the character of a deranged person, but was harmless'.[21] His second witness was Joseph Moser, an artist, prolific author of oriental tales and advocate of children's nurseries for the urban working class,[22] who would serve as a Westminster magistrate from 1808 and who lived in Romney Street, Westminster – Moser 'gave me the same intelligence'.[23]

The reports of Lush and Moser, added to Bickerton's behaviour and language during the examination, apparently satisfied Ford that his prisoner posed no immediate threat either to himself or to those around him. But he was equally satisfied that Bickerton was delusional and, without a member of his family to act as a surety for his good conduct or a credible undertaking from Bickerton himself, he could not be released. In normal circumstances, this might not have been the case – unfortunately for Bickerton, the circumstances of the autumn of 1803 were anything but normal.

Following the collapse of the Treaty of Amiens in May 1803, Britain was once again at war with France. More importantly, in the past few years there had been a number of instances of social unrest and attempted insurrection, most notably the Irish Rebellion of 1798. Then, in May 1800 had come Hadfield's attempt to assassinate the king. Against this background, anyone arrested while attempting to force his way into the presence of the king and armed with a sword, no matter how rusty, could not expect to be released back onto the streets.

Clearly, Ford remained convinced that Bickerton was a harmless lunatic rather than a murderous conspirator, but that conviction must be tested. To Thomas Stirling, he confided that the magistrates of the Middlesex Quarter Sessions 'will judge what is best to be done with him and I am happy the case is in such good hands'.[24]

For the time being, Ford's decision meant at least a temporary committal to a 'House of Correction [...] till he can be otherwise disposed of'.[25] Having been informed of Ford's decision, Bickerton was probably returned to the rather less than salubrious surroundings of the strongroom of the Brown Bear until such time as more hearings had been completed and more committals ordered.

In his *Chronicles of Bow Street Police-Office*, Percy Fitzgerald describes how 'there used to be a painful and not undramatic scene witnessed every afternoon in the street, which furnished a sort of excitement for the motley and uncleanly crowd which never failed to attend. This was the arrival of the funereal-looking prison-van.'[26] It was into a vehicle of this type – a small horse-drawn holding cell on wheels – that Bickerton and his fellow prisoners were then herded for their onward journey. Their destination, the notorious Coldbath Fields Prison: an institution known colloquially as the 'Bastille' or in the prisoners' own parlance, 'the steel'.[27]

5

The House of Correction

Jerry White, the historian of London, has commented, 'Of all the miserable places in which to die in eighteenth-century London none was more terrible than prison.'[1] By 1800, there were nineteen prisons in the capital to serve a population of a little over 950,000. Broadly speaking, prisoners might be divided into three categories: first, debtors, who were housed largely, though not exclusively, in eight dedicated prisons, such as the Fleet, the King's Bench and, most notorious of all, the Marshalsea; second, vagrants, rogues, vagabonds and misdemeanants – meaning those imprisoned for offences of a lower degree than felony, such as prostitution and petty theft – who were incarcerated in houses of correction, or 'Bridewells' as they were commonly known as a result of the first such institution having been established in Henry VIII's old home of Bridewell Palace; and, finally, felons – those whose crimes warranted sentences of penal servitude or transportation – who were committed to the convict prisons or, worse still, the rotting hulks on the Thames. However, the administrative and physical boundaries separating the different types of offender were all too often porous, with debtors, in particular, often living cheek by jowl with misdemeanants despite a law enacted during the reign of Charles II, which dictated that the two types of prisoner should be 'put, kept, and lodged separate and apart from one another, in distinct rooms'.[2]

Located in the heart of the old city, many of the prisons were of great antiquity, dating back to the medieval period, and most were poorly managed, insecure, decayed, filthy and overcrowded. The insanitary conditions in which prisoners lived often resulted in eruptions of smallpox and gaol fever, an often fatal form of typhus transmitted by body lice.

To some degree, Bickerton might count himself fortunate in that his destination was one of the newest of London's prisons. Intended for the short-term incarceration and reform of petty criminals and debtors and designed along lines suggested by the prison reformer John Howard, Middlesex's House of Correction at Coldbath Fields, Clerkenwell, had been erected as recently as 1794 – less than a decade prior to his committal. In his capacity as High Sheriff of Bedfordshire, Howard had visited his own county's prison in 1773 and had been so appalled by what he saw that he had become a committed advocate of reform.

Driven by his strong Calvinist faith and his sense of public duty, and benefiting from a considerable personal fortune, during the following months he travelled far and wide at his own expense, touring the prisons of Great Britain and Europe, and no doubt causing great consternation to many a gaoler as he poked his great hooked nose into every murky corner of their hitherto sacrosanct fiefdoms. 'Hearing the cries of the miserable,' he later wrote, 'I devoted my time to their relief. In order to procure it, I made it my business to collect materials, the authenticity of which could not be disputed.'[3]

The shortages of food, the nakedness, cupidity, cruelty, fraud, immorality and disease that he found everywhere and a death toll among prisoners far above what might reasonably be expected infuriated him and drove him to address his countrymen in impassioned prose:

> However sanguinary the wish of an angry creditor may be when he arrests and imprisons his debtor; there is no doubt but everyone who listens, not to his passions, but to reason, must know, and will own, that it is a flagrant crime to take away the life of a man for debt: and as to felony, a Gaol is not designed for the final punishment even of that; but for the *safe custody* of the accused to the time of trial; and of convicts till a legal sentence be executed upon them. The laws of England do not suffer private executions. No condemned malefactor may be secretly put to death; nor murdered in a prison directly or

indirectly: much less ought those to be destroyed whose sentence does not affect their life.[4]

Having described the multiple failings of the British prison system to a Select Committee of the House of Commons in 1774 – testimony for which he was called to the bar of the house and publicly thanked – three years later, Howard published his research and recommendations in *The State of the Prisons in England and Wales*.

Seeking to improve both the physical conditions and the moral wellbeing of prisoners, Howard advocated a systematic programme of refurbishment and replacement. Prisons, he argued, must not be located in the middle of towns or cities, but 'should be built on a spot that is *airy*, and if possible near a river, or brook'[5] to ensure a fresh supply of water for drinking and washing and to improve sewerage. Proximity to a river would also discourage the construction of dank subterraneous dungeons, 'which have been destructive to thousands'.

By placing prisoners' wards in free-standing buildings and on top of arcades, a triple benefit would be obtained: air would circulate more freely, a dry walkway would be created for use in inclement weather and security improved, as inmates would not be able to tunnel their way to liberty. Male and female prisoners should be segregated at all times and, on the basis that 'Solitude and silence are favourable to reflection; and may possibly lead them to repentance',[6] each individual should have a separate cell. Given the high levels of sickness in the dilapidated old prisons, each must have an infirmary, a bath and an oven, since 'nothing so effectually destroys vermin in cloaths and bedding, nor purifies them so thoroughly when tainted with infection, as being a few hours in an oven moderately heated'.[7] These, Howard contended, were basic requirements, not luxuries – unlike glass in cell windows, which he deemed an unjustifiable extravagance for any but the ill or pregnant.

Howard was equally clear on the critical importance of differentiating between convict prisons and houses of correction: while the former were designed for the long-term incarceration of those found guilty of serious crimes and were directly controlled by the government, the latter were intended to house only misdemeanants sentenced to short terms of from seven days to two years and were under the management of the local magistracy. Like those convicts sentenced to penal servitude, the misdemeanants must be made to undertake hard labour, the labour usually taking the form of wielding large mallets to beat hemp for the manufacture of rope, the prisoners 'twisting, rolling, rubbing, until their soft, thievish fingers grow red and sore, and afterwards hard by their contact with those stiff chunks of tarry hemp'.[8] Such labour, Howard believed, would have a salutary effect, convincing the prisoners of the error of their ways, and thereby encouraging them to turn from future wrongdoing. All too often, he argued, the inadequacies of the prisons, the gaolers who ran them and the authorities who inspected them had resulted in the two types of prisoner, the hardened criminals and the petty offenders, the incorrigible and the redeemable, mixing together with the corruption of the latter being the inevitable result. 'What is this,' he asked, 'but devoting them to destruction?'[9]

In terms of the regulations that should govern conduct within the prisons, some of Howard's recommendations seem truly extraordinary to the twenty-first-century reader – not because they are in any way absurd, but because he found it necessary to articulate what, today, seems blindingly obvious. That he had to make such suggestions serves to highlight the kind of abuses that were rife in the prison system of the late eighteenth century. A gaoler, he argued, should be sober; moreover, he and his turnkeys should not 'be suffered to hold the *Tap*; or to have any connexion, concern, or interest whatever in the sale of liquors of any kind'.[10] Gaolers should also be salaried, rather than reliant for a substantial portion of their income upon commercial transactions conducted within the prison, such transactions including the charging of rent for rooms and bedding, the sale of food as well as alcohol and the purchase of special privileges by prisoners. The gaoler should be fit and healthy and be expected to conduct personally daily inspections of the prison.

Each gaol should have its own chaplain, surgeon and apothecary – and crucially, each of these should be 'a man of repute in his profession'. No fighting, abusive language or gaming – 'the frequent occasion of them' – should be tolerated. Finally, Howard believed, to 'every prison there should be an Inspector appointed; either by his colleagues in the magistracy, or by Parliament'.[11]

In January 1777, Howard visited the old Middlesex House of Correction at Coldbath Fields, on the western edge of Clerkenwell. The name of the locality was derived from a privately run hydropathic establishment opened in 1697 by an entrepreneurial lawyer, Walter Baynes, who claimed, with the support of Dr Edward Baynard, a leading advocate of hot and cold bathing, that the local salt- and mineral-impregnated waters could ease a vast array of illnesses, including 'Dissiness, Drowsiness, and heavyness of the head, Lethargies, Palsies, Convulsions, all Hectical creeping Fevers, heats and flushings [...] disorders of the spleen and womb, also stiffness of the limbs and Rheumatick pains, also shortness of breath, weakness of the joints, as Rickets, etc'.[12] Originally on the periphery of the city, during the eighteenth century the fields surrounding Baynes' marble bath had been lost to rapid urban growth, with housing followed by a distillery in the 1730s and a smallpox hospital in the 1750s. Further to the south, the parish workhouse stood in Hockley-in-the-Hole, a disreputable neighbourhood celebrated for its bull- and bear-baiting.

The Bridewell predated all these developments, having been built during the reign of James I (1603–25), and by the time of Howard's inspection it exhibited many, though not all, of the shortcomings that had first provoked his ire:

> The Prison is much out of repair. It has not been so much as whitewashed for years [...] one person sick; a woman who lay on the floor. No straw. No Infirmary.
>
> Of the one hundred and eight in January last, above thirty were Fines, that is, Criminals committed for a term of years, five or six. Some of these, and of the others, were sick. They complained to me of sore feet, which the Turnkey said were quite black.[13]

One of the male prisoners' dormitories he found 'so crowded, that some Prisoners slept in hammocks hung to the ceiling', while the women slept in 'dark unwholesome night-rooms'.[14] In addition to the mixing of prisoner types, the prison's poor state of repair and its high levels of sickness, the gaoler's salary was little more than a pittance, making him reliant upon the money that he could extort from the inmates. All in all, the condition of Middlesex Bridewell offered a perfect opportunity to apply the principles of construction and management that formed the basis of Howard's new model.

The passing of the Penitentiary Act in 1779 – an Act which has been described as 'the most forward-looking English penal measure of its time'[15] – resulted directly from the advocacy of Howard and other vocal reformers. Under its terms, as drafted by the eminent legal commentator and judge Sir William Blackstone, two houses of hard labour would be erected somewhere in Middlesex, Surrey, Kent or Essex, one to hold 600 men and the other 300 women.

In fact, as historian of the Act Simon Devereaux has stated, 'No government-funded "penitentiary" of a scale commensurate with the scheme of 1779 came into being until Millbank was opened in 1816'.[16] But the demands for reform had become irresistible and the ratepayers of Middlesex became some of the first to foot the bill for improved prisoner accommodation at a local rather than the planned national level.

Purchased by the sitting magistrates for the sum of £4,350, the site for the new house of correction stood on Mount Pleasant, originally a muddy track running down to the Fleet River, which gained its ironic name and its physical elevation from the locals' habit of dumping cinders and other rubbish there until they had created a mountainous refuse heap. In 1728, Alexander Pope had written of the polluted Fleet with its 'large tribute of dead dogs',[17] and later in the nineteenth century, the journalist James Ewing Ritchie would observe, 'On a dull, dreary morning, it is anything but pleasant, that Mount, in spite of its name'.[18] Surely, then, there could hardly be a site more in keeping with the letter, but at the same time more in contrast with the spirit of Howard's suggestion that prisons should be located 'on a spot that is *airy*, and [...] near a river, or brook'.[19]

To reach the house of correction, the black prison van containing Bickerton would have headed north from Bow Street to join Broad Street, before heading west to climb High Holborn. It would then have turned left onto Gray's Inn Lane, up Mount Pleasant and through Dorrington Street to reach the prison's entrance on Coldbath Square. Through the tiny, barred window in the van's rear door, Bickerton probably saw little or nothing of the route they followed, and it is doubtful whether he even glimpsed the massive stone gateway, embellished with the County of Middlesex's coat of arms and great carved stone fetters on either side, as he passed beneath its archway. Only when the huge iron-studded gates clanged shut behind them would the guards have dismounted and released him.[20]

As their eyes adjusted to the light, probably the features that most struck Bickerton and the other new arrivals – at least those who had not previously been inmates – were the tall brick wall that surrounded the whole site and the looming mass of the prison buildings. But there were other sights. In his gossipy memoirs, P.G. Patmore, the friend of William Hazlitt, recalled visiting the prison in 1813 to meet the publisher John Hunt, who had been sentenced to a fine of £500 and two years' imprisonment for printing an article in which his younger and better-known brother, Leigh, described the Prince Regent as 'a violator of his word, a libertine over head and ears in debt and disgrace [...] a man who had just closed half a century without one single claim on the gratitude of his country'.[21] One of the things Patmore most remembered from his visit was the desolate garden next to the governor's house, a garden 'without a tree or a shrub in it; with nothing alive but long rows of sickly cabbages and lettuces, that seemed to be pining for the free air that passed hundreds of feet above their heads – an "unreal mockery" of a garden'.[22]

The prison had been built on a massive scale, and at the enormous cost of £65,650, 'the large outlay', according to the Victorian journalist Thomas Archer, 'being in proportion, not so much to the size or convenience of the structure, as to the thick walls, numerous and massy doors and gates, and winding passages, which were at that time deemed essential to a place for the punishment of criminals'.[23]

Leigh Hunt, imprisoned in Horsemonger Lane Prison, which followed the same pattern as Coldbath Fields, commented on the design not as a visitor, but as an inmate:

> At night-time the door was locked; then another on the top of the staircase, then another on the middle of the staircase, then a fourth at the bottom, a fifth that shut up the little yard belonging to that quarter, and how many more, before you got out of the gates, I forget: but

> I do not exaggerate when I say there were ten or eleven. The first night I slept there, I listened to them, one after the other, till the weaker part of my heart died within me.[24]

The main prison block consisted of four long galleries, forming a parallelogram by their junction, on the sides of which were ranged 232 cells – far too few, as it turned out. Less than a decade after its completion, Coldbath Fields House of Correction had become vastly overcrowded, with men, women, boys and girls routinely herded together without employment or strictly enforced rules, meaning that 'smoking, gaming, singing, and every species of brutalizing conversation and demeanour, tended to the unlimited advancement of crime and pollution'.[25]

And the crime and pollution were not limited to the inmates. In such an essentially lawless atmosphere, it was all too easy for some, at least, of those in authority to abuse their positions of power, with one report into the prison's management noting that 'in this place, originally destined for the improvement of the morals of petty offenders, a female prisoner [...] has been lately debauched by the son of the chief gaoler [...] and has since had a child, now, or at least lately, burdensome to the parish of Kensington'.[26]

Writing of his own early experiences of the prison, another reformer, Captain George Chesterton, who became the gaol's governor in 1829, described it as a sink of despair and degradation:

> Cleanliness scarcely seemed to be a necessary requirement; all care to ensure the space indispensable to common decency was deemed superfluous; the safeguards upon modesty were rudely cast aside, and shameless profligacy unblushingly prevailed. The lowest order of men only aspired to dispense the functions of a gaol, while the name itself was of evil omen, and its very sound became odious to those of honest and peaceful vocations.[27]

Unsurprisingly, Chesterton was at pains to emphasise the shocking conditions in the prison prior to the reforms he instigated, but other sources corroborate many of his claims; indeed, the prison became so notorious in the early years of the nineteenth century that Samuel

Taylor Coleridge even suggested that the Devil would happily take it as a model 'for improving his prisons in hell'.[28] In other words, many of the fundamental tenets of John Howard's reforms had already fallen by the wayside.

What would Bickerton have made of this atmosphere and of his fellow prisoners? And what did they make of him, this lean middle-aged man, with the air of a scholar and a mixture of fear and madness in his eyes? Writing of his own visit, Thomas Archer noticed how 'Many of the prisoners return the gaze of the visitor with an impudent look of careless or mocking bravado, others scowl darkly [...] and some go stolidly on without changing a muscle of their faces'.[29] Perhaps the very best that Bickerton could hope for was to be ignored.

There was, however, one man whose gaze Bickerton could not avoid – or at least not for long. That man was Thomas Aris, the prison's governor, and its evil genius. Born in 1744, Aris had followed the family trade and become a baker, opening his own premises at 5 Rosamond Street, Clerkenwell, just a few hundred yards from Coldbath Square. Ambitious and with a large family to support, he clearly wished to expand his business interests because, having already obtained the post of rates collector for his parish of St James, in May 1786 he applied to become supplier of bread to the old house of correction, describing his product as 'the best wheaten bread that can be made'.[30] The appointments committee, being 'satisfied with the character of the said Mr Aris', duly confirmed him as sole provider.

Seven years later, when the Middlesex Justices of the Peace reviewed the candidates for the post of governor of the new house of correction, Aris was among them, claiming that, as baker to the prison, 'he has had constant occasion to see the Prison [...] and thinks himself duly qualified to fill the office'.[31] He further assured them:

> That your Petitioner is fully aware of a rigid attention to cleanliness, Society, good Order, and due Labour in a House of Correction, and knowing how much it is the wish of the Magistrates to see the House of Correction Govern'd strictly according to Law, and their own Institutions, Solemnly pledges himself, that he will pay the most unremitting regard to those essential points of duty in such an Office [...]

> Your Petitioner begs leave to assure your Worships, that if he should be so happy, to be thought deserving of your Worships' favour, and be appointed, he will to the utmost of his Abilities, by a faithful, diligent, and Humane discharge of the Duties of the Office, endeavour to Deserve the Confidence reposed in him.[32]

He was also able to support his application with a glowing testimonial from the Governors of the Finsbury Dispensary who, with 'great Chearfulness', opined that Aris was:

> ... highly qualified to fill such Situation of Keeper, the said Governors having had an opportunity of judging fully of the character and abilities of the said Thomas Aris from the Institution of this Charity in the Year 1780 to the present period, during which time (now more than 13 years) he has been their Collector and Conducted himself with Fidelity, Honesty and Zeal.[33]

In selecting the erstwhile baker and confirming his annual salary of £300, presumably none of the members of the board of magistrates recalled that, two decades earlier, this same Thomas Aris had stood before them charged with having assaulted one Thomas Stone.[34] Given Aris' subsequent career, one might wonder whether justice had been served when he was found 'not guilty'.

The extent of Aris' mismanagement of the prison – and of his personal brutality – first came to light in 1798 when Sir Francis Burdett, Member of Parliament for Boroughbridge, and John Courtney, Member for Appleby, took up the cases of the sailors arrested and imprisoned after the mutiny at the Nore in May of the previous year, and of the radical campaigner Colonel Edward Despard. A scion of the Anglo-Irish ascendancy, a soldier who had served with distinction during the American War of Independence and a friend of Horatio Nelson, Despard had been arrested in March 1798 and detained under the terms of the Habeas Corpus Suspension Act (1794) because of his membership of the London Corresponding Society, an association seeking radical reform of Parliament, and his close connection with members of the insurrectionist United Irishmen movement.

Burdett and Courtney made the first of three visits to Coldbath Fields on 28 November, and they were disgusted by what they found. Courtney was the first to raise the issue of prisoner mistreatment in Parliament, telling the House on 21 December:

> Among the prisoners at Cold Bath Fields I saw [...] an officer distinguished in the Service and amiable in his character and manners – I mean Colonel Despard. He was confined till November 25 in a solitary cell, where even his wife was not allowed to visit him [...] These cells are so cold that at this season of the year it is scarcely possible to exist in them. The cold may in some degree be tempered by closing the wooden shutters; but if the unhappy prisoner wishes to be cheered by the air and the light of Heaven, he must admit the rain and the chilling blasts of winter at the same time [...] It is scarcely necessary to inform the House that the prison of which I have been speaking is that which is commonly called the Bastile [sic].[35]

The government's response was to forbid Burdett from continuing his visits because they adversely affected 'the Discipline and good Government of the Prison', and to instruct the supervising magistrates 'to make due enquiry into all the circumstances of the case'.[36] Not surprisingly, given that Burdett had accused them of gross negligence, the magistrates' report published on 5 March 1799 was a whitewash. William Mainwaring, one of their number as well as being MP for Middlesex, asserted in the House that Aris was a man 'remarkable for humanity'[37] and went on to publish a pamphlet in which he sought to ridicule the criticisms made of the prison and, by implication, Burdett and his supporters as well.

Visitors other than the honourable Member for Boroughbridge, Mainwaring declared, 'could not supress their astonishment at finding the prison in a state of such perfect health' and 'so perfectly inoffensive, so clean and so full of comfort'. If the magistrates of Middlesex had erred, he went on, it was for 'having done too much [...] for the benefit and comfort of the prisoners'.[38]

To further undermine Burdett, the government instructed a Select Committee to investigate the conditions in Coldbath Fields – the chairman of the committee being, by a convenient fluke, William Dundas, a kinsman of the Duke of Portland, the Home Secretary. Again, the prison's conditions were found to be more than adequate, with the cells 'dry and airy' and the health of the prisoners 'generally good'. As for Mainwaring and his colleagues, they could only be applauded for their 'laudable vigilance'.[39]

Burdett refused to be cowed, and over the course of the following months he gathered more and more compelling evidence of prisoner mistreatment – and, crucially, he ensured that his own findings were supported by the impartial testimony of a multitude of independent witnesses. In June 1800, he brought to Parliament's attention an inspection of Coldbath Fields made the previous month by the jury in a case of attempted rape. The jurymen had been horrified by the condition of the chief witness for the prosecution, the 14-year-old Mary Rich, who had been held at the house of correction prior to the trial of the man she accused and who had been so weakened by her month of confinement that she had been rendered practically incapable of sitting upright in a chair.

On questioning the child, they learned that she had been kept for four weeks 'without any allowance but bread and water to support her'.[40] Determined to get to the bottom of the matter and fearing that 'some misinformation' might be given by Aris and the prison doctor when interviewed, the jury decided to visit the prison themselves. Their subsequent report was not, perhaps, as damning as some might have anticipated. Indeed, 'from the cleanliness and good order preserved there', they considered it the 'best conducted prison we ever saw, for prisoners after conviction, the article of bedding alone excepted'.[41] For those imprisoned prior to conviction, on the other hand, they thought 'directly the contrary, inasmuch as no provision is made for them, but bread and water, and the difficulty, if not the impossibility, of obtaining admission for their friends to see them, renders it a melancholy and dangerous situation'.[42]

In fact, by sending individuals like Mary Rich and Bickerton to the house of correction, the Middlesex magistrates were in direct contravention of the 'Orders for Magistrates' of December 1799, which instructed Richard Ford and his colleagues 'not to send to the House of Correction in Coldbath Fields, any prisoners committed for re-examination'.[43] The reasons for this restriction were clear: the house of correction had been 'fitted up, arranged, and regulated uniformly as a Prison of Punishment',[44] making it wholly inappropriate as a place of detention for those convicted of no offence. 'So necessarily does this conclusion appear to us,' wrote inspecting commissioners in 1806, 'that we are led to apprehend, that those Magistrates who have acted contrary to it may have neglected to inspect, or otherwise to inform themselves of the real situation in which prisoners are placed by their commitments'.[45]

At the end of May 1800 another inspection was made, this time by the members of the Traverse Jury for Clerkenwell, a body intended specifically to determine questions of fact and, in this case, charged with reviewing the accusations made against Aris and the responsible magistrates. The prisoners first interviewed on this occasion were the sailors who had mutinied in May 1797. Finding that the mutineers dreaded the 'severity of the Governor in case he should know they made any complaint',[46] the jurors ordered the turnkeys out of the room before they began their questioning. Assured of the court's protection, the sailors stated that their allowance of food 'was not sufficient to support human nature; and they declared their suffering by cold during the winter was severe to the extreme; and many of them said, they had scarcely a bit of shoe leather to their feet'.[47] Proceeding to the cells, the jurors found a sick man named Jones lying on the floor with his head wrapped in a handkerchief. When asked the cause of his injury, he replied, 'cruel treatment', and went on to describe how he had been struck about the head by a turnkey wielding a heavy bunch of keys, 'which must have proved fatal if part of the keys had not hit against the wall'. The following morning Jones had again been attacked, but this time by Governor Aris himself:

> The Governor came up and beat him with a stick till he broke it to pieces; then he renewed the assault with his fists, and beat him in a cruel manner; after which, he took him to the yard and loaded him with irons, which were not taken off his limbs for several months after. And Jones declared to us that he never enjoyed an hour's health since he was so inhumanly beat by the Governor.[48]

As the tour of inspection continued, the jurors met many more half-starved prisoners, 'worn out by wretchedness and disease', ignored by the prison doctor and living on nothing but a small allowance of bread and some 'very poor broth'. A later inspection would reveal, too, that the bread the prisoners did receive was 'greatly deficient in point of quality [...] and, moreover, that the scales of the said prison were false and fraudulent',[49] indicating that Aris' experience as a baker continued to serve him well during his time as a prison governor.

Given the suffering they had witnessed, the jurors were surprised by – and increasingly suspicious of – the prison's apparent cleanliness. To investigate further, they visited again on 4 June, this time choosing to inspect the area inhabited by debtors, vagrants and paupers. 'That place,' they later reported, 'exhibited a *true picture of wretchedness, disgraceful to humanity.*'[50] In a corner of the first room reserved for debtors, they met a poor man 'with scarcely a rag to cover him'. The foreman of the jury, 'anxious to ascertain the real situation of the prisoners', approached the man, 'but was so overcome by the disagreeable stench of the place that he could hardly retire without fainting'.

Next, they proceeded to the wards occupied by those detained under the Vagrant Act. Here they discovered more scenes of abject misery: prisoners, emaciated, filthy and semi-naked, living on just a pound of bread and water per day, sleeping on an insufficient number of poor threadbare mattresses, and some of them 'tortured with vermin, which they caught from the filth of the place'. Not everyone suffered the same degree of neglect, however. The state prisoners – those held for trial on charges of treason or sedition – had generally fared better, but even they complained of shortages of food and of the rapacious behaviour of the turnkeys.

Astonishingly, despite the mass of evidence collected and presented by Burdett and others, Aris continued to enjoy the support of the magistrates and the government. He spoke freely of Burdett as a 'damned rascal'[51] and, when prosecuted in May 1801 for having mistreated a prisoner named Heron, he obtained sufficient support from the Middlesex magistrates to convince the court that 'there was no just imputation whatever on the conduct of Aris, either for his general government of the prison, or his treatment of this particular person'.[52] Of course, it helped that the judge in the case was Lord Kenyon, a strong supporter of the Tory administration, who went on to call the prosecution 'shameful in all its parts'.[53]

Protected by the magistracy and the government alike, Aris became so confident in his immunity that he even accused William Dickie, the foreman of the Traverse Jury, of slander and succeeded in having him arrested and imprisoned subject to payment of damages totalling an extraordinary £700.* The damages would never be paid, and the unfortunate Dickie died on 24 September 1808 after nearly five years in the Fleet Prison, leaving 'a distressed widow and four children still to lament his unfortunate offence and unhappy death'.[54]

In the event, it was not Aris' brutality but his corruption that brought about his downfall. In August 1810, the prisoners in Coldbath Fields included a man named Robert Roberts, an individual ostensibly of some education and wealth, who was being held prior to trial on the capital charge of forging banknotes – 'the cream of the counterfeit money-trade', according to Kellow Chesney.[55] In the early hours of the 28th, Roberts, with another prisoner named Harper (alias Smith), made their escape, having somehow managed to unlock all the intervening doors and gates before exiting the prison via a new lodge then under construction.

Unfortunately for the Aris family, a prisoner in a cell next to Roberts' had overheard a number of conversations between Roberts and Daniel Aris, the governor's son, which implicated the latter in the escape. Clearly, Thomas Aris had no more endeared himself to his staff than to the inmates because, during a number of examinations by the magistrates, which took place both before and after Roberts' recapture after a month on the run, turnkeys as well as prisoners lined up to give damning evidence against him and his sons.

Amos, a turnkey who was also Aris' son-in-law, stated that the younger Aris 'used to walk in the garden with Roberts, and he was a good deal with him [...] There was no other prisoner permitted the indulgence of walking in the garden but Roberts, and the Governor knew of these favours'.[56] For his part, Paull, one of the prison's watchmen, deposed that 'Governor Aris frequently conversed with Roberts,

---

* Roughly £79,000 today.

and he went out in his [Roberts'] chaise on the 18th of August'. Paull then went on to assert – irrelevantly, perhaps, but damningly – that two more of Aris' sons, Thomas and Charles, were nominally employed by the governor, 'the latter of whom had 23*s* a week, but he had not done any duty in the prison for two years'.

During the hearings, the thuggish Daniel Aris – an amateur boxer and of 'considerable note as a setter-to'[57] – did little to attract sympathy, 'biting his lip, and alternately boxing the palm of his hand with his fist',[58] until he was reprimanded for his indecorous behaviour. Nor did his father, once the darling of the Middlesex magistrates, obtain a more lenient hearing. One magistrate accused him of 'supineness',[59] and even Mainwaring, once Aris' most outspoken champion, called his behaviour 'shameful'. When Aris replied that 'he had never done an act in his life of which he was ashamed', another of his inquisitors took the opportunity to express his belief that 'Aris never did feel shame'.[60]

At the end of the proceedings, the chief magistrate informed Daniel Aris that he would be committed 'for feloniously aiding and abetting in the escape of Roberts and Harper' – a capital offence – and the amateur pugilist was taken away in chains. As for Aris senior, at the very least, he had been found neglectful of his duties and was further suspected of complicity in the jailbreak. In the circumstances, there could be no alternative to immediate dismissal.

Bewildered by the swiftness of his fall, Aris continued to petition the magistrates, pleading:

After devoting the last seventeen years of my life to the superintendence of the House of Correction [...] and conscientiously discharging the duty of Governor of that prison, I find myself removed from my situation at 66 years of age, which renders me incapable of obtaining other employment, without any charge having been made against me, or even [being] heard in my own defence [...]

Nor had I, on this trying occasion, the advice or consolation of a friend; for those who before treated me with kindness and attention, were the first to desert me without a cause [...]

I do most respectfully appeal to your justice and humanity for that protection and support, which I humbly conceive I am entitled to, upon this occasion; and I beg to assure you, that should I be restored again to the situation of Governor of the House of Correction, I will, by the most assiduous and unremitting attention to the duties of the office, endeavour to prove myself once more worthy of the confidence which was heretofore reposed in me.[61]

But the magistrates remained unmoved by Aris' eloquence and on 22 November they appointed as his replacement William Adkin, a Bow Street Runner.

Three years later, Aris found himself a witness at the Old Bailey where a young woman named Sarah Evans was on trial for her life, the indictment against her being that she 'not having the fear of God before her eyes, but being moved and seduced by the instigation of the Devil', had drowned her illegitimate 4-year-old son, George, in the New River, near Sadler's Wells.[62] Initially, Evans denied that the badly decomposed body was that of her child, insisting that he had been placed in the St Pancras Workhouse. Under sustained questioning, however, and in fear for her life, she eventually admitted that the boy was hers – and that its father was Thomas Aris. She went on to assert that her earlier lies were the result of 'the threats of Mr. Aris' and that he 'has threatened to shoot me three times'.

Gradually, her whole story tumbled forth: she had first met Aris some years earlier, when she was a prisoner in Coldbath Fields. On her release, he had employed her as a chambermaid and had fathered five of her children, whom he had supported with irregular subsidies. Having lost his post as governor, and in straitened circumstances – so straitened, indeed, that he was then a prisoner in the King's Bench Debtors' Prison and allowed out only on Sundays – he could no longer afford the children's upkeep. The solution to this problem, he had told Evans, was to send the boy into Buckinghamshire to live with his sister-in-law.

In compliance with his instructions, on 21 February in Gray's Inn Lane, Evans had delivered the boy into the hands of a woman sent by Aris. She had not seen the child again until his body was fished out of the New River on 14 March, a ligature made from a handkerchief around his neck and his body weighed down with half a brick. After the discovery, Aris had again spoken with her and had coached her in the story she was to tell if questioned:

I was to say that I had sent him to my own relations in the country. He said, if ever I told any person that he had taken the child he would surely be the death of me; and so he certainly would. He had threatened me many times.[63]

It was these threats, and Evans' conviction that Aris would carry them out, that had made her lie, 'and that only'.

When called to the witness box, Aris acknowledged that George Evans was his son – or at least that Sarah Evans had named him as the father. At first, he denied meeting the child more than once, when it had been in its mother's company, but then acknowledged that he had seen the boy 'half a dozen times'. He claimed to have been astonished when he read of the drowning in a newspaper, 'I think it was the *Daily Advertiser*, and seeing Sarah Evans in the paper, it struck me, good God, it cannot be this woman that I have known'.[64]

Under examination, he admitted that since his dismissal from Coldbath Fields he had been in want of money and he had been obliged to support eleven children, including at least three of Evans' – though he piously declared, 'I do not call it a burthen'. He also reminded the court that he was 'not under recognisance to appear' and that he 'came here voluntary today'. However, when questioned about the handkerchief, which Evans had sworn was one in his possession, his self-assurance began to slip. 'I never,' he declared, 'in all my existence, was possessed of such a handkerchief as that [...] I will swear it five hundred times.'[65] Finally, when asked whether he had met Evans, as she claimed, on Sunday, 21 February, Aris replied, 'Never [...] I passed that day with my family [...] It is my practice never to go out on Sundays'.

The next witness to be called was a Mrs Simpson who, herself a prisoner of the King's Bench, had washed clothes for Aris. Simpson had laundered a number of handkerchiefs for the ex-governor and had no hesitation in identifying the one that had been tied around the child's neck as belonging to him.

Simpson was followed by a policeman named John Matthews, who, when asked whether he ever saw Aris out on a Sunday, flatly contradicted Aris' earlier statement, replying, 'I did, about a quarter or ten minutes before ten in the morning. I spoke to him. It was about a month or six weeks before this affair [the discovery of the body] happened.'

And there, perhaps surprisingly, the matter ended. Evans, whom a number of witnesses described as a loving mother, was found 'not guilty', but there is no record of Aris having been charged with any crime. As the case was heard first by the Middlesex magistrates before being sent to the Old Bailey, some at least of Aris' erstwhile employers would have been aware of the case. Given its outcome and the suspicion thrown onto the ex-governor, they must surely have breathed a sigh of relief that they had not decided to give him a second chance three years earlier.

Aris' last appearance in the public records occurred on 20 April 1840 when *The Times* reported, 'Thomas Aris, who is nearly in the 100th year of his age, and was formerly governor of Coldbath-fields Prison' was listed as one of 168 persons, all of them 'descended from comparative affluence', receiving Gate Alms of 13*s* from the young Queen Victoria.

This, then, was the man to whose tender mercies the crazed and unworldly Bickerton had been consigned. With prison discipline reduced to little more than arbitrary brutality, with drunkenness and immorality rife, with prisoners herded into squalid dormitories or into three-man cells of just 6ft by 8ft, and with the entire prison system revolving on the principle that the strong should prey upon the weak, what possible chance could he have in such an environment?

Sir Richard Ford had ordered that 'proper care' should be taken of Bickerton until more suitable accommodation could be found – by which he presumably meant space in a private madhouse – but there seems very little reason to hope that he benefited from treatment any more humane than that meted out to the rest of the prison population. After all, he was caught in a system that made absolutely no provision for such care. In fact, the conditions in Coldbath Fields were more likely to send a man mad, as had been the case with a French nobleman, the Chevalier Charles de Blin, who served as aide-de-camp to the royalist General Dumouriez, then resident in England, but who was suspected of spying for Napoleon and who was 'deprived of his reason' while in Aris' care.[66] Homesick and melancholic, unable to speak English and prevented from communicating with other French-speakers, de Blin 'began to show the symptoms of insanity, and attempted to get over the wall which separates this yard from the female prisoners, throwing his money, linen, clothes and provisions over that wall'.[67] With his condition deteriorating, de Blin was eventually transferred from Coldbath Fields to St Luke's Hospital for incurable lunatics.

The cases of Mary Rich, the injured party in a rape case and the key prosecution witness, and of Colonel Despard, held on remand, prove beyond a shadow of doubt that innocence and presumed innocence offered no protection from abuse. Moreover, while commissioners who inspected the prison in 1806 asserted their belief that prisoners like Bickerton, who had been committed for re-examination, were 'entitled to every humane and every liberal attention which is consistent with their safe custody', the reality could not have been more different:

> No particular yard, room, or even division of cells, is appropriated to them [...] they have no access to fire, are kept in irons as sent by the committing Magistrate, have no other bedding than the ordinary prison allowance, and are not always separately accommodated with that. If they have money, it is generally proposed to them to have the better bedding, for the use of which they pay one shilling per night. They have no other allowance than a pound of bread per day, and if they enter the prison after the hour of delivery of bread in the morning, they have not this portion till the ensuing day.[68]

In reality then, if Bickerton did experience any amelioration in the conditions of his internment, that amelioration would almost certainly have found its cause not in the injunctions of the magistrate but in the contents of his own purse.

Although George Chesterton noted that the size of the prison meant that its 'numerous occupants were as diversified in disposition and pursuits, as were their features and stature' and its inmates often included 'some men of education, and erst of respectability',[69] background and education amounted to very little. Instead, status and treatment depended almost wholly upon ready cash. Even the biased commissioners appointed by the Duke of Portland to enquire into conditions at the prison had conceded that Aris 'has been sometimes tempted beyond what he has had fortitude to resist'.[70] Chesterton put it more bluntly, claiming that the 'first question addressed to a prisoner on his arrival, was, "had he money, or aught convertible into money, or would any friend, if apprised of its utility, supply him with money?"'.[71] If the answer to this all important question was 'yes', then the prisoner might be protected, to some degree, from the worst excesses of gaol life. But that protection would last only as long as his cash, and with spoliation and trickery everywhere, he would soon find himself reduced to dire straits, the weakest being defrauded even of their daily ration of bread.[72]

Fortunately for Bickerton, the size of the metropolitan area covered by the Middlesex Sessions was so large and the work it dealt with so voluminous that its magistrates met eight rather than four times every year. In theory, this meant that no prisoner should have to wait more than about six weeks to have his case heard by the magistrates at Thomas Rogers' classical Sessions House on Clerkenwell Green. Unfortunately, as the case of Mary Rich had demonstrated, six weeks in the Coldbath Fields House of Correction could seem a very long time indeed, even for those whom the law knew to be guiltless of any misdemeanour.

6

Lunatic?

In determining whether Bickerton should be further detained, and if so, where, the three magistrates of the Middlesex Quarter Sessions must first decide whether or not he was mad. According to the eminent medical historian Roy Porter, during the whole of the eighteenth century only two Acts of Parliament were passed that dealt specifically – though not exclusively – with the policing of the mad.[1] The Vagrancy Act of 1714 authorised two or more magistrates to arrest any person considered to be 'furiously Mad and dangerous' and to confine him 'locked up or chained […] for and during such time only as such Lunacy or Madness shall continue'.[2] The costs involved in such detention would be paid for 'out of the estate of such person if such person hath an estate to pay and satisfy the same over and above what shall be sufficient to maintain his wife and children if he hath any'.[3] As for dangerous lunatics not possessed of an estate, their costs would be met by the parish authorities. The provisions of the new Vagrancy Act, passed in 1744, developed the definition of the furiously mad to include 'those who by Lunacy or otherwise are so far disordered in their Senses that they may be dangerous to be permitted to go Abroad'.[4]

In 1800, in the aftermath of James Hadfield's attempt on the king's life, an additional law – the Criminal Lunatics Act – had been passed, dealing specifically with individuals charged with high treason, murder or felony but who had been found not guilty by reason of insanity. Crucially, it went much further than the previous Acts in that it instructed that such individuals 'be kept in strict custody, in such place and in such manner as to the court shall seem fit, until His Majesty's pleasure shall be known'[5] – and not just while they remained 'furiously Mad and dangerous'. It went further still, retrospectively authorising the continued incarceration of anyone who had been acquitted of such offences on the grounds of insanity *prior* to the passing of the Act – and by doing so, belatedly legalised the extrajudicial detention of George III's would-be assassin Margaret Nicholson, who had been held in the Bethlem Hospital since her arrest in 1786, and who would, as a consequence of the Act, remain there until her death in 1828.

British law certainly did *not* require that every individual categorised as insane should be brought under its control. In fact, the only non-criminal lunatics with whom it concerned itself were those who had the additional misfortune of being paupers. These were the sole responsibility of the guardians or other local authorities charged with the administration of relief to the poor.

By the terms of the Vagrancy Act of 1714, the destitute insane were placed in the same category as vagrants, vagabonds, rogues, beggars, gypsies, mountebanks and players – with one important exception: though liable to arrest and subject to being chained, the insane were not to be whipped. A final piece of legislation, the County Asylums Act of 1808 allowed – but did not compel – local justices of the peace to establish mental asylums to care for pauper lunatics, always supposing that they had both the will and the funds to do so. Until its passing, the fate of such paupers was to be immured in prisons or workhouses, which possessed neither the staff nor the facilities to care for them properly and where, according to the Bill's proposer, Charles Williams-Wynn, the MP for Montgomeryshire, 'they were precluded from all possible chance of recovery [... and] doomed to irremediable misery'.[6]

If then, as seems probable, the magistrates of the Middlesex Quarter Sessions agreed with Sir Richard Ford that Bickerton was deranged, they had a clear legal framework in which to operate. Given that the Acts of 1714 and 1744 referred specifically – and exclusively – to lunatics whose behaviour suggested that they posed a risk to others, and the Act of 1800 allowed for potentially perpetual detention, but only in those cases where an insane person had committed treason, murder or a felony, the next questions for the magistrates were first, whether his madness posed a threat to the safety of others, and second, whether by seeking admittance to the king's levee armed with a sword but not threatening to use it he had committed a felony. In the cases of violent and dangerous madness or commission of a felony while mad, he might be detained legally – but not otherwise.

Finally, if mad but neither dangerous nor guilty of a felony, was Bickerton a pauper? If not, he would be classed as a 'private lunatic', meaning someone with sufficient funds to support himself. The law took no interest in private lunatics unless, or until, they became dangerous to others. Instead, it left them to take care of themselves or to be taken care of by their relatives or friends.[7] In practice, for those whose families could afford it, this meant being placed in a private asylum or 'madhouse'.

The eighteenth century had witnessed a proliferation of private and completely unregulated madhouses and, inevitably, the care taken of patients varied enormously. At one end of the spectrum lay asylums run by competent physicians and 'mad doctors' with a particular interest in the study and cure of mental illness or by philanthropists concerned with the alleviation of the conditions in which the mad were kept. At the other were wretched hubs of neglect, cruelty and squalor. Some, then, were 'running sores of scandal', others, 'sites of therapeutic innovation'.[8]

All had one characteristic in common, however – they were discreet facilities where, as one typical advertisement assured the potential clientele among its readers, the 'most minute secrecy will be observed'.[9] In other words, these were places in which families fearing the taint of madness could hide their afflicted sons, daughters, wives or husbands. Afflicted or inconvenient, as Daniel Defoe pointed out in a tirade against those asylums where the palpably sane – specifically unwanted, disobedient or wilful women – were incarcerated at the behest of their designing and unscrupulous relatives, so that the latter 'may be more secure and undisturb'd in their Debaucheries'.[10] According to Defoe, this 'wicked Custom' had become so prevalent that it alone had caused the substantial rise in the number of private asylums, which – as early as 1731 – he believed to have 'considerably increased within these few Years'.

So little did matters improve over the course of the century that, eighty-four years later, in 1815, another reformer, the asylum-keeper

Thomas Bakewell, would make very similar accusations and contend that, all too often, brutal treatment of the insane resulted from the same mercenary motives, arising 'in general out of the absolute and uncontrollable power which relations may exercise over them [...] the means of recovery being delayed for the purposes of concealment, or prevented for the sake of possessing the property'.[11] If such unfortunates were not insane when they entered the asylums, argued Defoe, 'they are soon made so by the barbarous Usage they there suffer'.

A second characteristic – common, but not shared by every asylum – was that they were small, the majority housing no more than a dozen patients, almost invariably in what had begun as the private residence of the madhouse keeper. 'Thus,' writes Porter, 'the large private asylum was highly exceptional. Up to the end of the [eighteenth] century there were perhaps no more than three in the whole country, all huddled just beyond the City of London.'[12]

Private madhouses were an inevitable consequence of the poor and limited provision made at a county level, particularly as those asylums that were available were designed specifically for pauper lunatics, rather than for the deranged scions of the middle and upper classes. And there were offerings to suit every pocket, from a 'Young Man, who has been in the habit of attending upon Insane Gentlemen' offering to undertake the care – or, at least, the supervision – of 'One Gentleman'[13] at one end of the scale, to Dr Herdman's elaborate Edinburgh establishment, 'furnished with every requisite that can render it adapted for the cure or alleviation of mental diseases', including a 'delightfully and healthfully situated' villa and landscaped pleasure grounds, at the other.[14] Whatever their size, however, throughout much of the eighteenth century none of the private madhouses was subjected to meaningful regulation or scrutiny, with the result that abuses were commonplace.

In January 1763, an article in *The Gentleman's Magazine* drew attention to the 'many unlawful, arbitrary, cruel, and oppressive acts, which for some years past have been committed in places, generally called Private Mad Houses',[15] but the article writer and a Select Committee of the same year concerned themselves exclusively with the issue of the unlawful confinement of the sane in such institutions, and while the preparation of a Bill was ordered, no such Bill was brought before Parliament.

The broader issue of madhouse supervision was raised a decade later by Thomas Townshend, MP for Whitchurch, this time with more success. In 1773, he sponsored the Madhouses Bill which, despite some opposition in the House of Lords, received Royal Assent in May the following year. The Act's key provisions included requirements for all private madhouses to hold a licence issued by a special committee of the Royal College of Physicians, and for mandatory annual inspections by the same committee within London and by magistrates of the local Quarter Sessions for those outside the capital. Lastly, severe financial penalties were introduced for non-compliance with the licensing rules and for holding any patient without the appropriate order from a doctor.

But abuses continued. Indeed, it was the firm belief of George Rose, MP for Christchurch, that they remained both shocking and widespread. On 5 April 1814, he sought the House of Commons' permission to bring in a new Bill on the subject on the basis that the Act of 1774 'was now found to be very inadequate to prevent the evil':

> As a proof of this, he had a statement in his hand, concerning the situation of persons confined in some of these houses. In one instance, the apartments allotted for persons confined were found to be cells on the ground floor, nine feet long and five broad, the walls of which, as well as the ground, were wet with damp. The whole furniture consisted of a box containing some straw or blankets by way of a bed. The Act required the certificate of a surgeon, amongst others, before a person could be received into a private madhouse. There were actually cases in which it was found that the surgeon's certificate was signed by the keeper of the house.[16]

Just as had been the case in the campaign for prison reform in the 1770s, it was the evidence gathered by a private reformer, in this case a Quaker land agent named Edward Wakefield, that proved most compelling when published in the report of a Select Committee appointed 'to consider of provision being made for the better regulation of madhouses in England'. In the autumn of 1814, in company with fellow reformers Francis Place,

William Allen and James Mill, Wakefield had begun an entirely voluntary and self-funded tour of private madhouses – almost certainly being inspired to do so by the periodic mental illness of his mother, the writer and proto-feminist Priscilla Wakefield, who spent time in the Whitmore asylum owned and operated by Thomas Warburton, a madhouse keeper who, in the years to come, would become notorious for his ill treatment of the pauper lunatics placed in his care by parish authorities.

In his testimony to the Select Committee, Wakefield painted a very mixed picture of the conditions in which the mad were kept and of the treatment they received. Speaking, for instance, of Norman House in Fulham, a house run by Edward and Anne Talfourd, who would later care for the writer Mary Lamb during at least one of her bouts of violent insanity, Wakefield reported that he found in it:

> ... fourteen ladies, all of whom I saw, and was delighted with the manner in which they were treated, and with the degree of happiness which they appeared to enjoy; I remained with them nearly two hours; conversed with every individual; and could not find, that either hand-locks or leg-locks were ever used [...] I think it difficult to speak too highly of Norman House generally [...] there was the greatest kindness towards the patients.[17]

London House in Hackney, kept by Samuel Fox, a Member of the Royal College of Surgeons, he also thought 'admirably conducted', with men and women as well as violent and placid patients 'kept distinct and separate'. A trade card for this house claimed that its inmates 'are introduced to an agreeable family society; which is found in a great degree to dissipate the gloom and melancholy that pervades their Hours, when confined in dreary solitude',[18] and Wakefield learned that the house lived up to its advertising, with 'one lady, who conceived herself to be Mary Queen of Scots' acting 'as preceptress to Mrs Fox's little children'.[19]

Wakefield also took pains to emphasise to the committee that 'there is great merit due to many individuals for the humanity which they exercise to the unfortunate persons under their care' and that he would be 'very much hurt, if any observation that I made in any place should tend to injure the character of the business of a keeper of a Madhouse'.[20] No doubt he made these statements in part to recognise the commendable efforts that he saw being made in some of the houses he inspected – but, surely, also to ensure that he might not so offend madhouse keepers that they would forbid his visits in the future and thereby prevent his continuing to expose the vile abuses that he witnessed in so many.

For, if Norman House and London House stood as glowing examples at one end of the scale in terms of care and facilities, at the other things were very different. At a house in Hoxton, owned by Sir Jonathan Miles, Wakefield was refused admittance on the grounds, the keeper told him, 'that an inspection […] would be signing its death-warrant'.[21] And yet this was a house to which the insane of the Royal Navy, both officers and men, were sent despite outright condemnation of the prevailing conditions by both the Inspector of Naval Hospitals John Weir and John Veitch, Staff Surgeon of the Royal Navy.

The house contained 484 patients and in his evidence to the committee, Weir described how he found officers and men indiscriminately lodged with civilians of various ranks in life; the rooms they inhabited were overcrowded and in one instance, two men were forced to sleep in the same cot, despite the fact that one was wholly incontinent and the other 'cleanly in his habits'.[22] The most senior commissioned officer among the lunatics, a Captain Evans, he thought 'in a very critical state of health, much emaciated, and unless some sudden alteration should take place, he cannot live many months; the result, I conceive, of confinement and improper management'.[23]

For his part, Veitch thought the accommodation 'exceedingly bad; very ill calculated to give that bodily and mental relief, which is essentially necessary for the comfort and recovery of insane people',[24] and yet, despite these complaints, the madhouse at Hoxton would continue to receive the insane of the Royal Navy for many years to come. As an alderman of the City of London, Miles' influence was simply too strong to be easily overcome.

In Kingsland, where, in its more bucolic days, a youthful Samuel Pepys had once 'shot with my bow and arrows',[25] Wakefield visited a hovel where he discovered four patients confined to their beds in rooms 'without any ventilation, and almost more offensive than anything I ever put my head into'; at least one patient had not left her cot 'for many years'.[26] And at the village of Box, in Wiltshire, he was shown over the 200-year-old asylum, Kingsdown House, by its current proprietor, Charles Cunningham Langworthy, a Bristol surgeon. As well as treating wealthy patients from fashionable Bath and running a madhouse, Langworthy was a would-be medical entrepreneur who championed (and sold) 'Perkinean Electricity' or the 'Metallic Tractor', a device invented by an American quack named 'Doctor' Perkins, which he claimed could ease or cure – like all quack treatments – an astonishing array of ailments including 'rheumatism, gout, quinsy, pleurisy, tumefactions, scalds, burns',[27] and the effects of which he asserted, without a hint of irony, 'are so extraordinary, that the public cannot be called upon to credit them'.[28]

Unfortunately, Langworthy's supposed medical innovation did not stretch to his care of the insane. In an entirely dark cellar, sleeping in straw, Wakefield discovered women both naked and nearly naked – though Langworthy piously declared that 'in winter he sewed them up in a blanket' – and 'more in similar places making a great noise'. The male patients Wakefield was not permitted to see because, the keeper explained, 'it was not a day that the men were up', thereby indicating that they spent lengthy periods confined to their beds.[29] All in all, Wakefield declared, 'in the course of my visiting these places I never recollect to have seen […] so wretched a place'.[30]

It would be a mistake, though, to think that the conditions to be found in so many private madhouses were the worst to be endured by the deranged. Worse – often far worse – were those experienced by the pauper lunatics in the parish workhouses and the few asylums established for their care. By far the most famous – or notorious – of these was the Bethlem Hospital in Moorfields.

Originally founded in 1247 as the Priory of the New Order of Our Lady of Bethlehem on a site in the parish of St Botolph, Bishopsgate, the earliest indication that the priory housed the insane dates to 150 years later, an inventory of 1398 making reference to 'four pairs of manacles, eleven chains of iron, six locks and keys, and two pair of stocks' – the standard equipment of the madhouse keeper of the time.[31] Five years after that, visiting charity commissioners noted that the priory had in its care '*sex viri mente capti*', or 'six men who have lost their wits'.

From these small beginnings would develop the single largest charitable asylum in the kingdom. Relocated to a magnificent building purposely designed by Robert Hooke and built in Moorfields in 1676, by the end of the eighteenth century the hospital could home well in excess of 200 patients. But, despite its impressive façade, its spacious galleries and its unusually large and well-ventilated cells, the New Bethlem Hospital would become a byword for cruelty and degradation – that reputation being based largely upon the fact that the hospital's governors permitted paying visitors to view, and all too often to taunt, the patients within.

This practice appears to have become well established as early as the turn of the seventeenth century and may have originated much earlier. Certainly, Sir Thomas More, who lived close to the original foundation, noted how one might 'in Bedlam see one laughing at the knocking of his head against a post',[32] though there is no empirical evidence to suggest that More ever stepped inside the asylum.

Whatever date they first obtained entry, idle and curious sightseers could gain access throughout most of the eighteenth century. In his 'A Rake's Progress' of 1732–34, William Hogarth famously depicted fashionably dressed ladies watching Tom Rakewell in the asylum, and in 1753, *The World* reported that crowds of spectators 'were suffered, unattended, to run rioting up and down the wards, making sport and diversion of the miserable inhabitants'.[33]

In 1766, the hospital's court of governors finally decided, in the words of Catharine Arnold, the hospital's most recent historian, 'to close Bethlem to the public view',[34] but even then, it appears that the keepers continued to admit those willing to pay, as John Haslam, who was appointed apothecary to the hospital around 1786, later recalled, 'Within my own recollection Bethlem Hospital gratified the curiosity of the vulgar of both sexes', and noted, 'these visitors were most eager to penetrate into the recesses of the furious and naked maniac'.[35]

Wakefield first visited the Bethlem Hospital on 25 April 1814, and returned frequently over the following months. On this first occasion, in accordance with the regulations introduced following the criticisms of public opening, he went in the company of one of the hospital's governors, Alderman Robert Albion Cox. Unfortunately, according to

Wakefield's evidence, the alderman's feelings were 'overpowered before we had gone over the men's side',[36] and the visit came to an abrupt end.* It was hardly an auspicious start.

He returned on 2 May, this time to view the women's wards. In one side room he observed ten patients, each chained by an arm or leg to the wall, the chain allowing them merely to stand up by a bench fixed to the wall or to sit on it. All wore nothing but a 'blanket-gown', a kind of dressing gown made from coarse blanket material, with no means of fastening it in front; even their feet were bare. Wakefield went on to describe the plight of one particular inmate:

> One female in this side room, thus chained, was an object remarkably striking; she mentioned her maiden and married names, and stated that she had been a teacher of languages; the keepers described her as a very accomplished lady, mistress of many languages, and corroborated her account of herself. The Committee can hardly imagine a human being in a more degraded and brutalizing situation than that in which I found this female, who held a coherent conversation with us, and was of course fully sensible of the mental and bodily condition of those wretched beings, who, equally without clothing, were closely chained to the same wall with herself. Unaware of the necessities of nature, some of them, though they contained life, appeared totally inanimate and unconscious of existence.[37]

Wakefield acknowledged that the time he had spent with the unfortunate Mrs Fenwick did not allow him to form an accurate idea of what might be considered a proper level of restraint, but – in an unconscious echo of Defoe eighty-three years earlier – he unhesitatingly asserted that, in his opinion, 'her confinement with patients in whom she was compelled to witness the most disgusting idiotcy, and the most terrifying distraction of the human intellect, was injudicious and improper'.

---

* In 1824–25, Cox would be held up to very public ridicule after suing the actor Edmund Kean for criminal conversation with his wife. The case was widely caricatured by George Cruikshank and others. Cox was awarded £800 in damages.

Next, Wakefield proceeded to the male wards, where he found conditions much the same, with six patients closely chained to the wall, five being handcuffed and one locked to the wall by both his right hand and right leg. Like the women, all were barefoot and naked, except for the blanket-gowns, and those who could speak coherently complained of the cold. Again, individuals with different levels of mental debility were confined together, some apparently lucid and others 'dreadful idiots'. Overall, Wakefield told the committee, 'their nakedness and their mode of confinement, gave this room the complete appearance of a dog-kennel'.[38] He also observed that none of the cell windows, in either the men's or women's wards, were glazed.

Finally, Wakefield met a patient named James Norris whose condition seemed almost unimaginably deplorable. Enveloped in an extraordinary contraption made of iron bars and chains, Norris was unable to move more than a foot from the wall to which he was attached. 'It was, I conceive,' Wakefield told the committee:

> ... equally out of his power to repose in any other position than on his back, the projections which on each side of the waist bar inclosed [sic] his arms, rendering it impossible for him to lie on his side, even if the length of the chains from his neck and shoulders would permit it. His right leg was chained to the trough; in which he had remained thus encaged and chained more than twelve years.[39]

Norris' confinement was not, in fact, the product of an excess of arbitrary brutality on the part of the hospital's steward, Peter Alavoine, but resulted instead from his fits of extreme violence, during which he had stabbed two men, beaten another with a shovel and bitten off the finger of a fourth.[40] Catharine Arnold argues that while Norris' restraint appears barbaric, in reality it was 'understandable as a means of protecting the staff and other patients in the days before the "chemical cosh"',[41] but the Select Committee and the general public took a very different view at the time, and Norris' case became something of a *cause célèbre*, being widely reported in the newspapers and broadsheets, as well as being depicted by various illustrators. It is interesting to note, too, that John Haslam, the hospital's apothecary, had advocated an altogether different form of control, suggesting that Norris – whom he described as 'the most mischievous patient perhaps that I ever saw'[42] – be given two adjoining rooms, so that he could be confined in one while the other was cleaned and vice versa.

In light of the huge amounts of evidence it had collected – 147 pages in all, from a multitude of witnesses – unsurprisingly, the report of the Select Committee, issued on 11 July 1815, was unequivocal. 'Your Committee cannot,' it informed the House of Commons:

> … hesitate to suggest […] that there are not in the Country a set of Beings more immediately requiring the protection of the Legislature than the persons in this state [of insanity]; a very large proportion of whom are entirely neglected by their relations and friends. If the treatment of those in the middling or in the lower classes of life, shut up in hospitals, private madhouses, or parish workhouses, is looked at, Your Committee are persuaded that a case cannot be found where the necessity for a remedy is more urgent.[43]

In summary, the committee found that the madhouses routinely accepted far more patients than they could adequately accommodate, with the result that they might be considered 'better calculated for the imprisonment than the cure of patients'; the staff-to-patient ratio was almost universally inadequate, leading to patients being unnecessarily restrained; 'offensive' and incontinent patients were all too often mixed with the 'quiet and inoffensive'; medical assistance was limited to corporeal complaints, with little or no attempt to cure the insanity of patients; physical restraint was too frequently resorted to, and extreme in its nature; conditions for the pauper insane were particularly inadequate; despite earlier legislation, some sane individuals were still being confined; the certificate required for committal was not always completed; and programmes of inspection remained defective.

And yet, extraordinarily, even though George Rose's motion to bring in a Bill 'to repeal and render more effectual' the provisions of the 1774 Act was, according to Hansard, waved through the House of Commons 'without opposition',[44] and in spite of the popular revulsion caused by the revelations of the report of the Special Committee of 1815, opposition from various quarters prevented the passing of new legislation for another thirteen years. Some of this opposition was from those with vested interests, who were reluctant to see any greater scrutiny by or powers of enforcement granted to inspectors; but other opponents, including the highly regarded mad doctor and asylum-keeper George Man Burrows, were actuated by a genuine desire to see the draft legislation refined and its 'erroneous principles' amended.[45] Whatever the causes of the delay, however, each of these thirteen years was marked by the publication of yet more 'singular and shocking details'[46] in the newly instigated annual reports on madhouses.

Designed 'more effectually to provide for the care and maintenance of Pauper and Criminal Lunatics in England', the new County Asylums Act would finally become law in 1828. Its provisions required magistrates to send annual records of admissions, discharges and deaths to the Home Office; it allowed the Secretary of State to send a Visiting Justice to any county asylum, although the visitor couldn't intervene in how the asylum was run; and, in order to better facilitate the provisions of the 1808 Act, it granted counties new powers to raise money to build an asylum for the care of pauper lunatics.

In this regard, the Act would be highly successful and in the coming decades, more and more county asylums would open across the country. But, over time, the new asylums would replicate many of the problems of the eighteenth- and early nineteenth-century madhouses and, indeed, generate entirely new problems of their own.

Inevitably, perhaps, asylums remained a depository for those – all too often, and all too predictably, women – who, for whatever reason, failed to comply with society's conventions and expected behaviours. As the number of patients increased, it became increasingly difficult to deliver any form of personalised treatment in the overcrowded and understaffed wards, and close confinement, straitjackets and padded cells were resorted to with increasing frequency. With insufficient investment to maintain them, the built infrastructure of the hospitals began to decay and crumble, the ambitions of men like Edward Wakefield and George Rose dying in dank corridors and cells not unlike those they had sought to abolish. These, though, would be the challenges and ultimate failures of the Victorian rather than the Georgian age.

Poor Bickerton

After more than two centuries, it is impossible – or at least foolhardy – to attempt a retrospective clinical diagnosis of Bickerton's mental illness. However, it is perhaps feasible to determine how it might have been viewed by the physicians and, even more importantly, by the magistrates of his day.

At the turn of the nineteenth century, specialists still divided insanity into two broad categories – mania and melancholy – though it was understood that these seemingly very different manifestations of derangement were closely related and an individual exhibiting the signs of melancholy madness might well become manic, and vice versa. Moreover, within these divisions lay a plethora of often quite different forms of insanity, including monomania, theomania, demonomania, erotomania, suicide, lycanthropia, panaphobia and zoanthropia, to name but a few. Citing his many years' experience in treating the insane, as well as numerous authorities ancient and modern, George Man Burrows further asserted:

> Mental derangement assumes, successively and alternately, every possible form; that not only mania and melancholia, but fatuity also, is frequently complicated in the same case. In fact, any one of these mental affections may preserve its peculiar type unaltered for many years, and still be capable of interchanging one with another.[47]

Under the headings of mania and melancholy, then, madness was recognised to be not merely a many-headed Hydra, but also a chameleon capable of changing its form and symptoms at any moment. To complicate matters still further, the mad could experience periods of remission when their behaviour became, to all intents and purposes, entirely normal.

Despite reputational damage and financial ruin following his dismissal from his post as apothecary to Bethlem Hospital in the wake of the scandals of 1815–16, Dr John Haslam would become a respected and quite prolific writer on insanity, medical jurisprudence and on the reform of the treatment of the insane. In his *Observations on Madness and Melancholy*, he noted:

> Madmen do not always continue in the same furious or depressed states: the maniacal paroxysm abates of its violence, and some beams of hope, occasionally cheer the despondency of the melancholic patients [...] they conduct themselves with propriety, and in a short conversation will appear sensible and coherent.[48]

Although such periods of remission had been 'generally termed a *lucid interval*', Haslam disagreed with this application of the phrase because such *apparent* lucidity might simply mask the underlying malaise. 'Even in common society,' he observed, 'there are many persons whom we never suspect [...] to be shallow minded; but if we start a subject, and wish to discuss it through all its ramifications and dependencies, we find them incapable of pursuing a connected chain of reasoning.'[49] Similarly, a person might appear to be perfectly rational until the subject of their particular maggot was touched upon, at which point they would break out in all the baroque flamboyance of their delusion. On this basis, Haslam opined that a lucid interval would be more properly defined as 'a complete recovery of the patient's intellects, ascertained by repeated examinations of his conversation, and by constant observation of his conduct'.

Unfortunately, as he was at pains to emphasise – and as the illness of George III would illustrate – while a lucid interval might last for weeks, months or even years, unless a genuine cure had been completed, a lucid interval would remain just that – a period of sanity that must be, by its very nature, ephemeral. Madness was, then, a chimera, subtle and ever-changing. 'The most experienced,' wrote Burrows, 'will acknowledge the liability of being deceived, even where frequent opportunities of judging of the sanity of the mind have occurred.'[50] If this were true of expert doctors, what chance would the magistrates of the Quarter Sessions have of accurately determining the state of Bickerton's mind?

Even more significant was the absence of any meaningful legal definition of madness that might act as a signpost for judges, magistrates, lawyers and jurors. 'The information of the lawyer,' Haslam wryly observed, 'is principally deduced from the writings of those great legal authorities to which he refers with confidence; – although these grave authorities have laid down no definition of madness, nor given any directions how to discover it.'[51] The last jurist to attempt a definition had been Sir William Blackstone, author of *Blackstone's Commentaries on the Laws of England*, who would later draft the Penitentiary Act of 1779. Reflecting the ancient but still current belief that many abnormal behaviours including, but not limited to, irrationality, frenzy, alcoholism, epilepsy, somnambulism, suicide, homicide and arson were directly attributable to the phases of the moon, in 1765 Blackstone had described a lunatic, or *non compos mentis*, as:

> One who hath had understanding, but by disease, grief, or other accident hath lost the use of his reason. A lunatic is indeed properly one that hath lucid intervals; sometimes enjoying his senses, and sometimes not, and that frequently depending upon the change of the moon.[52]

But by the early nineteenth century, the law had been largely overtaken by medical science. Dr Francis Willis, grandson and namesake of the clergyman-physician who attended King George in his madness, observed in 1822 that the opinion 'formerly entertained, that persons of disordered intellects are influenced by the moon, and that symptoms of their state are more clearly manifested at the full and quarters of it, than at other periods [...] is now pretty generally exploded'.[53]

And if a legal definition of insanity was proving so elusive, what of the criminal liability of the insane? The seventeenth-century jurist Matthew Hale suggested that 'such a person as labouring under melancholy distempers hath as yet as great understanding as ordinarily a child of 14 hath, is such a person as can be guilty of treason or felony'.[54] But during the century and more since Hale published his 'rule', the courts had shown much uncertainty in its application.

When Edward Arnold was tried in 1723 for the attempted murder of Lord Onslow, whom he accused of torturing him with imps, Justice Robert Tracy instructed the jurymen 'not to fret over' Arnold's obvious derangement, telling them:

> It is not every kind of frantic humour or something unaccountable in a man's actions that points him out to be such a madman as is to be

exempted from punishment: it must be a man that is totally deprived of his understanding and memory, and doth not know what he is doing, no more than an infant, a brute, or a wild beast.⁵⁵

Tracy, then, erred on the side of believing that in spite of his insanity, Arnold retained the ability to make reasoned decisions which led, ultimately, to his attempt on Onslow's life – and his ability to make those decisions rendered his life forfeit. Not surprisingly, given the tenor of Tracy's summing up, Arnold was found guilty, though the death penalty imposed by the judge was later commuted to life imprisonment.

While Tracy's reading of the law aligned fairly closely with Hale's opinions, other judges expressed very different opinions. Seventy-seven years later, in the trial of James Hadfield for his attack on the king at Drury Lane Theatre, Lord Chief Justice Kenyon stopped the trial, advising the jury, 'If a man is in a deranged state of mind at the time, he is not criminally answerable for his acts'.⁵⁶ Although Hadfield – like Arnold before him – had fully understood what he was doing when he fired his pistol at the king, he was found 'not guilty, being under the influence of insanity at the time the act was committed'.⁵⁷

In a final example, at his trial for the murder of Prime Minister Spencer Perceval in 1812, John Bellingham was found guilty and sentenced to death despite clear evidence of his insanity. In summing up, the judge, Sir James Mansfield, told the jury:

> There is a species of insanity where people take particular fancies into their heads who are perfectly sane and sound of mind upon all other subjects; but that is not a species of insanity which can excuse any person who has committed a crime, unless it so affects his mind at a particular period when he commits the crime, as to disable him from distinguishing between good and evil.⁵⁸

There was, then, in the words of the mid-century Lord Chief Justice, John Campbell, 'a wide difference, both in meaning and in words, in [the] description of the law'.⁵⁹

Unlike Arnold, Hadfield and Bellingham, of course, Bickerton was not facing a capital indictment. Nonetheless, the key question facing him when he appeared at the Middlesex Quarter Sessions was how would the magistrates hearing his case interpret the law?

For once in his life, Bickerton seems to have been either lucky or fairly judged. Assuming that the Middlesex magistrates rapidly dismissed the possibility of his being a dangerous, even homicidal, political radical, they must next consider his state of mind. From his own statements to Sir Richard Ford, and from those given at the inquest into his death by those who knew him in his last years, it seems clear that he suffered from a form of persecution mania which left him convinced not only that he had been defrauded by a number of unconnected individuals, but that his very life was under threat. Indeed, it could be argued that he had displayed just those 'glaring exhibitions' and 'caricatures of disease' alluded to by John Haslam in his work *Medical Jurisprudence as it Relates to Insanity*.[60]

However, none of the surviving accounts make any reference to Bickerton raving or threatening or to his having used violence in resisting arrest. Indeed, the nearest indication of his having struggled with the Bow Street officers is the reference in the *St James's Chronicle* to their having 'forced the sword from him'. This being the case, he could not be described as 'furiously mad and dangerous'. Therefore, the provisions of the Acts of 1714 and 1744 did not apply. Nor did those of the newly passed 'Hadfield Act', because while its terms encouraged magistrates to arrest and confine individuals who were thought to be contemplating an offence in the vicinity of the king or of the royal palaces, there was no evidence whatsoever that Bickerton had contemplated such an offence, and the fact that he carried a sword would not, of itself, be sufficient grounds to convict him of a felony. Finally, Bickerton's resources meant that, no matter how deranged he might appear at times, he could not be described accurately as a vagrant or sturdy beggar, meaning that the laws allowing for the detention of such 'nuisances' could not legally be applied to his case.

Taken together, these facts meant that the Middlesex magistrates had no grounds upon which to order his continued confinement. We also know that Bickerton experienced lengthy 'lucid intervals', as is evidenced by his ability to complete his studies at St Edmund Hall and by the details of his career in the years following the incident in St James's

Palace. Perhaps his experiences in Coldbath Fields Prison produced just such an interval in time for his court appearance or, at the very least, a willingness to comply with Ford's request for 'some good security for his future conduct'. In the absence of any official records regarding the period of his confinement, all we can say with any certainty is that Bickerton was still being held 'at His Majesty's pleasure' on 27 October 1803, when Ford wrote to Thomas Stirling, and that, according to the record of future events, he had been released by the beginning of May 1804 at the latest. Thus, his maximum term of imprisonment was some seven and a half months.

Having been judged according to the law of the land and found, if not wholly innocent, then at least not culpable of any crime or misdemeanour, Bickerton's next move would be to the one place, above all others, where he might learn to better understand that very law.

7

Middle Temple to Hertford College

On Thursday, 3 May 1804, seven and a half months after his arrest in St James's Palace, 'JOHN BICKERTON, fourth son of Samuel B., late of Lee Brockhurst, Salop, gent., dead'[1] was admitted as a student member to the Honourable Society of the Middle Temple in central London. At the beginning of the nineteenth century, as now, the four Inns of Court – the Middle Temple, the Inner Temple, Lincoln's Inn and Gray's Inn – formed the hub of England's legal world, being the 'school' in which all barristers were trained, the location of the offices, or chambers, in which they practised and, for many, their home. With the Temple Church, their medieval halls and secluded squares and gardens, they also possessed the atmosphere of a separate, cloistered world within the great bustling city of London – in many respects, not at all unlike the Cambridge and Oxford colleges that Bickerton had left just a few years before.

Charles Lamb, whose father was servant to a barrister of the Inner Temple in the last quarter of the eighteenth century, called the Temple 'the most elegant spot in the metropolis', before going on to imagine the feelings of a stranger passing 'from the crowded Strand or Fleet Street, by unexpected avenues, into its magnificent ample squares, its classic green recesses!'[2] William Thorpe, a barrister practising in the second half of the nineteenth century, described the atmosphere and surroundings of the Middle Temple more specifically:

> On the south a pleasant and historic garden, on the north and west open spaces where the loiterer loves to linger 'mid the greenery of the trees, the shade of their branches, and the cool downfall of the long, straight jet of water [...] Benches are there, in which the idler – but twenty steps removed from the roar of Fleet Street, the tumult of the Strand, and longing to rest his tired eyes upon Nature's graceful curves and lines of beauty [...] can linger, in calm and placid repose of mind, and enjoy at leisure the finest town view in London.[3]

All in all, according to these accounts, it would be difficult to imagine a place contrasting more sharply with the squalid conditions of Coldbath Fields Prison, or one more likely to bring ease to a troubled mind. But not everyone described the Inns in such idyllic terms. William Makepeace Thackeray, who was admitted to the Middle Temple in 1831, wrote in *The History of Pendennis* of its 'dark alleys' and its 'various melancholy archways into courts each more dismal than the other'.[4] He also found the plumbing positively antediluvian, observing that while the 'poorest mechanic in Spitalfields has a cistern and an unbounded supply of water at his command', the residents of the Inns 'have their supply of this cosmetic fetched in jugs by laundresses and bedmakers, and live in abodes which were erected long before the custom of cleanliness and decency obtained among us'.[5]

Thackeray entered the Temple after Bickerton's departure, but the Inns had always been known for their literary men. John Webster, Sir Walter Raleigh, John Evelyn, William Congreve, Henry Fielding, Richard Brinsley Sheridan and Edmund Burke had all been admitted as Middle Templars. Tom Moore, Irish poet and friend of Byron, had left only the year before Bickerton's entry, and his direct contemporaries included Thomas Noon Talfourd, friend and biographer of Charles Lamb, and Thomas de Quincey, essayist and opium-eater. Lamb himself had been born in Crown Office Row in the Inner Temple and in 1804 was living with his sister, Mary, at 16 Mitre Court Buildings, in the shadow of Temple Church. Given Lamb's unerring and well-documented ability to attract eccentric and otherworldly waifs and strays, it is tempting to think that the two men might have met or at the very least been aware of one another. Unfortunately, besides their propinquity, there is no evidence to support such a delightful conjecture.

For Bickerton, admission as a student member of the Middle Temple meant that, at the age of 49, he intended to devote years to a kind of legal apprenticeship, studying in the Temple library with its vast collection of legal books and under the stewardship of whichever barrister saw fit to patronise him. Although 49 seems an extraordinarily advanced age to commence his legal studies, in fact he was not particularly exceptional, as Thackeray tells us that Arthur Pendennis' fellow students included 'gentlemen of all ages, from sixty to seventeen'.[6]

A prerequisite for all students was to obtain a position in the chambers of a practising barrister who would act as mentor and guide but, all too often, having once secured such a place, student members discovered that the indifference or preoccupation of their patron meant that they were obliged to learn through a process of osmosis rather than through the pursuit of a rigidly prescribed curriculum. Ben Jonson called the Inns of Court 'the noblest nurseries of humanity and liberty in the Kingdom',[7] but some student members were altogether less enamoured of the regime.

One such, William Ballantine, who would rise to become a leading practitioner at the Old Bailey, would later state, 'I have little to record of the two years I passed in these chambers amongst a mass of papers, copying precedents of pleading which were a disgrace to common sense, and in gossip with my brother students, most of them as idle as myself'.[8] Thackeray felt even less enthusiastic about his training, describing it to his mother as 'certainly one of the most cold-blooded prejudiced pieces of invention that ever a man was slave to' and overseen by 'old cold calculating codgers'.[9] Depending upon the abilities and conscientiousness of tutor and pupil in equal measure, the training might last anything from a handful of years to decades. Constantly distracted by gambling, high living and literature, it took Thackeray an extraordinary seventeen years to qualify.

When a student member was considered to have completed his studies and to have attended the required number of formal dinners in the Elizabethan hall with its vast hammer beam roof, where he would be expected to participate in learned debates, a final ceremony would take place in which he would receive his call to the Bar. Ballantine recalled his own call thus:

The batch to be 'turned off' were summoned to the bench table. We were each presented with a glass of wine, and a speech was made to us by the treasurer, giving us good advice and wishing us prosperity in our forthcoming career; and so we were launched upon the sea, looking then so calm, but, alas! too often engulfing pitilessly the brightest venture.[10]

Bickerton, though, never received this call – or, if he did, he failed to answer it. Indeed, it is very far from clear how seriously he ever intended to pursue a legal career.

The Middle Temple's supreme body is its Parliament, which is made up of the Benchers (judges and senior barristers), who are elected for life, and headed by a Treasurer, who is elected annually. The Parliament's minutes for 10 November 1809 – a full five and a half years after Bickerton's entry – cast serious doubt on his professional aspirations and suggest that, from the beginning, he was altogether more focused on pursuing his academic interests:

An application being read from Mr Bickerton J., a member of this Society, stating that his friends and old acquaintance being no more, the want of new obliged him to make his case known. He had the privilege of a virtuous parentage in Shropshire and education at Boarding and Grammar Schools and at last at the University of Oxford where he had taken a degree. That his inclination had been most for learning in which he had spent most of his time and never having been in any other way made him desirous to continue in the same the remaining part of his life. That he had been a Member of this Society about five years and a half and whose favour he was now necessitated to solicit in being proposed for the Bar this Term by some one of the Gentlemen of the Bench. It is ordered that he be referred to the order relating to Proposals.[11]

While it is difficult to be absolutely certain of the circumstances of Bickerton's application, it appears that having left Oxford following his graduation, and with no possibility of ordination, he originally wished to continue with his studies and decided that his best course was to enter the Middle Temple where, as a student member, he would enjoy unlimited access to its substantial library – a library stocked not only with legal texts, but with works on geography, topography, philosophy, theology and literature, the collection's range prescribed only by the interests and pursuits of those who had made gifts and bequests over the preceding centuries.

For more than five years he had pursued his chosen course, but then, in late 1809, for reasons that are unclear but which we might assume to have been financial, he had decided that he would, after all, seek a call to the Bar. His plan had been thwarted by the deaths of those members who knew him well enough to grant this favour, and he had hoped instead to obtain the call via an appeal to the Parliament. The picture becomes even more confused when we recall that in May 1808, Bickerton had been corresponding with the Duke of Portland over an unspecified post in Oxford. Was he keeping his options open at a period of financial necessity?

It is clear that his appeal to the Middle Temple's Parliament failed, because the minutes contain a second reference to Bickerton, dated 22 November 1822 – a full thirteen years after he asked to be proposed. This reference confirms that he had never been called to the Bar, while also casting further doubt on both his motivations and his levels of commitment:

> The petition of Mr Bickerton J. being read setting forth that he was specially admitted to this Society on the 3rd Day of May 1804 and having no intention of being called to the Bar prayed that his Bond might be cancelled. It is ordered accordingly.[12]

After almost twenty years as one of its members, Bickerton, now aged 67, had at last severed his ties with the Middle Temple. However, it is clear that he had long since turned his back on it, preferring instead to return to Oxford. His final petition to the Parliament made this decision irrevocable, denying to him forever the sanctuary he had once found beneath the arch of Christopher Wren's gatehouse on Fleet Street and among the chambers of Middle Temple Lane.

And yet those ancient precincts, and all they represented, clearly retained an important hold on his imagination, as his retention of his barrister's gown and wig makes clear. As *The Gentleman's Magazine* put it, by the time of his death, 'he had parted with every other comfort; but the emblems of that honourable rank, of which he imagined himself the possessor, he would not relinquish, except with life itself'.[13]

Although there is no record of Bickerton having demonstrated any aberrant behaviour during his years of study at the Middle Temple, it is quite clear that by the time he returned to Oxford his habits and demeanour had once again become distinctly odd. Writing in 1833, his obituarist in *The Gentleman's Magazine* noted:

> Between 20 and 30 years since [sic] he made his re-appearance in Oxford, with some money in his possession, and assumed the dress of a Master of Arts. He never walked in the streets without an umbrella, and always attended at the Assizes with a counsellor's wig on his head. At St Mary's Church it was his practice to seat himself near the pulpit, and to take his wig from his pocket, and gravely place it on his head. He usually called himself 'Counsellor Bickerton, Esq.' and in this name published a small pamphlet, full of incoherent matter. He was very loquacious, but perfectly harmless in his manners. He had no means of obtaining subsistence, at least none that were known, except the benevolence of some members of the University [...] At one time he purchased a chariot at an auction, removed the pole, and contrived to make it a one horse carriage. He purchased a horse also, and engaged in his service a youth, well known in Oxford, who was sent over the seas a few years since. Bickerton fitted up his carriage with cooking apparatus; and when the Judges left Oxford, he, dressed in his wig and gown, and accompanied by his man, followed them on the circuit. But his travelling the circuit was soon terminated, for the first time that he appeared in a court where he was unknown (it is believed at Gloucester), he was taken into custody, and afterwards sent from the place. During his journey, he regularly cooked his victuals on the roadside, and slept in his carriage. The only food furnished to his horse was what he could collect from green lanes and the sides of

ditches. At this period of Bickerton's life, he had taken up his residence at Hertford College, with Constantine Demetriades, the Greek.[14]

Bickerton's habit of assuming wig and gown to follow the lawyers as they made their circuit of the district's courtrooms is confirmed in a letter of 6 August 1814, written by the recently qualified barrister – and later Lord Chancellor – John Campbell, to his father, the Reverend George Campbell:

> There is a madman at Oxford of the name of Bickerton who has taken it into his head that he is a barrister-at-law. He has accordingly contrived to procure an old wig and gown, in which he travels about the country and walks into court, following us regularly from town to town. He is perfectly harmless, and people rather encourage his fantasy.[15]

Campbell concluded with the wry remark, 'If his going the circuit in this manner were to be considered conclusive proof of insanity, it might be very alarming to many of us'. More significantly, perhaps, the reference in *The Gentleman's Magazine* to Bickerton having taken up residence at Hertford College allows us to obtain greater clarity regarding the precise timing of his reappearance in and subsequent departure from Oxford following the end of his aborted legal career.

Originally known as Hart Hall, the college's history can be traced back to the late thirteenth century, when it served – like many halls in medieval Oxford – as a lodging house for both resident tutors and students, among whom the most notable were John Donne and Jonathan Swift. It was poor by the standard of many colleges and dominated by nearby Exeter College. Hart Hall did not receive its charter incorporating its principal and fellows until September 1740, when it became Hertford College, its incorporation having been engineered by the college's principal from 1710, Dr Richard Newton, an educational innovator whose arrogance and ambition led the antiquarian Thomas Hearne to dismiss him as 'a crackbrain'd Man, being mad with Pride and Conceit' and 'famous for talking much'.[16]

Under Newton's watchful eye, and with the benefit of the substantial sums that he invested personally, Hertford College did become renowned for its innovative approach to university education but also for a discipline so draconian that it led the contemporary satirist Nicholas Amhurst to describe Newton as 'a meer *tyrant* [...] not only monstrously whimsical with regard to his *own* œconomy and *method of living*; but likewise so *unreasonable*, as to expect the same individual *formalities* from all those under his power'.[17]

Crucially, despite the economy that he insisted upon, Newton failed to place the college's finances on a secure footing and its relative poverty made it unattractive to many of his possible successors. As a result, after his death in 1753, the post of principal fell to a series of men who, for the most part, lacked either the ambition or the energy to build on the foundations he had laid.

Though still capable of attracting wealthy students like Charles James Fox, who matriculated in 1764, the college fell into a terminal decline and, on the death of Principal Bernard Hodgson in 1805, no acceptable and suitably qualified replacement could be found. By 1810, new matriculations had ceased and after the graduation of the few remaining students the college's empty buildings were left to decay under the nominal stewardship of its senior fellow and self-appointed vice principal, the Reverend Richard Hewitt.

The son of a Manchester huckster,[18] Hewitt was an intelligent boy. He attended Manchester Grammar School and became one of just three or four out of fifty or so pupils to be awarded a school exhibition, or scholarship, to Oxford or Cambridge each year. With his status recorded as *plebeius filius*, or 'son of a common man', he matriculated at Brasenose College, aged 19, on 6 April 1796, graduating as Bachelor of Arts on 14 January 1800, and as Master of Arts three and a half years later, on 16 July 1803. His name was removed from the Brasenose College books on 9 February 1804, and it was probably at this date that he became one of only two fellows at Hertford College, just fifteen months before Principal Hodgson's death heralded the college's downfall.

Though terminal, Hertford College's decline was not swift, and Hewitt clearly believed that he was the man to reverse its fortunes. As the more senior of the two remaining fellows, he felt certain that he should be appointed as Hodgson's successor and he became increasingly frustrated at what he considered, not unreasonably, to be the unnecessary prevarication of the university's authorities. Exasperated by their continued inaction, he seems gradually to have slipped into something not far short of obsession and, convinced that the post of principal was being unfairly denied to him, he took to bombarding the vice chancellor and others with letters beseeching his appointment to a position for which, he asserted, he had been 'pointed out by the finger of God'.[19]

Finally, on 4 April 1814 – nearly a decade after Hodgson's death – he took matters into his own hands and 'nominated and admitted himself to the office of Principal'.[20] Of course, this self-appointment had no validity under the college's statutes, but Hewitt's perseverance did pay some dividends because when the college was finally dissolved in 1816, he was granted a pension for life, funded from the sale of the college's assets.

Hewitt would later be described as 'a man of some ability, but scarcely sane',[21] although this judgement seems unfair. There can be little doubt that his desire to be appointed as Hodgson's successor bore the hallmarks of monomania, but he had good cause for his frustration. Whether through arrogance or administrative incompetence, when he revised the college's statutes in 1747, Richard Newton had failed to properly formalise them, thereby leaving the 1739 statutes in force and creating a substantial degree of ambiguity over the college's future management – an ambiguity that its wealthy and powerful neighbours were more than willing to take advantage of in order to suppress Newton's upstart institution.

After 1805, Hewitt seems to have been perhaps the only individual genuinely concerned with assuring the college's future, and his letters on the subject to the chancellor of the university and others do not read like the ravings of a madman; nor, indeed, does his later correspondence on the subject of his pension. Instead, though eccentric, they are often passionate, humorous and well reasoned, commenting on people and events in Oxford, celebrating the passing of the Catholic Emancipation Act and expressing his enthusiasm for mathematics.

After leaving Oxford around 1818, the self-proclaimed principal lived for some years in rural Nechells Green, near Saltley in the West Midlands, before moving, in his last year, to live with his niece, Betsy, and her husband, William Greenhalgh, in Bamford, Rochdale, where he contemplated editing the works of the Swedish theologian and mystic, Emanuel Swedenborg – a project which he admitted to having 'very much at heart'.²² He died at Bamford on 29 November 1832, aged 57, and was interred in the burial ground of Bamford Chapel. Ironically, given his long if unsuccessful quest for preferment, in completing the burial register the chapel's clerk described Hewitt as 'Headmaster of Brazenose College, Oxford, late of Birmingham', meaning that in death he achieved an elevation beyond even his wildest dreams.

It was during the last years of Hewitt's fellowship that Hertford College's empty buildings became home to a peculiar collection of waifs and strays, who were unable or unwilling to find shelter elsewhere. Inevitably, the vast majority of these squatters are nameless, but there are a few exceptions to the prevailing anonymity: Thomas Roberson, Demetriades the Greek – and Bickerton.

First to take up residence was Roberson, an attorney who, according to Bickerton's Oxford contemporary, the gossipy memoirist and city coroner George Valentine Cox, installed himself and his family in the principal's lodging, 'at first by sufferance, on the plea of keeping the place decent, but not long after assumed a quasi "right of possession," with no one to say "nay"'.²³ In fact, far from being a pettifogging backstreet lawyer, Roberson was a well-respected figure in Oxford and a highly active member of the city's Corporation, becoming a Common Councilman in 1800, Chamberlain in 1803, and Bailiff in 1807. He had also served as a lieutenant in the Oxford Loyal Volunteers during the height of the fears over an invasion by Napoleon Bonaparte.²⁴ By 1802, he had become so prosperous that he commissioned the building of a grand three-storey house in a key location at the corner of Rose Lane, overlooking the eastern approach to the city.*

Perhaps this expensive building project overstretched his finances because *Jackson's Oxford Journal* confirms that in January 1811 Roberson was declared bankrupt. Beginning on the 15th of that month, the entire contents of his house were sold, including furniture, plate, linen and china; everything, indeed, from 'a set of the Statutes at Large from Magna Charta' to the fire irons and 'a Patent Mangle, nearly new, by *Baker*'.²⁵ Almost exactly a month later, the house itself was auctioned.²⁶

---

* The house still stands and is now Magdalene Gate House.

Roberson would survive the calamity and go on to become the Town Clerk of Oxford, but in its immediate shadow, he sought and found shelter in the vacant principal's lodging at Hertford College, using his knowledge of the law to maintain his occupancy until his finances recovered. That his finances were in a parlous condition is evidenced by Hewitt's recollection that, when they were both residents of Hertford College, he had made loans to Roberson of '£20 at a time' and that Mrs Roberson 'not unfrequently waylaid me when I went to the Buttery, and, with a large pitcher in her hand, begged the loan of some ale'.[27]

Perhaps emboldened by Roberson's success, other less-respectable drifters began gradually to occupy the rooms left vacant by the college's departing students. As a group, Cox thought them 'strange characters' and 'half-cracked',[28] and none, perhaps, was stranger than Chrysanthus Constantinides Demetriades, the Greek – though, as is the case with Bickerton, sometimes it can be difficult to distinguish the facts of his life from elaborately embroidered fiction.

Born to poor parents in 1754 or 1755 in Lepanto** on the north coast of the Gulf of Corinth, in his youth, Demetriades had become a *hieromonk*, or 'priestmonk' – a member of a monastic order ordained as a priest in the Greek Orthodox Church. At an unknown date, he travelled from Athens to Bucharest where he officiated in the Orthodox Church until an unspecified scandal or misdemeanour obliged him to abandon his post.[29] Having fled Bucharest, he next made his way to Trieste, on the Adriatic coast.

According to John Ward of Durham – a man who knew Demetriades personally, and not merely by reputation – it was in Habsburg-ruled Trieste that, 'falling in with Romish Priests, he was persuaded to forsake the Greek profession of faith, and adopt that of Rome'.[30] But this conversion proved to be only skin deep, because, having travelled to Malta on the advice of his proselytising friends, failure to obtain a promised pension from his newly adopted church caused Demetriades to voice certain heretical opinions which resulted in his temporary incarceration, probably in the Inquisition prison in Vittoriosa.

On his release, the Greek vowed to 'drop all farther connexion with the "Pope Devil"'[31] and choosing instead to try his luck in northern Europe,

---

** Modern Nafpaktos.

he reached Prussian-controlled Breslau* in 1795 and Berlin the following year. In the Prussian capital, he made the acquaintance of Dr Charles Brown, a Welshman who held the posts of Privy Councillor and Physician in Ordinary to Friedrich Wilhelm II. According to the American medical historian Guenter B. Risse, Brown had used 'Court intrigue and back channel connections' to assume the place of the intended appointee, the Scottish physician and creator of the Brunonian system of medicine, Dr John Brown, but by the time the imposture was detected, the interloper had fully established himself by successfully inoculating the king's children against smallpox. Clearly an opportunist of some experience, it was Brown who suggested that a man of Demetriades' particular talents might find gainful employment in Great Britain.[32]

By his own account, Demetriades reached England in 1796,[33] and he can be traced to Newcastle and thence to Durham, where he sought to establish himself as a teacher of modern languages. Unfortunately, in the opinion of John Ward, who was one of his pupils:

> His abilities as a teacher of languages were certainly moderate, and he did not procure more than three or four pupils here [...] Poor Constantine was perhaps 'below par' as a teacher of languages, but his misfortune was to be unconscious of this. He attributed his want of success, not to his want of abilities, but to the practices of some underhand enemies, against whom he was in the habit of inveighing for 'taking away his respect,' to use his own phrase. This idea, which had the full possession of his mind, together with the dread of being sent out of the country under the Alien Act,** or of coming to want while he remained here, produced alternate fits of irritation and depression, and may account for, if not entirely justify, his parsimonious habits.[34]

---

*   Modern Wrocław.
** The Act for Regulating Immigration into Great Britain (1793) was the first of a series of acts passed between 1793 and 1826 which granted the government broad powers of regulation over the country's resident foreign population. The powers included the authority to expel resident aliens and to keep aliens from entering the country and represent the first attempt on the part of the British government to regulate England's entire population of aliens. Its primary driver was the mass emigration of French nationals fleeing France after the French Revolution and the government's concern that these might include Jacobin agents disguised as refugees.

Other commentators were altogether less sympathetic, one accusing Demetriades of 'avarice and superstition, rarely, if ever, equalled', before going on to assert that 'the trade most congenial to his taste was that of exciting commiseration, and reaping the benefit arising from his miserable appearance and demeanour'.[35] Another took delight in claiming, 'In the course of his travels he had the misfortune to get a touch of syphilis',[36] while G.V. Cox called him 'a butt for the young men's jokes, a sponge for their eatables and drinkables, and a recipient of their loose silver'.[37]

Of Bickerton's relations with Roberson, Demetriades and their fellow residents at Hertford College we know very little, with most commentators preferring to dwell on the more absurd episodes. Of course, absurdity and truth are not mutually exclusive, and if the accounts of his exchanges with Hewitt are true, it is clear that despite, or perhaps because of, certain shared characteristics – as well as their general eccentricity, both men were obsessed with the idea that they had been defrauded – the two did not get along.

Ostensibly, the primary, if unconscious, cause of the friction between the two men seems to have been Bickerton's horse: a fact that comes as no surprise if stories of his having stabled his steed in the college's buildings are true, with one writer even claiming that the animal 'was sometimes seen looking out of a window on the second floor'.[38] The second bone of contention was the horse's dung, with Hewitt complaining bitterly at the filthy state of the quadrangle. Clearly Bickerton accepted the justice of the complaint because, 'In order to prevent the consequences of the indecorous behaviour of the horse, the counsellor regularly attended with his hat placed at the horse's tail'.[39]

On another occasion, it is reported that during a particularly cold winter, Bickerton, being in need of fuel, 'to procure it he contrived to climb into a tree that was in the quadrangle of Hertford College, seated himself upon one of its branches, and actually sawed the branch off between himself and the trunk, in consequence of which he fell to the ground and was much hurt'.[40] One can only assume that Hewitt, who remained extremely jealous of his assumed responsibilities, must have taken a very dim view of what, in his eyes, could only be considered wanton vandalism.

In 1811 the combined population of Oxford is estimated to have been 13,257, rising to 16,446 by 1821;[41] in a city this size and, moreover, one with a disproportionate number of wealthy and idle young men, it was only to be expected that misfits like Hewitt, Demetriades and Bickerton should attract attention. That these unusual men became, to some degree, notorious in Regency Oxford is proved by the number of contemporary and near-contemporary references to them, though the allusions to Bickerton far outnumber those to either Hewitt or Demetriades.

In *The Oxford Spy*, a verse satire on Oxford life published between 1818 and 1819, the Christ Church undergraduate James Shergold Boone mentions him on a number of occasions; but while Boone strikes unmercifully at the abuses rampant in the university, he treats Bickerton with kindness:

And thought shall turn, poor Bickerton, to thee!
While men, like moths, in quick succession bred,
Here shine their little season and are fled:
While all the young, the witty, and the gay,
Pass unlamented, and unmiss'd, away;
Thee, Oxford oft shall name, remember long,
As one, far separate from her vulgar throng;
No worldling thou, of dull lethargic breast,
In thoughts, words, feelings, moulded by the rest;
Thy manlier mind assumes no borrow'd tone –
Whate'er thy weaknesses – at least thy own!
What! Though strange visions fire thy wilder'd brain,
Thy dress disorder'd, and uncheck'd thy strain!
What! Though some pedant smile to see thee stray
With large umbrella in the clearest day;
Or lounge on Isis' banks; and feel no awe
To sit mid sages of the Church and Law!
Or, if thou lov'st in idly pensive mood
O'er human woes and vanities to brood,
And half to anger, half to mirth inclin'd,
Upbraid the crimes and madness of mankind;

> Should he, to make his own dull sense allow'd,
> Pity thy weakness, in that pity proud;
> Or dare, unconscious of his own estate,
> Insult with seeming sympathy thy fate;
> Still reason's self might bid thee not repine –
> If fame be worth our wishes thou hast thine!
> And oh! if radiant fancy's meteor gleam
> Can guild the colouring of thy darkest dream;
> If hope can cheer thee, till thou leav'st behind
> The loss of station, and the wreck of mind;
> If thou canst rest, while others seek the pole,
> To chase their languid listlessness of soul;
> If thou canst laugh, while all around are sad,
> And very reason drives the wisest mad;
> Oh, surely, then our feelings chang'd should be –
> Thou pity us – and we must envy thee![42]

Aside from its obvious gentleness, this contemporary portrait of Bickerton is interesting on a number of counts. First, Boone portrays his subject as a 'wise fool', mild-mannered and occasionally pensive, but still able, despite his 'strange visions' and 'wilder'd brain', to 'Upbraid the crimes and madness of mankind' – much in the style of a Shakespearian jester. Second, he acknowledges that Bickerton had become well known in his alma mater, 'Thee, Oxford oft shall name, remember long'. Finally, he appears to suggest – unlike most of those who wrote of Bickerton – that he was familiar with and sympathetic to his subject's 'loss of station, and the wreck of mind'.

Without further evidence, it would be wrong to assume that for Boone, Bickerton was anything other than a convenient poetic tool; a yardstick by which to measure the depravities and pretensions of his Oxford peers. If so, we can have no confidence that the portrait is accurate in any but its surface details, such as the umbrella, which Bickerton is known to have carried at this time. However, such suspicions are largely allayed by a footnote added by Boone beneath an earlier reference to 'unhappy Bickerton'.[43] In it, he states:

> Mr Bickerton is an original character, which, in most places, is of itself sufficient to cast upon a man the imputation of insanity. I once in the summer heard him inveigh with great indignation against the epithet here joined with his name. 'How,' he said, 'can anyone be unhappy, who breathes the air of heaven on a morning like this?' There is more philosophy in this single exclamation, than in all the gloomy denunciations of modern poetry.[44]

Within the context of the satire, this anecdote is unnecessary, and its very superfluity lends credibility. The details of Boone's own career also make it seem perfectly credible that he felt a genuine sympathy for the old man, perhaps recognising that they shared certain character flaws.

One near contemporary remembered Boone as 'the most promising man at Oxford [...] He could do everything and carry everything before him.'[45] And yet, despite winning an assortment of accolades, including the Newdigate Prize for English verse, he failed to take honours, apparently as a result of a fit of pique, and preferred instead to rile the authorities with his verse, which was later described as 'clever, dull, and hateful; a thing to read for two minutes and throw into the fire'.[46] After squandering various opportunities, he eventually took holy orders and became Vicar of St John's, Paddington, where, 'had he appeared in sackcloth and ashes he could not have made a more doleful or a more despicable figure'.[47]

Boone was not the only Oxford contemporary to depict Bickerton with sensitivity. Between 1818 and 1819, the portraitist Albin Roberts Burt made drawings of at least three Oxford eccentrics and notables, including Bickerton, Demetriades and the naturalist James Benwell, the first two drawings being etched by John Whessell,[*] and the last by Joseph Skelton.[**] Born in 1783, probably in Wales, Burt had begun his artistic career as an engraver and had studied under both Robert Thew and Benjamin Smith. As an artist in his own right, he exhibited at the Royal Academy in 1807 and pursued a peripatetic career, working in Bath,

---

[*] John Whessell (c. 1760–1820) was an Oxford-based etcher, engraver and mezzotinter.
[**] Joseph Skelton (1783–1871), an engraver and publisher probably best known for his engravings of the Oxford colleges, after line drawings by James Basire.

Worcester, Birmingham, Warwick, Chester, Southampton, Reading and London, as well as Oxford.

His sitters had included George III, Lord Nelson and Emma Hamilton, and he seems to have known both Nelson and Hamilton personally, the former because his brother, Henry, is reputed to have acted as Nelson's secretary, and the latter through his mother, who knew her as a girl. Not surprisingly, given his exalted clientele, his sensitive drawings exhibit none of the coarseness of the Rowlandson-like cartoon of Richard Hewitt made a decade earlier by an anonymous satirist,*** being realistic and clearly designed to engender sympathy rather than derision.

Regarding Burt's portrait of James Benwell, the latter's friend, the apothecary John Ireland, noted that copies of Skelton's etching were being sold entirely for the benefit of the sitter:

> In order to procure some trifling addition to his comfort and support during the remainder of his days, Messrs Burt & Skelton, two eminent artists now resident in this city, have kindly and gratuitously contributed their assistance, the former by furnishing a most correct and characteristic likeness of the old naturalist, and the latter by executing an engraving from it, with all his well-known taste. A specimen of the engraving is now to be seen at the house of Mr Wyatt, carver & guilder, in the High-street, where subscriptions will be very thankfully received on the following very moderate terms:- Proofs, 5s.; and Common, 3s. 6d.[48]

While there is no evidence that Burt and Whessell were practising the same philanthropy when they made and published the portraits of Bickerton and Demetriades, it is possible. Certainly, in their different ways, both subjects could be considered deserving of charity, though

---

*** Entitled 'A Great Northern Light', this anonymous cartoon shows a corpulent, red-faced and one-eyed Hewitt in the company of a scantily clad woman reclining on a couch, with an etching of Hertford College on the wall. Below the image is a line from Virgil's *Aeneid*: '*Monstrum horrendum, informe, ingens, cui lumen ademptum*' (trans.: 'A horrible monster, shapeless, vast, whose only eye had been taken'), followed by an original line '*de collo fistula pendet*' (trans.: 'pipes hang from the neck'). A copy of this etching is held by the British Museum (reference: 1868, 0808.7710).

their prior usefulness to society in no way compared with that of the ailing Benwell, a humbly born autodidact, who had spent four decades tending Oxford's Botanic Garden.

Whatever their motivations – whether altruistic or purely commercial – we know that the artists' efforts were not welcomed by the irascible and litigiously minded Demetriades, who is reported to have 'excommunicated them in the names of all the saints in the Greek Church; which written excommunication he caused to be exhibited in some of the shops of the City of Oxford'.[49] Either way, it is worth noting that Burt's portrayal of Benwell was described by an intimate friend as 'a very striking and characteristic likeness'[50] – praise which might lead us to suppose that Burt's depiction of Bickerton is equally accurate, with its large, sad eyes, gentle expression and tufts of grizzled hair escaping from beneath his oversized mortarboard. Certainly, contemporary accounts tell us that at this period, Bickerton usually wore a gown and mortarboard and carried a large green umbrella, 'confined about half way up by a large brass ring like a curtain ring',[51] and it is in this garb that Burt portrayed him.

Inevitably, the treatment that Bickerton received at the hands of his Oxford contemporaries was not uniformly benevolent. One correspondent of *The Gentleman's Magazine*, who had been an undergraduate at the time of Bickerton and Demetriades' residence, recalled the following 'ludicrous anecdote':

> ... of an entertainment given by a Jesus man to four strange characters at Oxford, viz. the old Greek Demetriades; a crazy being who called himself the head of Hertford College, long since dissolved, and was nicknamed Counsellor Bickerton, and a man grown music mad, and an Hebrew Jew. – These strange characters being thus amalgamated, became exceedingly obstreperous, and all quarrelled about their respective merits, each pretending that the other knew nothing about what he professed to discuss. The contest began between the Greek and the Jew. The gentleman who gave the entertainment then thought proper to anoint the head of Counsellor Bickerton with a quantity of grease, and then powdered it with the addition of flour, kicked him out, and shut the door. This was the only method of ending a

quarrel which lasted with great acrimony till a late hour, and it may be easily imagined what a *Babel* the commotion of four such choice spirits could create.[52]

However comical the anecdotist may have thought the episode, what strikes the modern reader is its cruelty: the deliberate bringing together, under a pretence of generosity, of four acknowledged misfits to mock, goad and, ultimately, physically assault them, the perpetrator resting easy in the knowledge that none of his victims could, or would, have recourse to the law. Was this, perhaps, the incident to which Boone referred when he spoke of someone 'unconscious of his own estate, Insult with seeming sympathy thy fate'?

Nor was this the only instance of victimisation. The same correspondent alludes to other occasions when students had deliberately made the usually abstemious Demetriades drunk, and even struck him in the street, while G.V. Cox asserts that he was 'thoroughly hated and sometimes roughly treated by the scouts'.[53] Perhaps the Greek's nationality, appearance and persistent importunity made him a particularly easy target, but it seems probable that Bickerton, too, would have received more than his fair share of indignities at the hands of a boisterous set of youths so confident in their supposed superiority.

As well as his umbrella, Burt's portrait shows Bickerton carrying a copy of *Multum Desideratum; or, a few Hints concerning the Bickertons* – the same publication that he is reported to have held when he attempted to enter the royal levee at St James's Palace fifteen years earlier. At fifty-five pages, this rather breathless account of his religious experiences as a young man in his early twenties is little more than a pamphlet and yet it appears to have retained significance for its author despite, or perhaps because of, the fact that his ambition to be ordained had been thwarted long ago. Four additional works, all short, bear the name 'Counsellor Bickerton' on their title pages, and all date to his years at Hertford College. They are: *An Address to the Literary Members of the University* (Oxford: Munday and Slatter, 1816), two issues of *The Farrago, or the Lucubrations of Counsellor Bickerton* (Oxford: Munday and Slatter, 1816) and *Lamentations for a Bad Use of Good Things* (Oxford: Printed for the Author, 1816).[54]

Poor Bickerton

In *Oxford During the Last Century*, John Green and George Roberson suggest that the *Lucubrations of Counsellor Bickerton* was written by someone else entirely, 'A Mr Tawney, we believe of Exeter [College]'. They go on to state, 'The Counsellor was not offended, but entered the publisher's shop, and seriously proposed a share in the division of the profits in recompense for the liberty taken with his name!'[55]

But the claims of Roberson and Green must be treated with caution as their brief article, which was published over a quarter of a century after Bickerton's death, contains a number of inaccuracies and is clearly based upon earlier publications rather than original research or first-hand knowledge, though Roberson was the son of Thomas Roberson, the attorney, and would almost certainly have seen Bickerton in the precincts of Hertford College when he was a boy. As for 'Mr Tawney', of the five Tawneys listed as students of Oxford in Foster's *Alumni Oxonienses*, none studied at Exeter College, and all matriculated too early or too late to be credible contenders for authorship.

The obituarist for *The Gentleman's Magazine* mentions Bickerton having authored 'a small pamphlet, full of incoherent matter', but it is unclear to which pamphlet he refers. *An Address to the Literary Members of the University of Oxford* might best be described as a prospectus for *The Farrago, or the Lucubrations of Counsellor Bickerton*, and while all three pamphlets exhibit whimsy, none can be described accurately as 'incoherent', as the following excerpt, in which Bickerton solicits submissions from his readers, proves:

> I shall use my own discretion respecting the admission of the Communications sent to me. The only subjects I have a real dislike to are Party Politics and Polemics. Writings in favour of the British Constitution, as established, or on National Œconomics, I earnestly solicit. I wish, however, my Correspondents to understand that I am not an admirer of the 'Vagabond' style. I think our own language is sufficiently copious and sonorous; I disapprove of that tasteless attachment to French words, which boys just escaped from their boarding-schools are so ridiculously fond of. Why in the name of common sense should we Frenchify the *Military Art?* Do not those

words sound as well as '*L'Art Militaire?*' I have no objection to quotations, but I am so true a John Bull that I most firmly believe we are as much superior to the French in our Language as we are in our Arms; and that the present vitiated taste for interlarding our sentences with Gallic frippery arises principally from the vanity of being thought adepts in that language.[56]

Bickerton goes on to state, 'I have in the Press *Memoirs of my own Life*', but there is no evidence that an expanded version of his account of his early years was ever written or printed.

On balance, there seems very little reason to doubt that Bickerton was the author of the publications that bear his name. The same cannot be said of an anonymous work with which his name has been linked: *The Letters of Junius*. Produced between 21 January 1769 and 21 January 1772, these letters gained widespread notoriety for their impudent and ferocious attacks on George III's ministers. Frustrated in its attempts to unmask the author, the government arrested publishers left, right and centre, including Henry Sampson Woodfall, owner of the *Morning Advertiser*, in which the letters first appeared, charging him with seditious libel. But for all its efforts, the identity of Junius remained a closely guarded secret – the secret itself becoming part of a lasting obsession as generations of critics and commentators sought to identify the gifted polemicist.

In fact, it has been convincingly argued that Sir Philip Francis, politician and colonial administrator, was the author,[57] though in the words of A.L. Rowse, 'that has not prevented fifty fools from putting forward fifty different people at various times as candidates for Junius, and a small library has been written to settle, or, rather, to confuse his identity'.[58]

The first suggestion that Bickerton and Junius were one and the same seems to have been made ironically by a contemporary of Bickerton's at Oxford – W. Lamb of Exeter College who, in his copy of the letters, observed in Rowse-like fashion:

Absurdity and improbability short of physical impossibility seem to be recommendations to the Junius-hunters. So far from being surprised that George III, Captain Allen, Dr Wilmott,* and Mr Suett,** having each had some supporters, I wonder they had so few, and that the superior claims of Mr Bickerton have found no advocate. Perhaps his own modesty keeps him from setting up against Sir Philip Francis.[59]

Despite his mocking tone, Lamb's suggestion was picked up by other 'Junius-hunters', including a correspondent to *Notes and Queries*, identified only by the initial 'L', who had acquired Lamb's copy of the letters and noted that he would be 'obliged by reference to any works in which the above claims are stated'.[60] Once the attribution had been made, no matter how humorously, it stuck – and continues to stick – largely as a result of its appearance in William Cushing's oft-reprinted *Initials and Pseudonyms: A Dictionary of Literary Disguises*,[61] Cushing clearly being unaware of the details of Bickerton's life and, in particular, of the fact that he would have been captivating his audience with his brilliant invective at the age of just 13.

---

*   James Wilmot (1726–1807), an English clergyman who was named as Junius by his niece, Olivia Serres (1772–1834), painter, writer and royal imposter.
** Richard 'Dicky' Suett (1755–1805), English comedian.

John Bickerton in Oxford, as drawn by Albin Roberts Burt and etched by John Whessell in 1818.

The Five Chimneys, the seventeenth-century pest house in which Bickerton died of starvation in October 1833. A lithograph dating to *c.* 1840, probably based on an engraving by C. Pye after E. Dayes, 1811.

'The Coroner's Jury Viewing the Murdered Body of Margaret Hawse' – an extremely rare, perhaps unique, image of an early nineteenth-century coroner's jury at work. From John Fairburn's chapbook of 1829.

St Edmund Hall, Oxford, where Bickerton took his Bachelor's degree in 1799. Photo-engraved by Emery Walker (published by Edmund Hort, 1920).

'An old English Gentleman pester'd by Servants wanting places' – James Gillray's cartoon of a St James's Palace levee, 1809. The figure in a coat and hat with his back to the viewer is George III; the gentleman to his immediate right is the Duke of Portland; and the figure bottom left with the bundle of petitions is John Townsend, the Bow Street Runner who arrested Bickerton at a similar levee on 14 September 1803.

The Bow Street Magistrates' Court as it appeared very shortly after Bickerton's appearance at the bar. Taken from Thomas Rowlandson and Augustus Pugin's *Microcosm of London* (1808–10).

Coldbath Fields Prison as it appeared at the time of Bickerton's incarceration.

A prisoners' dormitory in Coldbath Fields Prison. A woodcut from *The Criminal Prisons of London* by Henry Mayhew and John Binny (published by Griffin, Bohn, & Co., 1862). Although this image dates to a period somewhat later than Bickerton's incarceration, it serves to give an impression of the conditions he endured.

James Gillray's 'Citizens Visiting the Bastille' (1799) depicts the arrival of the campaigning Sir Francis Burdett at the gates of Coldbath Fields Prison. The troll-like gaoler is presumably the prison's governor, Thomas Aris.

The Elizabethan hall of the Middle Temple, London, where Bickerton studied from 1804. An illustration by Albert Henry Payne (published by E.T. Brain & Co., 1847).

The interior of Middle Temple Hall by Herbert Railton (an illustration for W.J. Loftie, *The Inns of Court and Chancery*, 1908). Bickerton would have taken his meals here, beneath one of the finest hammerbeam roofs in London.

OLD CHAMBERS IN MIDDLE-TEMPLE-LANE.

'Old Chambers in Middle-Temple-Lane', a woodcut illustration from *The Illustrated London News*, 1857. Bickerton may have resided here while he studied at the Middle Temple.

The exterior of old Hertford College, Catte Street, Oxford, much as it would have appeared during Bickerton's residence, *c.* 1810–20. Drawn and etched by John Whessell.

An anonymous cartoon of Richard Hewitt, self-appointed Vice Principal of Hertford College from 1805 until 1818 and Bickerton's rival for the post of principal.

Demetriades, the Greek, Bickerton's fellow squatter in Hertford College, as drawn by Albin Roberts Burt and etched by John Whessell in 1819.

Title page of Bickerton's *Address to the Literary Members of the University*, 1816.

The first page of Bickerton's letter of appeal to the Court of Claims, 20 June 1820.

York Street (formerly Petty France), showing Van Dun's Almshouses (from Edward Walford, *Old & New London*). This drawing was made in 1820, during the period of Bickerton's residence.

George Cruikshank's 1838 cartoon, 'Battle of A-gin-court (Petty France)', shows the seamier side of the neighbourhood.

The façade of Whitecross Street Debtors' Prison, painted by Thomas Hosmer Shepherd.

The courtyard of Whitecross Street Debtor's Prison by an unknown artist. Bickerton was imprisoned here on the suit of the mysterious Mr Dance of Edward Street, probably in the late 1820s or early 1830s.

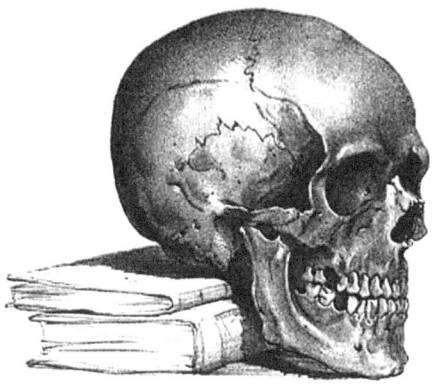

A Greek.

Above: 'Resurrectionists' by Hablot K. Browne ('Phiz'), from Camden Pelham's *The Chronicles of Crime* (1887). Like almost all images of its kind, this picture does not accurately reflect the *modus operandi* of the resurrectionists.

Left: The skull of Demetriades, whose body was anatomised by Oxford medical students in 1825 – a fate that Bickerton only narrowly escaped.

This 1866 engraving of the unkempt Bunhill Fields burial ground gives a reasonable impression of how the burial ground of St John the Evangelist, Horseferry Road, Westminster, looked at the time of Bickerton's interment in 1833.

The garden of St John the Evangelist, Horseferry Road, Westminster. Once the burial ground of the church of the same name, this is the last resting place of John Bickerton. (Photograph by George Haddelsey)

8

Place-Seeker

We can't be certain of the exact date upon which Bickerton left the old Hertford College but on 27 May 1820, *Jackson's Oxford Journal* advertised the sale of 'Capital Fine Old Oak and other Building Materials, now pulled down and in lots, On the premises, at Magdalen Hall, and Hertford College, Oxford'. Moreover, the advertisement declares that the 'Girders, Lintels, and Scantlings […] Doors, Sashes, and Frames; several Thousands of good Slates […] must be cleared off the premises immediately, on account of the plan of the new buildings'. In fact, the catalyst for this sale was the collapse of the neglected medieval frontage of Hertford College into Catte Street – a potent symbol, if any were needed, of the institution's decline and fall. It also meant that Bickerton no longer had a roof over his head.*

The *Oxford Herald* describes the old man as he appeared during his last days in Oxford:

> Poor Bickerton was perfectly harmless; he possessed that sort of cunning which often accompanies aberration of intellect; was always moderate in drinking; would never take more than two glasses of wine; he would eat heartily, provided he could do so gratuitously; he never paid attention to cleanliness; he was full of

---

* In August 1874, Magdalen Hall was incorporated as the second Hertford College, which exists to this day.

fantasies, and we believe, in spite of apparent misery, was contented and happy.¹

Thanks to *The Gentleman's Magazine*, we also know something of his movements after the demolition of Hertford College:

> He purchased a small boat, and for some time lived upon the Isis. After his aquatic residence he left Oxford, but occasionally paid it a visit. Several times within the last few years he was relieved at the Oxford Anti-Mendicity Society.² At one time he was completely re-clothed; but in a few months he returned, again wrapped in rags, and covered with vermin. He gave an incoherent account of his losing the clothes given to him, but there is reason to believe that he had sold them. At that time he rode on a donkey, and stated that he was travelling to collect his rents. Several gentlemen of the University and City, at these visits, gave him money and clothes.³

If this picture is accurate, during the last decade or so of his life, Bickerton had become a suppliant for charity, but there is no evidence that he ever became one of the 250 inmates of the Oxford Workhouse – an institution which, given his later aversion to St Margaret's Workhouse on Dean Street, Westminster, he seems likely to have avoided at all costs. In addition, his ability to pay for the printing of his pamphlets, his purchase of a pony and 'chariot', a houseboat and, latterly, a donkey, all indicate that he retained an income – probably derived from his ownership of properties which he then rented to lodgers. But it is also clear that either his income became insufficient to meet his needs or his declining mental health made it impossible for him to manage it effectively.

In addition to the handful of whimsical publications that appeared under his name during the course of 1816, one letter survives that is indisputably in Bickerton's hand. Written at No. 8 York Street, Westminster, it is dated 20 June 1820 and is addressed to 'The Right Honourable, the Court of Claims'. As the only known surviving example of Bickerton's correspondence, and providing as it does a number of clues as to his movements and preoccupations during his years at the Middle Temple and in the period immediately succeeding his final departure from Hertford College, it merits quoting in full:

> John Bickerton, Graduate, and Compounder of Oxford, presents his most respectful compliments, and is happy to have an opportunity of relating my Right to Hertford College, Oxford, which is founded on the grant of His Grace, the Duke of Portland, late Chancellor of the University of the aforesaid, Oxford; and obtained in the following manner.
>
> Having lost a place in the country through the Death of a relation, soon after I entered at St Edmund Hall, who was my Father; and not long after, losing my place at St Edmund Hall, through Dr Dowson, the principal, being no more; occasioned me to endeavour to make my case known to His Grace, by writing to, and calling upon Him, at His house in Piccadilly, as much as I could, when residing in London, This being continued for the space of five, or six years, when notice was given to me by the Porter, 'to go to Oxford, there being plenty of places there, and His Grace had kept one for me on purpose'.
>
> While I was preparing to go, the servant, in Livery, brought a Letter to my Lodging, near the Temple, from the Duke, to order me to go to Oxford, to a place which He had kept for me; a part of which Letter I now have, and have found the Person who brought it; but could not get it believed at Oxford. This was done after the time when Dr Hodson [sic], Principal of Hertford College was no more. About which time, His Grace the Duke wrote to Dr Thompson, successor to Dr Dowson, Principal of St Edmund Hall, to know whether a Person of the Name of John Bickerton belonged to Oxford, as I have been informed, and being answered in the affirmative, refused to let anyone have the aforesaid Hertford College, though diligently sought by many.
>
> Having stated my Right to Hertford College, to the Lawyer Robertson [sic], who has the keeping of Hertford College; and the new grant; and informing him of the measure of removing Hertford College, to one called St Mary's, where there are two places of

Worship, a Church and a Chapel; and plenty of Room for both Colleges, occasioned him to promise to vouch for me.[4]

Perhaps the immediate reaction to Bickerton's lengthy petition is to dismiss it as the product of an unsound mind. We might also question the motives behind the encouragement apparently offered to him by Thomas Roberson – a man whose integrity Richard Hewitt certainly questioned, claiming that the lawyer 'was notorious of old for appropriating his client's monies to relieve his own necessities'.[5] And yet a closer reading reveals that some, at least, of Bickerton's statements bear more detailed scrutiny.

At the heart of the letter is his claim that the Duke of Portland – Chancellor of the University of Oxford from 1792 until his death in 1809, and prime minister in 1783 and again between 1807 and 1809 – had offered Bickerton an appointment at the university. Reading the letter in isolation, it is difficult not to conclude that following years of unwelcome importunity, the great man had instructed one of his flunkeys to dismiss the eccentric but persistent suppliant with a vague and meaningless promise of a place kept for him at Oxford 'on purpose'. But, if Bickerton's account is to be believed – and there seems little enough reason to doubt his sincerity – the verbal promise was followed by a letter reiterating the offer. This was the letter retained by Bickerton and later examined by the jurors and reporters at the coroner's inquest a quarter of a century later. What was the nature of that promise? Clearly, Bickerton believed it to have been the principalship of Hertford College, vacant since the death of the previous incumbent, Dr Bernard Hodgson, in May 1805.

There is no doubt that when he wrote to Bickerton on 28 May 1808, the duke knew the post of principal was unoccupied; indeed, after Hodgson's death, he had been actively involved in attempts to fill it, personally nominating Henry Phillpotts, later Bishop of Exeter. But when Phillpotts declined the principalship, in accordance with the college's statutes, the right to nominate its head passed from the chancellor to the Dean of Christchurch, Dr Cyril Jackson – and Jackson, in the words of the historian of Hertford College, had 'made up his mind to allow the College to die a natural death'.[6] To achieve this end – which would enable the surrounding colleges to acquire Hertford's land and buildings – all he needed to do was refrain from appointing a principal, leaving the college to wither on the vine as its remaining students graduated.

Without the text of Portland's letter, we can only speculate regarding what he offered Bickerton – if anything. Since he no longer held the power to nominate the new principal, perhaps his letter was intended as one of introduction, suggesting to Dean Jackson and others that the bearer seemed a suitable candidate for the role. But on what basis could he make such a suggestion?

Portland had made enquiries regarding Bickerton's background, writing to George Thompson, the Principal of St Edmund Hall, to ask about his membership of that institution, but Thompson had been appointed in 1800, the year after Bickerton's graduation, while Isaac Crouch, who would have known Bickerton much better even than Thompson's predecessor, had left Oxford to become a parish priest in 1807. That being the case, in answer to his enquiries, Portland is unlikely to have received anything much beyond confirmation of Bickerton's attendance and subsequent graduation; hardly enough to qualify him for a senior role he might inhabit for decades to come.

On balance, if Portland understood – as surely he must – that Dean Jackson had no intention of resuscitating the dying college, and that he knew little or nothing of Bickerton's capabilities, it appears that the duke was being, at best, somewhat disingenuous if he led Bickerton to believe that, through his influence, he might be offered such an appointment.

In this scenario, the letter that so raised its recipient's hopes would seem to have been nothing but a convenient means by which to dispose of a tiresome petitioner. But perhaps this is to do the duke a disservice. Though far from being one of the age's intellectual giants – the MP George Selwyn dismissed him as 'jolterheaded'[7] – Portland was honest, industrious and conscientious. Moreover, as prime minister and Chancellor of Oxford, he would have been inundated with requests from men seeking to benefit from his influence – and yet he did initiate investigations into Bickerton's claims, following which he wrote a letter on his behalf. Given that by 1808 the duke was 'old and feeble, and unequal to his great duties',[8] this was perhaps far more than might reasonably have been expected.

Poor Bickerton

Aside from the light that it casts on the reasons for Bickerton's return to Oxford, his letter to the Court of Claims is interesting because it tells us that by 1820 he was once again resident in London: at No. 8 York Street, Westminster. Running between James Street to the west and Broadway to the east, and parallel with Birdcage Walk to the north, prior to the middle of the eighteenth century, York Street had been known as Petty France, probably as a result of French wool merchants having settled in the area in the fifteenth century.* In 1781, Richard King, the 'Modern London Spy', had described the area as 'a nest of little streets and lanes [...] Many [...] inhabited by wretches who were a disgrace to humanity, while in the neighbourhood, as in that of St Giles's, some hundreds of the industrious poor were scattered up and down'.[9]

A woodcut engraving of 1820 shows the sixteenth-century almshouses founded by Queen Elizabeth's Yeoman of the Guard, Cornelius Van Dun, while to their left can be seen more cottages of a similar date. Eighteen years later, in his comic illustration of the 'Battle of A-gin-court', George Cruikshank chose to depict the street's seamier and more boisterous life – a far cry from the cloistered atmosphere of the university colleges and precincts of the Middle Temple that Bickerton had known. But Petty France in the seventeenth century, and York Street in the eighteenth and nineteenth, were not without their more respectable, wealthier and notable citizens. No. 19, for instance, had been home to John Milton and James Mill and would later be occupied by James' son, John Stuart Mill.

Between 1813 and 1819, the same house was rented by the irascible essayist William Hazlitt. His landlord, the philosopher Jeremy Bentham, lived next door and could often be seen 'shuffling about in dishabille, his shirt open at the neck, the strings of his knee-breeches hanging loose, his coat too large for his shrunken frame, his shrill, chirpy voice fluting forth an endless succession of ideas to some companion'.[10] Frustratingly, we don't know precisely when Bickerton took up residence on York Street,

---

* The name Petty France was restored to the street in the mid-1920s and has been retained to the present day.

but it is impossible not to wonder whether he and Hazlitt ever came face to face on its pavements, and whether the aging eccentric recognised in the sharp-featured man of letters the son of the Presbyterian minister who had tended to his family's spiritual needs at the chapel in Wem. He might also have observed Charles and Mary Lamb on their way to or from No. 19, where they are known to have taken part in more than one convivial gathering of like minds.[11]

With his petition to the Court of Claims eliciting no reply – a fact that is hardly surprising given that the court was an obsolete creation of the seventeenth century, its sole function being to resolve land disputes in Ireland in the aftermath of the Civil Wars and the restoration of the monarchy** – Bickerton moved again, this time to Wych Street, close to the Strand, where he sought to embark on a new career as a schoolmaster.***

In the early nineteenth century – as now – many neighbourhoods in London had a very mixed occupancy, with the very wealthy often living, if not cheek by jowl, then within close proximity to the abject poor and to every gradation of society in between. Westminster, for instance, as well as containing the king's court at St James's Palace, the Abbey and Palace of Westminster, was home to the fashionable and political elite living in their elegant townhouses, a large and growing middle class and whole communities of urban poor. While Bickerton had been residing at No. 8 York Street, his neighbours had included craftsmen and traders, philosophers, writers and, at No. 6, General Sir Charles Asgill, Equerry to the Duke of York and hero of the so-called Asgill Affair during the American War of Independence.

** Bickerton's familiarity with the Court of Claims may have been a product of his reading when attempting to claim lands from Lord Cholmondeley in 1803. Certainly, it seems unlikely that he planned to address his petition to the alternative Court of Claims, which was founded in the fourteenth century and still exists today, as the duties of this court are strictly limited to the management of elements of a new monarch's coronation. Bickerton's letter was neither received nor read by any government department as it bears a superscription stating, 'Refused to Pay the Postage at the House of Lords – Not Known in the South West Divisions'.

*** Wych Street was located where Melbourne and Australia Houses now stand on Aldwych. It ran west from the church of St Clement Danes on the Strand to the southern end of Drury Lane.

Wych Street, too, housed an eclectic mixture of people and businesses in its Elizabethan buildings – rare survivors of the Great Fire – with their wooden jetties teetering towards one another across the narrow roadway. The author and publisher John Nichols, for instance, remembered that, a few years before Bickerton took up residence, the Shakespeare Head Tavern was a favourite haunt of well-known booksellers including Thomas Cadell, James Robson, Thomas Longman and Thomas Evans, among others, who 'warmed not heated with the genuine juice of the grape, have unreservedly poured out their whole souls in Attic wit and repartee'.[12] When the members of that club died out towards the end of the eighteenth century, the Club of Owls took their place, so called on account of the late hours kept by its members, their meetings no doubt kept orderly by hard-hitting 'Dutch Sam', the pugilist under whose protection the landlady conducted her business.[13]

The presence of two Inns of Chancery, New Inn, where Sir Thomas More had studied and which was attached to Middle Temple, and Lyon's Inn, where the jurist Sir Edward Coke was a reader in 1578, also meant that lawyers were frequently to be seen in their black robes – a sight that would no doubt have made Bickerton feel very much at home. Not all the buildings were ancient, though, with the most notable of the newer examples being the Little Drury Lane Theatre, originally built in 1806 as the Olympic Pavilion by the riding master Philip Astley, reputedly from the timbers of the French warship *Ville de Paris*, and described by one theatre-goer as 'a queer, low-browed little building with a rough wooden portico before it [...] and with little blinking windows, very much resembling the port-holes of a man-of-war'.[14]

As well as the lawyers frequenting the Inns of Chancery, Wych Street was home to a wide variety of respectable tradesmen and women including booksellers, scriveners, a stationer, a truss-maker and a cabinet-maker. In the first decade of the century, the premises of Mr Dawson, woollen draper to the Prince of Wales, were also to be found here.

The presence of these reputable businesses tends to undermine the suggestion of one mid-century writer that the street 'had borne an evil name for centuries',[15] but it is also true that it – and particularly the squalid and unhealthy courts hidden behind the shopfronts – had their less-respectable denizens. Up one dreary little court branching to the north, the notorious petty criminal and prison-breaker 'Honest Jack' Sheppard had served his apprenticeship to a master carpenter in the first quarter of the eighteenth century. More recently, sellers of pornographic literature had become both commonplace and sufficiently bold to attract the ire of one correspondent to *The Times* who deplored the fact that the windows of shops in Wych Street and nearby Holywell Street were full of 'books and pictures of the most disgusting and obscene character, and which are alike loathsome to the eye and offensive to the morals of any person of well-regulated mind'.[16]

The theatres in the area also attracted prostitution. The author and publisher John Diprose remembered nearby Newcastle Court as a particular den of iniquity where might be seen, 'in the broad glare of day, sitting at the parlour windows of nearly every house, abandoned women, young and old, decked in tawdry finery, bloated with gin and debauchery, lavishing enticing smiles, and bandying obscene expressions to entrap the unwary passer-by'.[17] When the parish authorities were at last stirred into action by the complaints of the residents and the women were evicted, some immediately resumed their trade in Wych Street. According to Diprose, who could ill conceal his delight, one of this 'frail sisterhood, whose magnitude of height and rotundity may be better conceived than described, when we state that her weight was above twenty stone, bore the cognomen of "The City Barge"'.[18] Certainly, the local watchmen had little enough reason to thank the authorities whose actions had caused the migration because it now fell to them to bring an end to the nightly scenes in Wych Street, which one correspondent of the *Morning Chronicle* described as rendering 'it not only unsafe, but also disgusting, for persons of decent character to pass and repass after ten o'clock in the evening'.[19]

On 26 April 1801, another kind of public disturbance occurred which proved too riotous for the watchmen to handle unaided. That evening, some boys who had been playing outside the empty Queen of Bohemia Inn declared that they had seen 'some persons through the key-hole employed in cutting up human bodies'. When a number of bystanders broke in, they were horrified to discover several corpses partly dissected, as well as several tubs filled with offal. 'The stench was so great,' wrote a reporter for *Jackson's Oxford Journal*, 'that many were glad to return without viewing the disgusting scene, and many who went in were seized with sickness.' The inn had, it seems, been used as an illicit anatomy theatre and such was the abhorrence with which anatomists were generally viewed, the student surgeons were lucky to have escaped undetected, leaving their instruments behind them in the shambles.

We don't know precisely when or why Bickerton abandoned teaching, but the testimony of Daniel Friend at the coroner's inquest indicates that he had probably closed his school by the time he purchased the freehold of the Five Chimneys around 1827.[20] What does seem clear is that his habitation of the tumbledown Hertford College under the jaundiced eye of Richard Hewitt and his move to the damp and inconvenient timber-framed Elizabethan buildings of Wych Street is indicative of a gradual decline in his circumstances; a decline that would end in the derelict Five Chimneys among the very poor. We also know that during his time in Wych Street, or shortly afterwards, Bickerton suffered a calamity experienced by large numbers of his contemporaries from all ranks of society: imprisonment for debt.

9

Debtor

Few of the details of Bickerton's imprisonment for debt can be traced – the date of its commencement, its duration and the sum for which he was seized all being lost to time. What we can say with confidence, based upon the statements made by his neighbours at the inquest into his death, is that Mr Dance, a broker, lived in one of Bickerton's houses on Edward Street, Vincent Square; Bickerton 'seized upon Mr Dance for rent'; and Dance 'replevied, and threw the deceased into Whitecross-street Prison'.[1]

The interpretation of these few bald statements must be a matter of conjecture, but it appears that Bickerton or his agents distrained, or seized, from Dance goods or property to the value of the unpaid rent. By replevying, Dance offered security for the alleged debt to the Court of Requests – a local court which dealt in a summary fashion with small claims – and obtained in return an order for the provisional restoration of his goods. Thereafter, the three commissioners of the court* would have determined on the rights of the case.

Both Bickerton and Dance would have been required to attend the hearing so that, as one anonymous legal commentator wrote at the time, the parties might 'be examined and cross-examined in the presence of each other [...] as nobody can know so much of the transaction

---

* Judgements in the Court of Requests were made not by judges and juries or by magistrates, but by three commissioners who, under the terms of an Act of 1752, must be householders and possessed of an income of at least £20 per annum. No other qualifications were required.

in question as they do'.² Failure to attend by either party would have resulted in an automatic verdict in favour of the opposing party.

What may have happened in this instance is that the commissioners found against Bickerton's original seizure and ordered him to pay damages and costs. If he was unable or unwilling to do so – and damages and costs could amount to substantially more than the original disputed sum – the court would have issued a writ for his arrest by the beadle of the court and his detention until he either paid the debt or served the sentence handed down by the commissioners.

That Bickerton had become a debtor was in no way surprising or unusual. As Jerry White makes clear in his history of the Marshalsea Debtors' Prison, 'Everyone was a debtor in eighteenth- and nineteenth-century London'. He goes on:

> If everyone was a debtor for a time it was not necessarily through inability or unwillingness to pay, for deferred payment on credit was the way business was generally organised [...] During much of the eighteenth century, specie – ready coin of the realm – was in such short supply, especially in small denominations, that it suited buyer and seller to allow an account to accumulate till it could be paid in silver or gold or, more rarely, by banknote or draft [...] An account or tally would be run up with the grocer, baker, butcher or milkman, all on the credit of an address given, confirmed by the tradesman's delivery. Something ought to and might be occasionally paid on account, but otherwise the bill was rendered after a time thought reasonable by both sides: on the four quarter days, for instance.³

However, if payments were routinely missed or a rumour of financial difficulties should gain currency – the result, perhaps, of a doubtful speculation or the failure of someone to whom money was known to have been loaned – a creditor might choose to obtain immediate payment, and if one so chose, then others would almost certainly stake their claims in order to avoid being last in the queue. In these circumstances, the usual process would be for the creditor or creditors to swear an affidavit quantifying the sum owed; this affidavit would then be put before a judge and an arrest warrant issued.

On the whole, very little stigma was attached to imprisonment for debt; after all, during the late eighteenth and early nineteenth centuries some 10,000 individuals were imprisoned for debt each year, with over half of the entire prison population being debtors.[4] Nonetheless, many felt that the threat of incarceration in a debtors' prison hung like the sword of Damocles over their heads. What they feared was not indebtedness or the stain of imprisonment *per se* – debts, if sufficiently large, might almost be worn as a badge of honour and would certainly not negatively impinge on claims to gentility – but the stigma that was associated with and the conditions to be faced in particular prisons.

Just as being arrested on the orders of small claims courts, such as the Court of Requests, carried with it an indelible mark of shame because the debts were so small and therefore utterly lacking in dignity, so too did detention in the Marshalsea or Newgate prisons. And the conditions to be endured in these institutions gave debtors very good cause to be fearful, as was revealed by the radical publisher, reformer and Sheriff of London, Sir Richard Phillips, who described the debtors' wards of Newgate Prison in his 1808 publication *A Letter to the Livery of London*.

Originally built in 1188 during the reign of Henry II (1154–89), Newgate was one of London's oldest prisons and despite many refurbishments, extensions and rebuilds over the ensuing centuries, it had not aged well. By the early nineteenth century, the single most pressing problem was overcrowding – an issue so acute that Phillips felt it could best be illustrated by comparison with the conditions endured on the *Brookes*, a slave ship that had become notorious during the 1780s when an engraving showing its slave decks was widely circulated:

> To convey a just idea of these yards, and of the wards in which the prisoners live and lodge, the most apt comparison will be the engraved representation of a slave ship, which, a few years ago, was circulated through England with so much effect. When the prisoners lie down on their floors by night, there must necessarily, at least in the women's wards, be the same bodily contact, and the same economical disposition of heads and legs, as were represented in that drawing of the deck of a slave ship [...]

> In these common wards, the situation of the debtors is little better [...] For example, in the ward called the long ward, 35 feet in length and 13 feet in breadth, there are usually 30 prisoners, which affords a breadth of only 26 inches to each prisoner, allowing space for door-ways and fire-places. The horrors of such a situation, during the night, when the prisoners are all locked up in their respective wards, especially during the heat of the summer, may be better conceived than described.[5]

Although Phillips' impassioned advocacy would eventually lead to change, the process was not a quick one and in December 1813 – five years after the publication of his pamphlet – George Eden, the MP for Woodstock, told the House of Commons that where no more than 100 individuals should be secured in Newgate's debtors' wards, in November there had been no fewer than 340, 'most of these were in want of clothing and bedding, and [...] the rain beat upon them'.[6]

And the problem was not restricted to the debtors. When a newly appointed Special Committee of the House of Commons visited the prison in April 1814, it found that, with a theoretical capacity of 427 prisoners, including 110 debtors, Newgate actually held 486, of which 160 were debtors. In January of the same year, it had housed an extraordinary 822.[7]

The debtors were accommodated in two yards, one for men and one for women, with the men's yard containing three buildings: the Master's Side, the Cabin Side and the Common Side. The poorest debtors inhabited the last of these, while for admission into the two former, prisoners paid a fee of 3s, the occupants having, in the words of the committee, 'the advantage of living in better society'. The prisoners' rooms were about 15ft wide and 23–36ft in length, with each containing between ten and fifteen men, day and night, when the prison was not crowded, and sometimes double that number during busy periods.

Reflecting the fact that the debtors faced no criminal charges, they were, to a substantial degree, self-governing and allowed to elect their own 'steward', whose job it was to preserve order, see the food allowances weighed, examine offerings made via the poor box and superintend the receipt and distribution of charitable donations. By way of payment for the fulfilment of these duties, the steward would receive small gratuities and an additional allowance of provisions.

If guilty of misconduct, prisoners could be punished by removal to the Disorderly Ward, where they would be locked up an hour earlier than their fellows and, if that punishment failed to reform their manners, the prison's governor, or keeper, could order their confinement in a cell.

Although visiting was permitted any time between nine in the morning and nine at night – and sometimes as many as 200 visitors a day took advantage of these regulations – the prison's overcrowding meant that the inmates could enjoy no privacy when meeting family, friends or creditors – a lack which one prisoner told Sir Richard Phillips caused them to 'suffer exceedingly'.[8] As well as enjoying, to whatever degree was possible, the company of family and friends, debtors could buy wine and beer for which they paid the same price as that charged by public houses. Though limited to the purchase of only one bottle of wine or one quart of ale on any single occasion, the total number of occasions was not restricted, 'a regulation', the committee noted drily, 'which little tends to preserve sobriety and order'.[9] It also observed that the 'Act of Parliament against the introduction of spirituous liquors* is conspicuously hung up, and all pains are taken, though sometimes ineffectually, to see that it is enforced'.

Many would sympathise with the prisoners' recourse to the anaesthetising effects of alcohol. The prison authorities provided no coals or candles for warmth and light and no mops or pails to prevent conditions becoming squalid. All must be bought by the prisoners themselves. They also received no beds or bed linen, meaning that the poorest debtors had no option but to sleep on the bare floorboards, their only coverings the two coarse rugs given by the City. The wealthier, meanwhile, hired beds at sixpence per night from outside suppliers, who no doubt paid a commission to the keeper and his turnkeys in return for the business.

As for food, the debtors each received 14oz of bread a day, and 8 stone of meat to be shared among them every week. However, since the same weight of meat was provided no matter how numerous the inmates, the prisoners' portions could vary enormously. The committee also noted that:

---

* The Sale of Spirits Act 1750 (the Gin Act).

> The manner of distributing the bread, which is given on every alternate day, is liable to this objection, that the prisoner is tempted on the first day to eat the allowance which is meant also to support him on the second; and that a person brought to prison immediately after the hour of distribution, receives nothing for forty-eight hours, and may be six days without receiving any meat.[10]

All in all, the committee thought the prisoners' rations 'barely sufficient, without the assistance of their friends, to support life'.

A notorious feature common to most, if not all, debtors' prisons was the practice of demanding a fee, or 'garnish', on a debtor's admission to the prison, and further fees on their discharge. At Newgate in 1814, the garnish varied from 13s to 1 guinea, depending on the ward to which the prisoner found himself allocated. An unwillingness or inability to pay would incur a variety of penalties such as preventing the defaulter from warming himself by the fire or receiving any portion of charitable donations intended for all prisoners. 'It is a disgraceful and oppressive custom,' the committee observed, 'and ought not to be permitted to exist [...] and your Committee have it in evidence from the gaoler of Newgate, that a very small allowance as a compensation, and a positive order from the magistrates, would cure this evil at once.'[11]

It was generally agreed that the only way to address the serious problems at Newgate, particularly the overcrowding, was to build an entirely new prison to which all the debtors from Newgate and the Giltspur Street, Poultry and Ludgate compters would be transferred. In fact, this realisation had been reached long before the Select Committee presented its report – so long before, indeed, that by the time it presented its findings to the House in May 1814, the construction of the new prison was already far advanced, despite vocal opposition from residents who objected, in particular, to the plans for a high perimeter wall.

It was to this institution, the Whitecross Street Prison, that Bickerton was sent by order of the commissioners of the Court of Requests. Designed by the Clerk of the City Works, William Montague, work on the new prison had begun in 1813 on a plot of land between Whitecross Street, which gave it its name and onto which its entrance opened, and Red Cross Street, Cripplegate.* Located just to the north of the Church of St Giles-without-Cripplegate, until very recently part of the site had been occupied by the hall of the Worshipful Company of Framework Knitters who, ironically enough, had been forced to sell it because of the parlous state of their finances. Just like Coldbath Fields, then, the prison in which Bickerton now found himself was fairly new, being between five and thirteen years old at the time of his arrival. Unfortunately, according to John Wade, a reforming journalist writing anonymously for the *Morning Chronicle*, it had been built 'upon a worse plan than any other perhaps in the Empire':

> The preparations made fourteen or fifteen years ago for constructing a 'perfect prison' were very great. Some of the Aldermen, the City Surveyor, and others connected with the City, visited all the prisons worth examining in the Empire, took notes of the various excellencies [sic] and defects of each, and Whitecross-street Prison sprung out of these materials, and remains a complete blot upon the judgment of those deputed to investigate.[12]

Wade was not the only critic. During its investigations, the Select Committee had been invited to inspect the plans for the new prison. It had not liked what it had seen and deeply regretted that 'any improvement now suggested could [only] with difficulty be adopted'.[13]

In particular, the committee members thought the area of the prison far too small. Intended to contain 544 prisoners, the outer wall enclosed a space of just 1 acre, with much of this being 'little beneficial to the prisoners, it being left as an interval between the outer wall and the prison'. They also noted that the prison building:

> ... is not fire-proof, and is otherwise faulty, in having the gaoler's house placed at one extremity, from which the access to some parts

---

* Neither Whitecross Street nor Red Cross Street have survived to the present day. The Barbican Centre now stands on the approximate site of the Whitecross Street Prison.

of the prison is distant and inconvenient. The rooms, too, are many of them too large; a greater number of small rooms would tend not only to the comfort, but to the order also of those confined in them.[14]

When, on 10 February 1818, the aldermen had the audacity to seek a further £30,000 in addition to the £100,000 already granted in order to complete the prison, Henry Grey Bennet, the MP for Shrewsbury and a keen advocate of the abolition of gaol fees, could hardly believe his ears. 'Of all the gaols in England,' he declared, 'that in Whitecross-street was the most unfit for its object, and the most incommodious for the prisoners, while it was by far the most expensive in its construction.'[15] And yet, despite its myriad faults and the colossal sums involved, the House would eventually support the raising of more cash. After all – nearly five years into the build – what choice did it have?

Time would soon prove that the prison's failings were, indeed, manifold and covered practically every aspect of its daily functions, from its management to its sanitary arrangements. Of course, some of these inadequacies were fairly typical of debtors' prisons as a whole, but others were peculiar to Montague's supposedly model facility.

At the time of Bickerton's incarceration, Whitecross Street Prison was divided into four: the Ludgate side for those who could produce a certificate called a *douçee* proving them to be Freemen of the City of London; the London side for all other debtors arrested within the jurisdiction of the City; and the Middlesex side – the side in which Bickerton was held – for those arrested in any other part of the county, including Westminster. Finally, there was a separate ward for women, whether from the City or the county.* Although each division was essentially self-contained, with no communication permitted (in theory at least) between the inmates of each, there were no distinctions within the divisions, with those from the higher echelons of society and those from the lowest, the temporarily embarrassed and the long-term detainee, the devoted family man and the rake, the honest and the fraudulent expected

---

* In later years, the total number of divisions would increase to six, including the Middlesex Ward, the Poultry and Giltspur Street Ward, the Ludgate Ward, the Dietary Ward, the Remand Ward and the Female Ward.

to rub along together as best they might. As Professor Margot Finn has remarked, this social promiscuity was a characteristic almost unique to the prison and stood 'in sharp contrast to the genteel exclusivity associated with the other London debtors' prisons'.[16]

This lack of classification was considered by many commentators to be one of the new prison's chief flaws – just as Phillips, among many others, had considered it to be a major fault of the old, where prisoners were corralled together 'without regard to their difference of education, to their various habits of life, or to their degrees of religious or moral feeling!'[17] Classification, John Wade argued, was 'as necessary in prisons for debt, as in felons' gaols' and failure to implement such a system in the Whitecross Street Prison meant that 'greater injury has arisen from blending decent persons with reprobates in this gaol, than in any other in the Empire'.[18] Many inmates agreed, particularly gentlemen and respectable traders who found themselves forced to consort, as one prisoner expressed it, with those 'whose only ambition was to prove they never were any other than the lowest order of society'.[19]

The same complaint was made by William Hepworth Dixon, who visited the Middlesex Ward while researching his book on London's prisons. Though initially impressed by its spacious yard, which he described as 'flagged, clean, and airy – considering the dense part of the city in which the prison stands',[20] his positive impressions were quickly dispelled as his tour continued. The day room, which he thought 'the best, perhaps, in the whole establishment', was nonetheless redolent of some of the city's cheaper coffee houses, with benches and tables positioned against the walls and a bank of pigeonholes or small cupboards in which the prisoners might lock their tea, coffee or bread. Despite these facilities and the large fire at the end of the room – above which, according to George Augustus Sala, the motto *dum spiro, spero*** had been painted[21] – he found the atmosphere 'anything but agreeable':

> Store-room, cooking-room, sitting-room, dining-room, reading-room, and smoking-room, for about forty to sixty persons – it is necessarily full of many scents, and is all but as foul as the streets

---

** 'While I breathe, I hope' – a classical phrase of uncertain origin.

of Cologne. Yet every man who is sent hither [...] is compelled to take his share of the crowd and stench. There are no private apartments – no means of getting either quiet or privacy. The gentleman occupies the same day-room and night-room as the vagrant. There is no distinction of persons in Whitecross-street gaol. The unfortunate soldier, barrister, or merchant, is compelled to eat, herd, and sleep with the lowest vagabonds of his sex. There, in the day-room, is a man half buried in a mass of papers: he is a solicitor by profession, and has been accustomed to live and move in good city society. The two coarse fellows sitting near him, making the noise which seems to distract him so much, are coal-heavers. He cannot escape from them. They dine from the same bench, and sleep in the next bed. That man would give a finger, probably, to have quiet and to be alone.[22]

Up a flight of stone stairs, Dixon found the dormitories poorly ventilated and seriously overcrowded, with between sixteen and eighteen men to a room – and yet, at the time of his visit, prisoner numbers had declined by as much as 50 per cent since the 1820s.* 'When the prison is full,' he observed, 'it must be horrible to sleep in them.'

To complete his inspection of the Middlesex Ward, Dixon put his head round the door of the water closets – and immediately regretted doing so. He thought them 'disgraceful' and ideal candidates for a visit by the newly created Metropolitan Sanitary Commission. 'There is abundance of water,' he fumed, 'yet, for want of a little machinery there is only one flushing a-day, sometimes not that. The stench is exceedingly disagreeable.'[23] The problems with the prison's plumbing were nothing new because in 1828 – a decade before Dixon's visit – a prisoner had complained to the city's aldermen that 'the place through which water for the purpose of mixing with food was communicated, was abominably polluted' and 'calculated to poison the whole prison'.[24]

Depressing though these conditions were, worse in some respects was the all-pervading ennui. In having some form of meaningful occupation, the solicitor whose plight Dixon describes so feelingly was exceptional. Though the prison's regulations allowed them to work, few debtors

---

* Based upon prisoner numbers quoted by Wade in 1828 and Dixon in 1850.

did so, simply because they struggled to obtain employment from the outside world: with tailors, cobblers, clergymen and scriveners aplenty beyond the walls of the prison, who would go to the trouble of seeking the services of those immured within? As a result, the prison possessed an atmosphere of 'suspended animation', the lives of its inmates on hold for weeks, months, years – or, in some cases, forever. In Dixon's view:

> One had much better be transported than sent to this prison for seven or ten years. In Australia, by industry and good conduct, a convict may redeem himself, may recover a position, and amass wealth. All that is quite impossible here. The poor debtor can do nothing but waste his time – which, to an active nature, is also a consumption of the brain as well.[25]

And here was to be found the ultimate failure of imprisonment for debt: even those with the very best of intentions towards their creditors found it impossible to meet their obligations because the system that punished them not only made it utterly impracticable for them to earn and pay but also caused them to accumulate yet more debt merely to survive. Caught in this vicious circle, it is not surprising that the other pervasive feeling was one of melancholy.

Little wonder, too, that the prisoners should make the most of whatever opportunities presented themselves for diversion. If Charles Dickens is to be believed – and there seems little reason to doubt him, given his intimate knowledge of London's debtors' prisons – Whitecross Street Prison's visiting hours were much more limited than was commonly the case. Mr Perker, the benign lawyer in *The Posthumous Papers of the Pickwick Club*, tells his eponymous client that 'the bolt's on, sixteen hours out of the four-and-twenty',[26] meaning that the main prison gate was locked for that period, with no person allowed in or out.

But there were other diversions. Some prisoners attended the daily services in the chapel; some played chess or read, with books being 'admitted at discretion';[27] and despite the prohibitions against it, others gambled with seemingly carefree abandon. On 2 October 1828, for instance, *The Times* reported that a complaint had been made against a prisoner named List 'for that he [...] kept a gaming table'. On further enquiry by Alderman Sir Peter Laurie, it was suggested that the gaming, though strictly forbidden, should be ignored since it was, so the accused averred, 'only for farthings "amongst a select party of gentlemen for their own amusement"'.[28] Laurie, a keen advocate of prison reform who would later author two books on the subject, disagreed, strongly supporting the determination 'not to countenance the introduction of gaming under the plea of amusement'.

Another sore temptation was drink. In a society notorious for its bibulousness from the king downwards, each male prisoner was permitted just a single pint of wine per day – and no spirits. The predictable consequence was smuggling.

In a typical example, on 19 March 1827, 'a respectable looking female'[29] named Sarah Allen faced a charge of having attempted to introduce a gallon of spirits into the prison. Though previously suspected and searched, it was not until the 19th that a bladder of rum had been discovered concealed within her basket of potatoes and another containing gin found on her person. In her defence, Allen, the wife of a crown prisoner convicted of operating an illegal still, pleaded extreme distress 'in consequence of having been so long deprived of her husband's company, and from having had every particle of property seized'.[30] Alderman William Thompson, apparently without querying how the supposedly destitute wife of an illicit distiller had laid her hands on the alcohol, and taking into consideration the facts that her husband would remain in gaol for some time to come and that her visiting rights would be suspended, which he 'considered as amounting to some punishment', sentenced her to a week's imprisonment in Bickerton's old place of detention, the Middlesex House of Correction at Coldbath Fields.

Less than three months later, the prison governor detained two more women, Anne Pearce and her sister-in-law, Mary, when they sought to enter the prison carrying 4 gallons of gin and rum hidden beneath their skirts in twelve long skins. When examined at the Guildhall Justice Room, the alderman on duty was inclined, like Thompson before him, to accept Pearce's claim that pecuniary distress had driven her to make the attempt, but when her story began to unravel in the face of further investigations, he sentenced her to three months' imprisonment.

Believing her young accomplice to be merely 'an ignorant country girl', she received a lesser term of six weeks.[31]

As is the case with all smuggling, no matter how much contraband is confiscated, it can reasonably be assumed that much more escapes the attention of the authorities. In a lengthy letter published in the *Morning Chronicle* on 7 October 1824, a correspondent writing under the pseudonym 'Humanitas' described his own mercifully brief experiences in the London side of Whitecross Prison. In the day room, which was furnished with twenty-six benches and thirteen deal tables, he found himself consorting with a motley group of debtors, variously occupied in smoking, drinking and playing cards and dominoes. Every class of society was represented and none dared stand aloof on the basis of his rank outside the prison walls. Anyone suspected of doing so would be 'voted a bore' and 'subjected to every annoyance the ingenious minds of the vulgar in such cases are so happy in devising'.[32]

As the evening progressed, so did its boisterousness, 'Humanitas' discovering that most of his companions were 'in a state of intoxication'. At ten o'clock, the prisoners went to their dormitories, but here he found that another ceremony must be gone through:

> ... which was to give a glass of liquor to each man in the room. I then laid myself down on the bed, and for two hours was doomed to hear every sort of language which, in so mixed a company, and the majority inebriated, may be more easily imagined than described.[33]

It is difficult to believe that such levels of drunkenness, apparently a routine feature of prison life, could be sustained on the regulation pint-a-day of cheap prison-issue wine.

A combination of boredom, frustration, hopelessness, gambling and alcohol inevitably led to outbreaks of violence in all debtors' prisons; add overcrowding to these factors and the prison began to resemble a tinderbox. By the 1820s, Whitecross Street Prison had become the second most populous of London's debtors' prisons,[34] and by far the largest of its divisions was the Middlesex side.

When John Wade wrote his condemnatory article in 1828, the Giltspur Street Yard, allocated to the Londoners who were not freemen, generally contained no more than thirty prisoners, the Ludgate Yard between twenty and thirty, and the Female Yard usually around twenty-five. The Middlesex Yard, in contrast, contained around 400, and often in excess of that number.

An uneven distribution had been predicted but seriously under-estimated when the prison was built, with the result that the area of the Middlesex Yard was only a third larger than that of the Giltspur Street and Ludgate Yards. This miscalculation had led not only to serious overcrowding but also, all too often, to the flaring of tempers, with assaults being perpetrated not by gaoler upon prisoner, as had been the case in Coldbath Fields Prison under the malevolent sway of Thomas Aris, but by prisoner upon prisoner. In fact, conditions had become so poor that, according to Wade, all the acts of violence and insubordination committed within the prison walls could be traced to the Middlesex Yard. 'So ill regulated, indeed, is the place,' he declared, 'that when any individuals become offensive to the other prisoners, there is no place to which to remove them, except the infirmary, where they may exercise their disposition to annoy in the presence of those who are least able to bear it.'[35]

But violence was not merely the spontaneous product of the intolerably cramped conditions, it was built into the daily rituals of the debtors – and, to a large degree, policed by them, with Dixon noting, 'In point of fact, the governor and officers of this gaol have little or no power over their charges beyond what is absolutely necessary to their safe custody'.[36] Like all societies, over time the debtors had created their own customs and regulations – most notorious among which was that of 'catting', a practice that would produce more than its fair share of newsprint during Bickerton's day. According to a debtor named John Duncomb Bentham, catting was common to many if not all debtors' prisons. 'It was the custom in the gaol,' he told a visiting magistrate:

> ... and had been so, he believed, from its first erection, for the prisoners in every separate ward, to subscribe the sum of 16s to the expenses of the ward, for coals, wood, swabbers, &c., and on failure of payment, or giving some property to the steward of the ward as security for that sum, to 'cat' him.[37]

To 'cat' meant to seize by force that which had not been voluntarily surrendered by the new arrivals, the term being derived from the habit of those involved to mew like cats when signalling their purpose to one another, their business usually being conducted at night. Such seizures were committed by prisoners from a ward different to that of the intended victim, and they further protected their anonymity by adopting disguises, such as blackening their faces and wearing cowls made from their bedding. Not unnaturally, the prisoners who had been unwilling or unable to pay the subscription, but who were possessed of sufficient strength and will, often resisted these attempts on their already meagre property.

One such prisoner in the Middlesex Ward was Captain William Frederick Kelly, 'late of Brighton',[38] an Irish naval officer who, by his own account, 'had served His Majesty, by sea and land, more than forty years'.[39] Kelly was also a serial debtor, having spent (and going on to spend) many of the years following the resignation of his commission in 1815 in debtors' prisons, often on account of matters relating to the turf, including distinctly dubious horse-dealing. In later years, he would also abscond from the King's Bench Prison.[40]

Despite serious doubts regarding his probity in financial dealings, however, Kelly would not fail to uphold the honour of the Royal Navy when it came to close-quarter actions. On Tuesday, 24 June 1823, at least five disguised prisoners had entered his ward in company with its steward. Understanding that they intended to cat him, Kelly initially offered them his snuffbox, which he told them had cost him a guinea. But when the steward rejected the box as being of insufficient value, the captain became 'extremely violent', took up a quart pot and, in the best manner of a character from an early story by the Anglo-Irish novelist Charles Lever, swore 'by the Holy Jaysus' to break the head of any man who dared approach him.[41]

When a prisoner named Robert Cauch wrested the tankard from his hand, Kelly drew his penknife and, according to the testimony of his opponents:

> … with dreadful imprecations vowed he would stab the first man that touched him. Upon this there was a push forward, and one or two

of the foremost were shoved upon Kelly, who immediately struck in all directions with his knife, and wounded several. He was at length overpowered, the watch called, and the Governor alarmed, who had him conveyed to the strong room for the night.[42]

During the affray, Kelly had managed to stab four of the 'cats' and Thomas Milner Wadd, the prison's surgeon, declared that he must have used his penknife 'with great violence, the blade alone not being of sufficient length to inflict so deep a wound as that on the loins of Sutton. A part of the haft must also have entered his body.'[43]

When brought before Alderman Robert Waithman, Kelly remained defiant, demanding 'with much warmth, what right had they to force into his room, and rob him of his property?' Despite the fact that the cats had entered Kelly's apartment with the avowed intention of taking his property, that he was outnumbered by at least five to one, that the first real act of aggression had been committed by Cauch when he forced the tankard from Kelly's hand, and that the Irish captain had himself been left with a long contused wound on his forehead, Waithman sided with Cauch and his accomplices and ordered that a commitment be made out against the Irishman, telling him that 'he would have felt great sorrow if death had ensued through his violence'. Given that Kelly had vowed to 'rip the guts out of anybody' who attempted to steal from him, Waithman may have misjudged the fiery captain's potential for repentance.*

In contrast to Waithman, Newman Knowlys, the Recorder of London and therefore the Senior Circuit Judge of the Central Criminal Court, took an altogether dimmer view of the cats' activities, siding with the intended victim rather than the perpetrators and finding serious fault with Governor James Spencer for turning a blind eye to such practices. According to a prisoner named Valentine Musson, on 20 November 1826, a group of eight men in disguise had entered the ward of a fellow inmate named Mapleston, intent on stealing his bedding 'and otherwise maltreating him'.[44] Although they had armed themselves with brooms

---

* According to a report in *The Standard* of 2 October 1828, Captain Kelly was still an inmate of Whitecross Street Prison more than five years later, when he complained to Sir Peter Laurie about fleas in his bedding and the lack of privacy allowed to prisoners when receiving visits from their loved ones.

and sticks, clearly indicating that they were fully prepared to resort to force, their intended victim, like Kelly before him, put up a stout defence and the witness testified to soon seeing 'the chamber utensils, with their contents, flying from his room'. After one of the 'cats' was knocked down, his companions retreated, but they quickly regrouped and returned to the charge, at which point, Mapleston began to shout, 'Murder!' 'He was', according to Masson, 'dreadfully beaten, and they left him with the blood flowing profusely from his wounds.'[45]

When Governor Spencer was called to give evidence regarding the brawl, the Recorder 'censured him with great severity for not having acted with more energy to prevent the outrage'. The humiliated governor attempted to defend himself by explaining that catting was the established custom, but Knowlys was having none of it:

> A custom, Sir! No, do not let the Court hear of such a defence. Robbery on the highway and picking pockets have been customary from time immemorial. The public will not hear of taxes levied except by authority of Parliament, or of any taxes levied in such a manner. You must put a stop to it, Sir, and cause notices to that effect to be given to those under your care [...] do your duty by putting an end to the practice.[46]

He was no more accepting of the defence counsel's suggestion – supported by the jury – that the perpetrators should be treated leniently as the levying of the 16s tax was 'an ancient observance, which had been anciently enforced by the practice now complained of' and that it had been 'connived at by the authorities who had the charge of the prison'. Knowlys responded that if the offence had been a mere personal insult, such as pulling off Mapleston's bed clothes, 'the Court would have listened to the humane suggestion of the jury, but it was violence, approaching almost to murder. The inmates of that gaol would think themselves countenanced, if the defendants now convicted received but a slight punishment'. He sentenced them all to six months' hard labour in Giltspur Street Compter.[47]

In claiming that the practice of catting had never received 'the slightest sanction or connivance' from the prison authorities, the judge was quite mistaken. The custom was very well publicised. Time and again, its consequences had been brought to the notice of the Middlesex Magistrates and they had done nothing to suppress it.

Indeed, on hearing of another case of catting less than two years after Knowlys' pronouncements, Alderman Sir Peter Laurie would merely remark that 'he could afford the complainant no redress. There was a description of freemasonry in operation in the prison, which he could not put a stop to.'[48] Supine the aldermen may have been, but it was also true that the 1812 Act of Parliament that had paved the way for the erection of the new prison had explicitly stated that the inmates would be 'subject to the same Regulations, Management, and Controul, and shall enjoy and be entitled to the same Rights, Privileges, Charities, Gifts, Benefits, and Advantages whatsoever as [...] the Prisoners would have been under and subject to [...] if the said Prisoners [...] had not been removed [to Whitecross Street]'.[49]

Supported by this legislation, the imprisoned debtors jealously guarded the ancient privileges and customs that had been a part of life in prisons like the Fleet, the Marshalsea and the King's Bench, and the City's mayor and aldermen had neither the will nor the inclination to challenge them. Besides, were they to push through a programme of reform, they might well find themselves worse off because, as Margot Finn has pointed out, 'the City freeman of today might well be the imprisoned debtor of the morrow'.[50]

Governor Spencer may have been weak, and he was certainly unwilling or unable to challenge or remedy the longstanding customs of his prison, but he appears to have been guilty of neither the overt corruption nor the arbitrary brutality of men like Thomas Aris. According to the testimony of the debtors in his care, he was a kindly, even charitable man – and, ironically, it was the consequences of his benevolent inclinations that would eventually force him to resign his post and its salary of nearly £700 per annum.

On Saturday, 27 September 1828, a committee of five aldermen met at the Guildhall to consider a number of charges brought against the governor, the most serious of which was that he had misappropriated money donated by the Society for the Discharge and Relief of Persons Imprisoned for Small Debts, more usually known as the Craven Street

Society. Convinced that imprisonment for debt was 'infectious both to body and mind',[51] the society routinely contributed funds to offset against the small sums for which many debtors had been imprisoned but, believing that creditors had a moral duty to work compassionately with debtors rather than against them, funds would be contributed only on the understanding that creditors would compromise with their debtors and not seek repayment in full. The debtors themselves must owe no more than £200 in total and no more than £60 to any single creditor, and they must also be sober, industrious and of good character. The maximum amount to be paid by the society to any creditor was £20.[52]

The man recruited to negotiate with the creditors of the Whitecross Street Prison inmates was Governor Spencer and when the society studied their accounts for the year 1827–28, they found discrepancies between the amounts they had advanced and the amounts he had paid to creditors, but with no money returned to the society's coffers. As a result of their further investigations, the society submitted a memorial to the Court of Aldermen 'complaining that an extraordinary and gross violation of integrity and confidence had taken place'.[53]

The committee of five aldermen were now tasked with investigating the discrepancies. What they discovered during the course of their inquiries probably surprised and pleased them in equal measure because, in place of the usual sordid story of embezzlement for personal gain, they found that while Spencer had undoubtedly used the society's money in an entirely irregular fashion, he had given it to the debtors about to be released, being 'under the impression that a few pounds would be of important service to the latter in again beginning the world, and that the creditors would not feel the loss'.[54] In addition, a number of witnesses came forward to inform the committee that Spencer had 'given 50*l* or 60*l* a year out of his own pocket to ameliorate the sufferings of some of the unhappy creatures in the prison over which he presided'.

As if to further cement his reputation as a man of integrity, when the governor resigned after being asked to account for his actions, the Court of Aldermen received a petition 'signed by almost every one of the unfortunate debtors now confined in the prison, declaring that they one and all bear testimony to the humanity of Mr Spencer, and praying that he should be immediately reinstated'. For their part, the aldermen declared that the governor was 'completely exonerated from all moral censure, although he is considered blameable in having, under any circumstances, applied the contributions of the society in a different manner from that intended'.⁵⁵

Overall, the committee can hardly have been more satisfied with this unexpected outcome to their investigations into a case of fraud. The prisoners, though, would be disappointed in their attempts to have Spencer reinstated and his job was given instead to Deputy Governor Barrett, who would remain in post until his death in 1842. This decision on the part of the aldermen not to reinstate Spencer suggests that there was, perhaps, more to the case than was reported – and that, in testifying to the misguided kindness that motivated the governor's misdemeanour, the aldermen were seeking to deflect attention and avoid blame, just as the Middlesex Magistrates had sought to shield themselves from criticism by speaking of Thomas Aris' humanity in the discharge of his duties. Certainly, Margot Finn believes Spencer to have been very far from the angelic character described in the newspapers, and points to his having acted as an unofficial pawnbroker within the prison, 'advancing sums on debtors' watches and plate, while conniving with debtor Solomon Neate to dispose of a chaise, harness and Newfoundland dog belonging by rights to Neate's creditors'.⁵⁶

On 21 September 1829, *The Times* complained that warrants issued by the Court of Requests were 'daily crowding' Whitecross Street Prison and went on to cite the case of one Elizabeth Caisley, 'a poor woman [...] arrested for the sum of 1s 3½d, and locked up. The costs amounted to five times the amount of the debt, and the prisoner was actually, when she entered the prison, without the means of buying a morsel of bread.'

If the destitute Elizabeth Caisley stands at one end of the spectrum in terms of sums owed and the costs awarded, at the other end stands the rotund, bespectacled, good-humoured but outraged figure of Mr Pickwick, found guilty of breach of promise and made to pay an eye-watering £750 in damages to Mrs Bardell in Chapter 33 of *The*

Pickwick Papers. Bickerton is likely to have fallen midway between the fictional Mr Pickwick and the all-too-real Elizabeth Caisley.

Unable to pay her debt, Caisley was sentenced by the Court of Requests to a term of twenty days; unable or unwilling to pay his, Bickerton's sentence would have been of longer duration (up to forty days), assuming, as seems probable, that the disputed sum plus damages and costs exceeded 20s.[57] Like Pickwick, Bickerton may have declared to Dance or his lawyers, 'not one farthing of costs or damages do you ever get from me, if I spend the rest of my existence in a debtor's prison'.[58] But, also like Pickwick, perhaps circumstances and experience taught him to compromise in order to regain his liberty — though William Hutton, historian and commissioner of the Birmingham Court of Requests, admitted to knowing 'many an obstinate defendant lie the stated time in prison, merely out of revenge to the plaintiff; when, with a small degree of prudence, he was well able to pay him'.[59]

Either way, assuming that Bickerton believed his original claim to be just and bearing in mind the nature of his experiences in the Whitecross Street Prison, we can understand why Dance's 'treachery' remained an *idée fixe* right up to the time when he lay, confused, starving and close to death in the early days of October 1833.

10

Death and Resurrection

In the Crown & Sceptre, the clock on the wall of the make-do courtroom stood at a little past 10 p.m. Coroner Higgs and his jury had devoted over two hours to examining the circumstances around the miserable death of John Bickerton; now they must agree on a verdict.

To all intents and purposes, it was an open and shut case; after all, several of the jurors had themselves seen Bickerton 'pick up the heads of mackerel and other fish off dunghills, and take them home to eat',[1] so his hand-to-mouth means of subsistence were known to them all. Yes, the parish authorities appeared to have failed in their duty of care, but even here there were mitigating circumstances as Bickerton was reputed to have 'always pertinaciously refused going into the hospital'.[2] This being the case, and in the absence of any evidence of foul play or suicide, the jury rapidly – and reasonably – concluded that 'the deceased died from the want of the common necessaries of life'.[3]

This verdict must have come as a significant relief to the parish overseers, in particular. The decision on whether to pay a coroner for his time depended on his ability to convince his paymasters – the local Justices of the Peace – that a death was potentially violent, suspicious or unexplained. Higgs clearly felt that Bickerton's death fell into at least one of these categories and that an inquest was, therefore, justifiable. If such a case were to be considered at a modern inquest, then it is quite probable that the apparent failings of those responsible for poor relief would have led to an open verdict, which leaves unanswered the question of who was ultimately responsible for a death or deaths; it suggests that insufficient information has been made available in order for the coroner to reach any alternative verdict, and implies that important questions remain unresolved.

While an open verdict does not mean that a misdemeanour has *definitely* been committed, it leaves open the possibility that blame *could* be attributed and culpability demonstrated, if more evidence were forthcoming. In October 1833, the jury examining Bickerton's case had no such option, and the overseers could breathe a collective sigh of relief. In conclusion, Higgs thanked the jurors for their service and confirmed that he would write to the High Bailiff to take care of the property of the deceased until it could be delivered up to his next of kin – whoever that might be.

Given that Bickerton had told Charles Rice and John Hastings that he had left his property to his niece, Elizabeth Wood, it seems unlikely that the claim made by Richard Palin Bickerton would have been recognised, especially as he was a more distant relative than Mrs Wood. However, the parish of St Margaret and St John may not have been too scrupulous in the matter as his offer to foot the bill for Bickerton's burial would save the parish both the trouble and the expense. Perhaps they passed responsibility for the body to the surgeon and left him to argue the rights and wrongs of the case with his aunt. What we do know is that the matter was quickly resolved, because on 10 October, two days after the inquest, Bickerton was interred in the burial ground of St John the Evangelist on Horseferry Road, just a few hundred yards from the banks of the Thames.

Designed by Thomas Archer and consecrated on 20 June 1728, St John the Evangelist was one of a proposed fifty churches intended to accommodate the estimated 200,000 Londoners who, in 1711, lacked any permanent place of worship.[4] According to legend, its unique design, with a tower at each corner, was the result of a petulant intervention by Queen Anne who, when asked by the architect what design she would favour, kicked over her footstool and uttered the imperious words, 'Like that!' In fact, Archer added the towers to prevent subsidence – 'that the whole might sink equally'[5] in the swampy ground of Millbank – but whether the product of royal whim or astute civil engineering, the church's unusual appearance had its detractors, most famously Charles Dickens, who thought it 'very hideous [...] generally resembling some petrified monster, frightful and gigantic, on its back with its legs in the air'.[6] Whatever its merits or demerits, however, it was not the church but its burial ground that caused the greatest consternation among the Georgian congregation of St John's.

By the turn of the nineteenth century, overcrowding in the capital's churchyards and burial grounds had developed from a long-running scandal into an outright crisis. Between 1801 and 1831, the population of London is estimated to have grown by 73 per cent, from 959,000 to 1,655,000[7] and with poor sanitation, high population density and diseases such as diphtheria, cholera and scarlet fever all contributing to an average life expectancy of around 40 years, burial plots were at a premium. In 1834, it was calculated that during each of the previous three years, burials within the Bishop of London's diocese had averaged 22,548 in graveyards that totalled just 103 acres. This meant 219 burials per acre, per year. But this was just the average. In some grounds, the number of interments was as high as 891 per acre.[8] What this meant in real terms was described by the Reverend John Blackburn of Pentonville, 'Heaped soil, saturated and blackened with human remains and fragments of the dead, exposed to the rude insults of ignorant and brutal spectators'.[9]

Seeking to address the issue of overcrowding, in 1802 the gloriously named Anthony Florian Madinger Willich, a German-born medical writer and author of the *Domestic Encyclopaedia*, recommended that 'the privilege of being deposited in a coffin (whether kept above or underground), in towns shall be conferred only on those who have rendered themselves worthy of such a distinction, by virtuous and patriotic actions' and 'all others [...] shall either be buried at a certain distance from inhabited places, or at least twenty feet deep'.[10] Of course, as Willich knew full well, in the vast majority of urban cemeteries it would be absolutely impossible to excavate graves 20ft deep.

Burial outside the city's periphery, however, was a much more practical proposition and this strategy was adopted by the authorities of the overcrowded parishes of St Giles-in-the-Fields, St George, Hanover Square, St James, Westminster and St Martin's-in-the-Fields. At the time of their acquisition, these newly consecrated patches of land were relatively isolated and separate from any buildings, whether commercial or domestic, but with the juggernaut-like expansion of the city it was not long before they were swallowed by new developments. And with the continuing growth of the local population, the demands placed upon the burial grounds became ever greater.

The issue was not simply one of acreage. The proximity of the closely packed living to the even more closely packed dead gave rise to serious concerns over health and sanitation. On 12 April 1830, *The Times* reported:

> The practice of interring the dead in the midst of the habitations of the living has long excited the surprise and horror of strangers, and could not be endured in a state in other respects so 'well-policed' as ours, but that long custom has rendered the great majority of the people insensible to the disgust which so revolting an usage is calculated to produce.[11]

Whatever the supposed opinions of the 'great majority' – and, of course, that majority seldom found an effective voice – an influential cadre of social reformers was speaking out against ancient customs with ever-increasing vehemence. One such was George 'Graveyard' Walker, a Nottingham-born surgeon and campaigner who spent two years examining the disgusting conditions in the tightly packed burial grounds of London before publishing the first of his many works on the subject, *Gatherings from Graveyards*, in 1839.

If the title suggested to some readers an anthology of quirky epitaphs collected by a mild-mannered antiquarian with a penchant for visiting churchyards, they were to be swiftly disabused. Walker did not pull his punches, and in the opening passages of his book he expressed his astonishment that 'London, the seat of science, the arena of inventions, the vast amphitheatre where all that is great, good, and noble; all that is conducive to the comforts and the pleasures of life [...] should bear upon its breast those plague spots, the burial grounds'.[12] In vivid, impassioned prose, he wrote of the worst being 'saturated, absolutely saturated with human putrescence',[13] and of those unfortunate enough to live close by being constantly assailed by putrefying effluvia, foul smells, bloated flies or 'body bugs', and sickness.

Certain vested interests – in particular, the vestries that earned fees from each interment – accused Walker of having 'outrageously overstated'[14] his case, but the overwhelming consensus of critical opinion was that by drawing to its attention the risk of 'diseases of a fatal nature, such as malignant, putrid, and exanthematous fevers',[15] he had done society a notable service. The following year, he was asked to present the evidence that he had gathered at considerable personal risk to a Select Committee of the House of Commons and his testimony and his continued campaigning proved so compelling that another champion of public health, Edwin Chadwick, took up the case.

A barrister by training but a reformer by instinct, today Chadwick is best known for his work on Poor Law reform and for his highly influential and best-selling *Report on The Sanitary Condition of the Labouring Population of Great Britain* (1842), but the following year, he published a supplementary report dealing exclusively with the practice of interment in urban areas.[16] He described the problem in great detail and in equally stark terms:

> It is fully ascertained and well recognized that the alluvial soil, or whatever soil that receives the exuviæ of animal matter, or the bodies of dead animals, will become rich in general; it will abound in animal matter; and the water that percolates through the soil thus enriched will thus become injurious to the health of the individuals using it [...]
>
> In the metropolis, on spaces of ground which do not exceed 203 acres, closely surrounded by the abodes of the living, layer upon layer, each consisting of a population numerically equivalent to a large army of 20,000 adults, and nearly 30,000 youths and children, is every year imperfectly interred. Within the period of the existence of the present generation, upwards of a million of dead must have been interred in those same spaces.[17]

Going on to describe innumerable instances of graveyards knee-deep in putrid slime, people living cheek by jowl with the dead, open graves beneath bedroom windows, bodies being disinterred while flesh still clung to the bones, exploding coffins and poisoned congregations – and with all of his findings backed up by the kind of detailed statistical analysis for which he was famed – Chadwick's case was irrefutable and would lead, ultimately, to the 1851 Act to Amend the Laws Concerning the Burial of the Dead in the Metropolis. It would take a few years more for the Burials Act, as it came commonly to be known, to take full effect, but Walker, Chadwick and their supporters had won an important victory, bringing to an end centuries of urban burial.

That Bickerton's last resting place, the burial ground of St John the Evangelist, was overcrowded did not, then, make it in any way exceptional. Originally consecrated in 1731, the site on Horseferry Road had soon proved much too small for the population it served but exorbitant land costs rendered the purchase of a new plot unaffordable. Instead, the parish paid for extra earth to be spread across the graveyard to a depth of 3ft – a practice so common and longstanding that it had caused the diarist John Evelyn to remark in the previous century that many of London's churches looked as though they had been 'built in pits'.[18] Additional soil was deposited twice more in the coming years, with the result that it became necessary to embank and wall the perimeter of the graveyard in order to prevent earth and cadavers slipping into the public highway – a risk exacerbated by the ground conditions which, due to the proximity of the Thames, were later described as 'very damp' with the water flowing in 'abundantly'.[19]

The problem of overcrowding at Horseferry Road was somewhat alleviated in 1823, when the neighbouring landowner, Lord Grosvenor, finally agreed to sell a plot of land adjoining the original burial ground for £2,050, with compensation for the loss of leasehold interests fixed at a further £2,258.[20] But with the population of London continuing to rise exponentially, the solution could be only temporary.

To deter bereaved families from choosing Horseferry Road as the last resting place for their loved ones, the cost of interments was also regularly increased but, even so, by the end of the first quarter of the nineteenth century, a surveyor employed by the parish reported:

Death and Resurrection

The part of the ground allotted for the poor is buried all over four or five deep; that 5,126 graves had been dug in ten years; that 5 or 6 coffins are placed in every grave where eight feet in depth can be obtained, and that many of the bodies are less than two feet from the surface.[21]

Placed in such shallow graves, it was inevitable that the dead would be disturbed, not merely by gravediggers – a class whose 'surreptitious modes' of disposing of half-decayed bodies Chadwick described as abhorrent[22] – but by rats, dogs and crows scavenging for food. Most notorious among the disturbers of the dead, though, were the 'body snatchers' or 'resurrection men'.

In Great Britain, the illegal trade in bodies for dissection had its origin in the early eighteenth century when the great London hospitals of St Thomas and St Bartholomew began to teach anatomy; a precedent soon followed by an increasing number of private medical schools, which required no licence to open and advertise for students. Prior to this development, the dissecting of human specimens had been the preserve of the Company of Barbers and Surgeons, a body to which, in 1541, Henry VIII had granted the right to 'have and take without cõtradiction foure persons condempned adjudged and put to deathe for feloni [...] for their further and better knowlage instruction in sight learning and experience in the said scyence or facultie of Surgery'.[23]

Inevitably, with hospitals and private lecturers competing for students, the demand for fresh subjects grew exponentially. In 1752, the problem was addressed, albeit somewhat indirectly, by a new law which placed the corpses of all executed murderers in the hands of the anatomists, 'because the crime of murder has been more frequently perpetrated than formerly [...] and [...] it is thereby become necessary that some further terror and peculiar infamy be added to the punishment of death'.[24] But in an age when science was finally throwing off the shackles of ages-old Hippocratic and Galenic medical theory, the gallows simply couldn't keep pace with demand – particularly when methods of preservation were poor and even the freshest subjects spoiled quickly.

The first to attempt to meet demand by committing grave robbery were not criminal gangs but anatomy students and hospital porters stealing for their own use or to supply their professors. It was not long, though, before what one eminent surgeon described as a 'set of wretched, clever, unprincipled rascals'[25] recognised the potential to develop a lucrative new trade and by 1828 the London police believed that, while there were probably only ten individuals living almost exclusively on the profits of the trade, these were supported by a further 200 who were occasionally employed.[26]

With the anatomy schools competing for bodies, prices naturally rose, and for those willing and able to supply fresh corpses the rewards could be substantial. In 1811, for instance, Joseph Naples, a resurrectionist working with the infamous Borough Gang, recorded in his diary that he had received '£4/4/0' for an adult's body and a further '£1/10/0' for that of a child,[27] and this at a time when a skilled worker, such as a plumber, might earn just £0 4s 6d for a day's labour.[28] Naples also noted that, during the year 1810–11, his gang had sold 305 adult corpses and forty-four 'small'; another thirty-seven had been sold to the Edinburgh schools. This would equate to an annual income for the gang of over £1,500.

For particularly unusual specimens, the prices could be extraordinarily high, with John Hunter, the pioneering anatomist, famously paying £500 (roughly £60,000 today) for the skeleton of the 7ft 7in Charles Byrne, the 'Irish Giant'; indeed, so anxious was Hunter to possess Byrne's body that he paid accomplices to steal the corpse while it was en route to Margate to be buried at sea.[29] On another occasion, resurrectionists exhumed and then decapitated the body of a young woman whose head had grown to nearly twice its normal size because of 'an immense secretion of osseous and cartilaginous substance'[30] resulting from an infected dental cavity. Dismemberment of a body in situ was itself a highly unusual occurrence and may indicate that, like the theft of the Irish Giant, this exhumation had been especially commissioned.

By 1828, the average price of an adult specimen had risen to 8 guineas, with anatomists and their students, in the words of the surgeon Sir Astley Cooper, 'completely at the feet of the resurrection men'.[31] For such potentially substantial rewards, the risks were relatively insignificant – at least in terms of the penalties handed down by the courts. The only Act of Parliament bearing any relevance to the matter had been passed as long ago as the reign of James I (1603–25). That Act had made body snatching a felony – but only if the corpse had been stolen specifically for the purposes of witchcraft. Moreover, according to English law, a dead body belonged to no one, not even the next of kin; therefore, a prosecution for felony could be pursued only if goods other than the body itself were taken – the coffin, for instance, or the shroud.

Knowing this, body snatchers were careful to ensure that they replaced in the grave everything but the corpse. If taken in possession of a body, they could be charged only with a misdemeanour and, if found guilty, faced a penalty no more severe than a fine or a short term of imprisonment in a local gaol. So much for the law.

When brought before the court of public opinion, on the other hand, body snatchers could expect to be very roughly handled, and in January 1828, a hospital porter named Luke Redmond was murdered for his supposed part in the trade.[32] For this reason, the resurrection men often went armed 'with bludgeons, and other offensive weapons'.[33]

In terms of the exhumation of corpses, the robbers' methods were well established and have been described by the surgeon John Flint South who, as a medical student at St Thomas's Hospital in the second decade of the nineteenth century, acknowledged that he had benefited directly from their labours:

> The mode in which the exhumation was performed by the adepts was not, as might have been supposed, by digging out the newly-filled earth from the not very deep grave, and exposing the coffin lid, and, after removing, to take out the corpse, but they found it most convenient to dig down at the head of the grave, knock in the end of the coffin, and drag the body out. It was then disrobed from the shroud, which was most carefully put back in the coffin [...] The subject was then doubled up into the smallest possible compass, and either thrust into a coarse sack or an orange basket – if in season – and laid aside till as many graves as were convenient had been despoiled.[34]

Time and time again, suspicious carts or carriages would be stopped by police constables or watchmen and multiple bodies discovered 'doubled up, like fish in a barrel',[35] and burial grounds and churchyards were found to have been stripped of all the bodies which the robbers thought sufficiently well preserved to be of use to their customers.

Of course, to obtain knowledge of recent burials, the resurrection men relied upon a network of informants, including paid watchers, but also gravediggers who, according to evidence given in 1795, could expect to receive 5s for every corpse removed.[36] After all, with such potentially substantial rewards, the grave robbers could afford to be generous with their bribes.

In the words of one magistrate, what could be more agonising for a bereaved parent or spouse to anticipate than that the tombs of their loved ones 'would be violated, and their persons stripped, exposed, cut to pieces, and divided'?[37] And the reports from magistrates' courts are full of the horrified testimony of men – and it was almost invariably men who gave the evidence – whose family graves had been pillaged. But, in the face of such organised, extensive and determined criminality, how could they hope to foil the body snatchers?

Inevitably, just as the demand for anatomy specimens had given rise to the illegal trade in cadavers, so that trade in turn generated opportunities for entrepreneurs of a different stripe. One such was Gabriel Aughtie of Cheapside who, in July 1796, patented a reinforced iron coffin 'that will perfectly secure the body therein; it being so securely bound with iron internally, and the lid fixed on with springs and screws, which, when fixed on, it will be impossible to take it off again'.[38] Priced at 5 guineas, Aughtie's coffin was beyond the reach of all but the wealthy, but cheaper alternatives included coffins banded with iron or bound with chains.[39]

In Scotland, particularly in the neighbourhood of the anatomy schools, 'mortsafes' – external cages made of iron or iron and stone – were popular, with some churches earning extra income from the hiring out of reusable models. Also in Scotland, one bereaved parent is recorded as having placed a 'deathful apparatus' on his child's coffin. This device, filled with 'a large quantity of gunpowder', was intended to explode if the coffin were disturbed – destroying the body and almost certainly injuring the depredators.[40] Most effective of all, though, was the placing of a reliable guard or guards who could ensure that a grave remained undisturbed until the natural processes of decay rendered the body beyond use: a period that might last up to six weeks. Of course, the key to this approach was locating someone whose integrity could be relied upon – and that usually meant a member of the family.

With demand remaining constant and vigilance increasing, the body snatchers soon expanded their activities far beyond the immediate neighbourhoods of the anatomists' demonstration rooms, whether in England or Scotland, and the newspapers of the period recount multiple instances of body snatching in the provinces, though the vast majority of the corpses still found their way to the anatomy schools in London and Edinburgh. Of course, transportation across the country of fairly large numbers of bodies presented additional difficulties, and one of the earliest and best historians of the trade has described the methods adopted:

> It was the custom of the resurrection-men, when they had bodies to send from the country to London, to forward them so that they should, in outward appearance, correspond with the class of goods exported from the place where the bodies had been obtained. If the goods usually came to London in crates, crates were used by the body-snatchers; if ordinary packing-cases, then the bodies were enclosed in like receptacles. The proceeds of the exhumations at Yarmouth were probably packed in barrels, and came through Billingsgate [fish market].[41]

The movement of corpses over long distances increased the risk of decomposition while they were in transit and, in October 1826, 'a horrible stench' emanating from three casks labelled 'Bitter Salts' resulted in the discovery of eleven bodies on the quayside at Liverpool. A further twenty-two were found, also packed in casks, in a nearby cellar.[42]

These bodies, which were destined for Edinburgh, were thought to have been taken from the burial ground of the local workhouse. However, a more usual source for the Edinburgh anatomy schools were the cemeteries of Ireland where the majority of the population were simply too poor to afford mortsafes, iron coffins or cemetery guards. The Irish trade was mostly conducted by smugglers who landed their wares from small boats on the lonely parts of the coast, usually that of Ayrshire, whence they would be taken by cart to the Scottish capital. One entrepreneurial ex-naval captain in Dublin was so enterprising that he raised a public fund to pay graveyard watchers to prevent exhumation, but then used the fund to pay the watchers to become resurrectionists themselves.[43] So profitable did this route become that the anatomists of Dublin and Belfast found themselves devoid of subjects upon which to practise, 'home grown' or otherwise.[44]

Unlike Manchester, Liverpool and Yarmouth, and despite its long history as a centre of anatomical research, Oxford does not appear to have been regularly targeted by the resurrection men. In fact, while dissections had been conducted regularly in the basement of the Old Ashmolean Museum from 1683 onwards, by the end of the eighteenth century, the university's medical faculty attracted very few students. It continued to be one of just two English universities entitled to confer medical degrees (Cambridge being the other) but it seldom did so, with all but the most fashionable students preferring to pursue their studies in Edinburgh, where the courses were cheaper, of shorter duration and open to men who were not necessarily communicants of the Church of England, or in Paris where, in 1828, it was estimated that 200 English students of anatomy were pursuing their courses of instruction and paying no more than 3–12 francs for each body they dissected.[45] Occasionally, bodies were snatched in the neighbourhood of the university, as is evidenced by a case reported in *Jackson's Oxford Journal* of 28 November 1829, but they were relatively few and far between and the stolen bodies were more likely to be sent to London or Edinburgh than to the anatomists in Oxford itself.

With so few corpses being exhumed in the city, most of those dying in its environs could feel confident that their bones would be allowed to rest in peace. One such was Bickerton's old friend Constantine Demetriades, who died at his lodgings in the parish of St Peter-le-Bailey, Oxford, in August 1825.[46] His confidence would prove sadly misplaced.

After the partial collapse and subsequent demolition of Hertford College, the now homeless Demetriades had moved, temporarily at least, to a house on Pigney Lane in Reading. In the early years of the nineteenth century, the county town of Berkshire remained largely

Death and Resurrection

medieval in character. Its centre felt crowded, with even the wider and more fashionable streets pierced by the mouths of dark passageways leading to grim and unsanitary courts and alleys. Its lanes, which wound seemingly without plan, were encumbered by stalls, barrows and refuse, making them impassable to most wheeled vehicles, while in Butcher Row, carcasses overhung the footway and the gutters ran with blood and offal.[47]

Yet, in spite of appearances, and like so many towns across England, Reading stood on the cusp of great change. Between 1801 and 1821, the population had grown by more than a third to 12,867, and by 1841 it would exceed 19,000. The development of the iron and brewing industries had driven much of this growth and they had long since overtaken the town's ancient cloth trade as the mainstay of the local economy. But cloth remained an important product and one of its leading manufacturers was Demetriades' new landlord, Musgrave Lamb, who specialised in a sail cloth that was remarkable for its strength and whiteness and whose 140 looms could produce cloth 6 or 7 yards in width.[48] Lamb's principal customers were the Royal Navy and the East India Company, and the navy purchased so much of his sail cloth that locals – no doubt encouraged by Lamb himself – quipped that the Battle of Trafalgar had been won at his manufactory in Katesgrove Lane.[49]

The exact nature of the relationship between the down-at-heel language teacher and the affluent entrepreneur is uncertain, but it appears to have been based on more than the routine commercial transactions to be expected between landlord and tenant as, in January 1822, Demetriades appointed Lamb the sole executor of his will. Moreover, the terms of the will that Lamb agreed to administer were both unusual and complex. Specifically, Demetriades bequeathed his entire estate to:

> … the four holy fathers or patriarchs of the Eastern Christian Church of the Orthodox Christians at a place called Anari [?] in the City of Constantinople equally, share and share alike, and I desire my executor to transmit the said […] instructions in the Greek language which are attached to this my will to the said four holy fathers through his Britannic Majesty's Ambassador at the Ottoman Porte, whom I request to take this trouble upon himself, it being a safe medium especially in

these perilous times when so violent a persecution rages against my devoted fellow countrymen in Turkey; and I further desire that they, the said holy fathers, will put down the names of my father, mother, myself, brothers and sisters [...] to be repeated every Saturday and Sunday in their prayers for one hundred years commencing at the time of my decease or thereabouts.[50]

For his onerous role in converting Demetriades' estate, 'whatsoever and wheresoever and of what nature or kind soever', into ready cash, transmitting it the 2,000 miles to Constantinople and recruiting the British Ambassador to treat with the Orthodox Patriarchate, Lamb was to receive nothing. The acceptance of such a responsibility must surely, therefore, have been the act of a friend, and a close one at that – a supposition supported by the fact that Musgrave accompanied Demetriades' corpse to its grave on Tuesday, 23 August, the only other mourner being 'a gentleman of the University, who had taken considerable interest in him'.[51]

We do not know when Demetriades left Reading to return to Oxford, the exact location of his lodgings in the poverty-stricken parish of St Peter-le-Bailey or the cause of his death at the age of 70 or 71, but given the detailed provisions of his will, it comes as no surprise to discover that he left precise instructions regarding the treatment of his remains:

If I should die in England I desire to be interred in that part of a church yard where no other person has been before or at a future day may be buried in, with my face towards the East and with the Greek Testament which I carry constantly about me to be laid on my breast and an Ecclesiastical cloth ornament with Gold crosses which will be found in my chest, the cloth to be suspended from my neck to my feet.[52]

There seems to be no reason to doubt that Demetriades' wishes were fully complied with when he was interred in the burial ground of St Peter-le-Bailey, nor that the costs of his burial were kept below the carefully stipulated figure of £8. Unfortunately, he expressed no desire that his body should be encased in one of Gabriel Aughtie's patented iron coffins nor that any other precautions should be taken to protect his corpse, and not long after his interment resurrection men dragged Demetriades from his grave and sold him for dissection.

The local newspapers carry no report of the desecration or of any body snatchers being tried for the offence, so we don't know who exhumed the Greek or to whom they sold him. However, very unusually, it seems that the receiving anatomist knew precisely whose corpse lay on his dissecting table because by 1841 Demetriades' carefully labelled skull had been placed on public display in the museum of Dr Richard Smith, senior surgeon at the Bristol Infirmary.[53]

As far as the resurrectionists were concerned, the bodies they sold were anonymous merchandise, devoid of personality and history. Only in very rare instances – such as that of the gigantic Irishman, Charles Byrne – were specific individuals required by their customers. So why should Demetriades' body have retained his name? There was nothing exceptional in his appearance: he was neither a dwarf nor a giant and, according to Albin Burt's drawing of 1819, he did not suffer from any marked deformity – and surely such an abnormality would have been mentioned by his mocking obituarists – so it seems highly improbable that his particular body would have been especially desired by a latter-day John Hunter with a passion for unusual skeletons.

More probably, Demetriades' identification was a product of happenchance: just as the corpse of the novelist Laurence Sterne had been recognised, quite by accident, on the slab of an anatomist at Cambridge in 1769.[54] If Demetriades was recognised in this fashion, then it seems likely that his body had been sold to an anatomist in Oxford where his eccentricities and his appearance had made him a well-known butt for undergraduate humour. If this was the case, then it is quite possible that his body was dissected by the eminent John Kidd, who resided in Oxford throughout Demetriades' period in the city and became Reader in Anatomy at the university in 1816.

Although the burial ground of St John the Evangelist had been targeted by resurrectionists so frequently that an armed patrol had been instituted in 1814 and the perimeter wall raised, by the time of Bickerton's death, the gruesome trade of body snatching was a thing of the past. Most ardent for change had been the surgeons and teachers who argued that the existing laws not only made malefactors of them all but also rendered body snatching an absolute certainty if anatomical knowledge and surgical practice were to be advanced for the benefit of mankind. As Thomas Southwood Smith, surgeon, reformer and colleague of Edwin Chadwick, put it:

> At present, exhumation is the only method by which subjects for dissection can be procured; but subjects for this purpose must be procured; and be the difficulties what they may, will be procured; diseases will occur, operations must be performed, medical men must be educated, anatomy must be studied, dissections must go on. Unless some other means for affording a supply be adopted; whatever be the law or the popular feeling, neither magistrates, nor judges, nor juries, will, or can put an entire stop to the practice.[55]

The law, then, was an ass, hampering medical research and exasperating the public against resurrection men and anatomists alike. Various solutions were proposed to address the problem by increasing the supply of subjects. Some, for instance, recommended that all those who died when engaged in 'immoral pursuits' – and not only murderers – should be anatomised, including prostitutes, prize-fighters, duellists and drunks. Others suggested that people still living should be allowed to sell their bodies for dissection after death – though the means by which the movements of such individuals might be tracked during their remaining years of life remained unclear.

So great was the demand for change that in 1828 the House of Commons appointed a Select Committee 'to enquire into the manner of obtaining subjects for dissection in the Schools of Anatomy, and into the state of the law affecting the persons employed in obtaining and dissecting bodies'.[56] Those called to give evidence included not only the presidents of the Royal College of Surgeons and the Royal College of Physicians, but surgeons, apothecaries, lecturers, demonstrators, church wardens and no fewer than three active or retired resurrectionists, whose identities were concealed for their own protection. Their testimony proved compelling – revealing not only the anatomists' total reliance upon the body snatchers and the disadvantages of the English schools when compared with those on the Continent, but also the critical role that the study of anatomy played in the advancement of medical science.

In the opinion of Sir Astley Cooper, the most famous surgeon of his generation, 'without dissection there can be no anatomy [...] anatomy is our polar star, for, without anatomy a surgeon can do nothing, certainly nothing well'.[57] With hardly a dissenting or equivocal note in the 108 pages of evidence – even in that provided by the resurrection men themselves – the committee could draw only one conclusion: that the 'state of the law is injurious to students, teachers, and practitioners, in every department of medical and surgical science, and appears to the Committee to be highly prejudicial to the public interests also'.[58] So much for the problem. What was the solution?

In making its recommendations to Parliament, the committee described in detail the manner by which the anatomy schools in Paris were furnished with sufficient cadavers, 'because it approaches most nearly to the plan recommended by most of the witnesses for adoption in this country'.[59] In brief, if the body of anyone who died in one of the Paris hospitals or institutions for the maintenance of paupers remained unclaimed twenty-four hours after death, that body was sent automatically to one of the two public dissecting schools in the city, l'École de Médecine or the neighbouring Hôpital de la Pitié (there were no private schools in France). The bodies were treated respectfully, being accorded all the usual rites of the Roman Catholic Church before being sewn up in clean cloth prior to transportation in a covered wagon to the dissecting school. After dissection, each body was interred in the nearest consecrated burial ground.

As a result of this policy, 'exhumation is wholly unknown, and the feelings of the people appear not to be violated'. Given its success in France, argued the committee, why should this method of supplying the anatomy schools not be adopted in Britain? In support of the idea, statistics for the year 1827 showed that of the 3,744 persons who died in the workhouses of the City of London, Westminster and Southwark, 3,103 were buried at the parish's expense, with 1,108 being sent to their graves without any relatives in attendance.⁶⁰ Such a source of supply, the committee believed, would far outstrip the demand of all London's medical schools combined and render the body snatchers redundant almost overnight.

In March 1829, the Select Committee's chairman, Henry Warburton, the Radical MP for Bridport, obtained permission to introduce into the House of Commons a Bill 'for preventing the unlawful disinterment of human bodies, and for regulating the schools of Anatomy'. The most important element of this Bill was that seventy-two hours after death, all unclaimed bodies from hospitals and workhouses would be made available to the schools of anatomy. Other clauses stipulated prison sentences of up to two years for those found guilty of exhumation and confirmed the right of individuals to direct that their bodies be dissected.*

Unfortunately – and surprisingly, given the efforts that the committee had gone to in order to gather expert opinion – the wording of the Bill was not agreed with those who were to be its primary beneficiaries, the anatomists. As a result, many opposed it, their main concerns being that the Bill appeared to benefit the London schools at the expense of those in the provinces, which might be driven out of business; its provisions did not cover Ireland; and those whose bodies would be offered for dissection would be overwhelmingly from the poorest echelons of society. This last would remain a highly contentious issue, with one vocal critic, William Roberts,** claiming that one of the Act's main objectives 'was to *victimize* a certain class [...] The intention of those who drew it up, was – to the utmost extent possible – to lay their hands upon the bodies of those, who might be driven by penury, disease, or accident, into our Poor-Houses, hospitals and infirmaries'.⁶¹

After lengthy debate, the Bill was passed by the Commons but rejected in the House of Lords. In the opinion of historian Sarah Wise, it had been defeated by 'a broad coalition of a number of Tories who [...]

---

* It was accepted that there was no legal property in a corpse so bodies could not be bequeathed in the manner of other possessions.

** According to his own testimony to Earl Stanhope, Roberts had 'attended before the commissioners and tendered his evidence, which was of great consequence, but they refused to hear him'. He also claimed to have invented an 'antiseptic process' for keeping anatomical subjects fresh 'for an indefinite period'.

foresaw the potential for further civil unrest if such a socially divisive act were to be passed; and Radicals, who believed the poor should never become fodder for middle-class self-betterment'.⁶²

Warburton tried again in December 1831, and this time his timing could not have been better judged. The preceding month, three men, Thomas Williams, John Bishop and James May – the last two being well-known resurrection men – had been apprehended when they attempted to sell to the anatomists of King's College the body of a 14-year-old Italian boy named Carlo Ferrari, for which they asked 12 guineas. The appearance of the body, which seemed never to have been buried, immediately excited the suspicions of the hospital porter and the demonstrator of anatomy, and it was they who sent for the police.

At their trial, which took place at the Old Bailey between 2 and 3 December, the three men were found guilty of murder, 'being evil disposed persons and not having the fear of God before their eyes',⁶³ and sentenced to death by hanging. In their subsequent confessions, made on 4 December, Bishop and Williams admitted to enticing the boy to their house in Nova Scotia Gardens, where they had made him drunk before throwing him headfirst into a well. They had then sold his teeth to a dentist for 12s before hawking the body around the London hospitals in search of a buyer. They also admitted to the murders of Frances Pigburn, an indigent, on 9 October, and a boy named Cunningham on 21 October.

These crimes, the subsequent trial and the executions on 5 December*** generated enormous public interest, with a crowd of upwards of 30,000 gathering to witness the hanging of Bishop and Williams, who were dubbed the 'London Burkers' after the notorious resurrection man and murderer, William Burke, who had been executed in Edinburgh in January 1829. Of course, the crimes of Burke and his accomplice, William Hare, and of Bishop and Williams were the exceptions rather than the rule, with the vast majority of resurrection men keen to ensure that their activities could be categorised as no more serious than

---

*** The confessions of Bishop and Williams cleared May of the charge of murder and his sentence was commuted to penal servitude. He died at the penal settlement of Port Arthur, Australia, in 1834.

misdemeanours, but it was now generally accepted that there could be no further delays in addressing the issue.

In the words of James Blake Bailey, Librarian of the Royal College of Surgeons and historian of the body-snatching trade, 'as has happened frequently in legislation, the absolute necessity for a change in the law was brought within the range of practical politics by a crime of a most diabolical character'.[64] In introducing his amended Bill just ten days after the executions, Warburton took full advantage of the febrile atmosphere surrounding the trial of the London Burkers and saw it pass safely through both Houses of Parliament.

The new Act for Regulating Schools of Anatomy received Royal Assent on 1 August 1832. Under its terms, the unclaimed body of anyone who died in a public hospital or workhouse would be passed to the anatomists, unless that individual had expressed the wish, either in writing or before two witnesses, that they should not be dissected. The bodies could be released only to those holding a licence to practise anatomy and not until forty-eight hours after death – a certificate stating the cause of death must also be issued. Finally, bodies must be removed in a 'decent coffin or shell',[65] interred with the appropriate religious rites and a certificate of interment issued to the appropriate authority.

Prior to its approval, the wording of Warburton's original Bill had been subject to a number of important amendments to make it palatable, in theory at least, to those who had previously objected. Overall, perhaps the most obvious alteration was that body snatching was not made a specific criminal offence, the legislators being convinced that the trade would collapse as a result of the other provisions within the Bill. In this assumption they were largely correct, and within a few years, body snatching had been consigned to history.

Other claims made for the Act were more suspect, at least in the early years. As far as the provision of corpses was concerned, in April 1834 – twenty months after the Act came into force – Dr James Somerville, the first Anatomy Inspector appointed for England and Wales, gave evidence before the Parliamentary Select Committee on Medical Education. According to his testimony, anatomy subjects were being received in a much fresher condition and in much greater numbers: 600 in the first year after the passing of the Act, compared with an estimated 300 previously. But the supply fluctuated. In 1838–39 the number fell to 430, while in 1845–46 it was just over 300.⁶⁶

More importantly, the Act did nothing to abate the widespread loathing for both the practice of anatomy and the anatomists themselves; indeed, given that its provisions resulted in the vast majority of subjects being taken from the poorest parts of society, many considered the Act to be part of a wider plan to further oppress the worst off. In June 1838, for instance, Peter Bussey, the Yorkshire Chartist leader, told a meeting at Bradford that the Anatomy Act and the New Poor Law of 1834 were part of the same oppressive system: 'If they were poor they imprisoned them, then starved them to death, and after they were dead they butchered them.'⁶⁷ It would take many decades more before anatomy and the benefits it undoubtedly bestowed became broadly acceptable to society as a whole.

Although the benefits of the Anatomy Act were not necessarily as overwhelming or as immediate as some claimed, by October 1833 there was only the remotest possibility of Bickerton's body being exhumed by resurrection men. There would, however, have been a near certainty of his being anatomised, as had been recognised by the outraged reporter for the *Morning Post* who had fulminated over the parish authorities' neglect, their desire to hush the matter up and their wish to send 'the unfortunate deceased [...] to the dissecting-room'.⁶⁸

In fact, under the terms of the Act, Bickerton would have ended up under the anatomist's knife no matter how promptly the parish overseers had acted in moving him to the workhouse infirmary. Had dissection occurred, what was left of him would eventually have been interred – but, again in the words of William Roberts, those remains would no longer constitute what could be described as a body:

> In most cases little else remains than an assemblage of disconnected bones, well-nigh denuded of the flesh; which, having soon become one mass of corruption and putrefaction, has been day by day removed and put out of sight. Such is the ordinary havoc and waste, that what is still called 'the body', and is ultimately deposited in the coffin or shell, does not upon an average weigh more than one-fourth, and certainly less than one-third, of what it did when it was first delivered over for 'anatomical examination'.⁶⁹

According to Roberts, even the promise of burial with the appropriate religious rites could not be relied upon, as he had himself witnessed 354 dissected bodies being buried in unconsecrated ground in Globe Fields, Stepney, with the undertaker's man acting as clergyman. Even worse, he claimed to have seen 'many hundred weight of human flesh thrown into heaps, and in that way allowed to rot'.[70]

It was, then, perhaps the supreme irony of Bickerton's strange, sad story that it was his very neglect – and the publicity it caused – that saved his remains from the indignity of public dissection. Had the manner of his demise not given rise to interest among the newspaper men and to an inquest, Richard Palin Bickerton might never have heard of his death and claimed his body, thereby preventing him becoming an anatomical specimen.

Unsurprisingly, there is no surviving eyewitness account of Bickerton's burial on 10 October, but there is no reason to suppose that his last rites were conducted in anything other than the 'respectable manner' that his great-nephew had promised. However, there was very little that could be described as 'respectable' about the burial ground of St John the Evangelist. The additional land acquired from Lord Grosvenor in 1823 had proved only a temporary expedient; the cemetery was once again close to overflowing and precisely the same scandalous methods of accommodating yet more bodies were being adopted. In these circumstances, we might be forgiven for taking Dickens' account of the burial of Poor Jo, the crossing sweeper in *Bleak House*, as being to some degree representative:

> Then the active and intelligent [beadle ...] bears off the body of our dear brother here departed, to a hemmed-in churchyard, pestiferous and obscene, whence malignant diseases are communicated to the bodies of our dear brothers and sisters who have not departed [...] Into a beastly scrap of ground which a Turk would reject as a savage abomination, and a Caffre would shudder at, they bring our dear brother here departed, to receive Christian burial.
>
> With houses looking on, on every side, save where a reeking little tunnel of a court gives access to the iron gate – with every villainy of life in action close on death, and every poisonous element of death

in action close on life – here, they lower our dear brother down a foot or two: here, sow him in corruption, to be raised in corruption: an avenging ghost at many a sick-bedside: a shameful testimony to future ages, how civilization and barbarism walked this boastful island together.[71]

Perhaps Richard Palin Bickerton paid for a headstone to mark the last resting place of his great-uncle; perhaps not – we have no way of knowing. What we do know is that, just as in life, in death Bickerton kept eclectic company, as the parish records reveal that those interred in Horseferry Road include Christopher Cass, a master mason who worked on Blenheim Palace, a Native American chief who had been brought to England in 1734 but died of smallpox, John Johnson, spectacle-maker and Lord Mayor of London, James Caldwell, an artist and engraver of portraits, and no fewer than seven centenarians.[72]

The burial ground's gates were finally locked in November 1853, with Lord Palmerston, the then Home Secretary, observing that 'the ground had had deposited in it about six times the number of bodies it was properly fit to hold, and had become a great public nuisance'. The site was subsequently stripped of its headstones and memorials and converted into St John the Evangelist Garden, which was opened in 1885. It remains a place of recreation to this day, an unassuming spot surrounded by looming office blocks, where civil servants from the nearby government departments, businessmen and tourists might eat their sandwiches, unaware that the bones of Poor Bickerton lie beneath the grass at their feet.

Notes

Introduction

1 *The Standard*, 10 October 1833.
2 John Wight, *Mornings at Bow Street: A Selection of the Most Humorous and Entertaining Reports which have Appeared in the Morning Herald* (London: Charles Baldwyn, 1824), pp. iv–v.

1. A Death in Westminster

1 To reach the Five Chimneys from the Crown & Sceptre, Higgs and his jury needed only to cross Chapter Street in the direction of the Thames. The Five Chimneys is clearly marked on a plan dating to 1796–1803 within the Pelham papers held by the British Library (British Library: Tothill Fields, Westminster. Pelham Papers. England; circa 1796–1803). Though not marked on later maps, the Five Chimneys is thought to have stood on a site which became Five Chimney Court (later, Douglas Gardens), where Douglas House now stands on the junction of Douglas Street and Chapter Street. See J.E. Smith, *St John the Evangelist, Westminster: Parochial Memorials* (London, 1892), p. 316.
2 8 Hen. VII, *c*. 1 [reconfirmed 1751–52], quoted in Yvonne King Fisher, 'Coroners in London and Middlesex, *c*. 1820–1888: A Study of Medicalization and Professionalization'. Unpublished PhD thesis (2019), The Open University, Open Research Online.
3 See Yvonne King Fisher, 'Coroners in London and Middlesex …' (2019).
4 William Darton's *Entire New Plan of the Cities of London & Westminster, & Borough of Suffolk* (London: William Darton, 1 January 1817) shows neither Douglas Street nor the building thought to be the Crown & Sceptre. Both are present in *C & J Greenwood's Map of London, Made from an Actual Survey Made in the Years 1824, 1825 & 1826, Extended and Comprising the various improvements to 1830* (London: Greenwood &

Co., 31 August 1830). This suggests that the Crown & Sceptre must have been built between 1817 and 1830.
5 John Stow, *Survey of London, Written in the Year 1598* (London: Whittacker and Co., 1842), p. 176.
6 Charles Lethbridge Kingsford (ed.), *Chronicles of London* (Dursley: Alan Sutton, 1977), p. 148.
7 George A. Aitkin (ed.), *Jonathan Swift, The Journal to Stella* (London: Methuen, 1901), p. 212.
8 See William Blackstone, *Commentaries on the Laws of England*, Vol. III (Oxford: Clarendon Press, 1768), Appendix I, 5, pp. iii–v.
9 John Wykeham Archer, *Vestiges of Old London* (London: David Bogue, 1851), quoted in Edward Walford, *Old & New London: A Narrative of its History, Its People & Its Places – Westminster & The Western Suburbs*, Vol. IV (London: Cassell, no date), p. 14. For additional references to Wigtoft's career, see William Page (ed.), *The History of Yorkshire, The Victoria History of the Counties of England*, Vol. 3 (London: Constable, 1906–14), p. 22, and C.R. Cheney, *From Becket to Langton: English Church Government, 1170–1213* (Manchester: Manchester University Press, 1965), pp. 64–65.
10 William Stubbs (ed.), *Chronica Magistri Rogeri de Houedene*, Vol. IV (London: Longman, 1871), p. 15.
11 John Wykeham Archer, *Vestiges of Old London*, quoted in Edward Walford, *Old & New London*, p. 14.
12 See John Keevil, *Hamey the Stranger* (London: Geoffrey Bles, 1952), p. 85.
13 James Heath, *A Chronicle of the Late Intestine War in the Three Kingdoms of England, Scotland and Ireland* (London, 1661), quoted by Edward Walford, *Old & New London*, p. 15.
14 See Charles Edward Banks, 'Scotch Prisoners Deported to New England by Cromwell, 1651–52', *Proceedings of the Massachusetts Historical Society* (October 1927), pp. 17–18.
15 Edward Walford, *Old & New London*, p. 15.
16 Nicholas Culpeper, *Complete Herbal* (London: Richard Evans, 1814), p. 132.
17 *The Mirror of Literature, Amusement and Instruction*, No. XLV (30 August 1823), p. 233.
18 Gregory Smith (ed.), *Diary of Samuel Pepys*, 18 July 1665 (Globe Edition, London: Macmillan, 1905), p. 327.
19 Daniel Defoe, *The History of the Great Plague in London in the Year 1665: containing observations and memorials of the most remarkable occurrences, both public and private, during that dreadful period, by a citizen, who lived the whole time in London* (London: John Offor, 1819), p. 372.
20 *The Mirror of Literature, Amusement and Instruction*, No. XLVII (13 September 1823), pp. 263–64.
21 *The Mirror of Literature, Amusement, and Instruction*, No. XXIV (London: Limbird, 1835), pp. 200–01.
22 *The Mirror of Literature, Amusement and Instruction*, No. XLVII (13 September 1823), p. 264.
23 *The Builder* (1832), quoted in Walford, *Old & New London*), p. 15.
24 'Death from Starvation', *The Standard*, 10 October 1833, p. 3.
25 *Morning Post*, 8 October 1833.

26 'Death from Starvation', *The Standard*, 10 October 1833, p. 3.
27 *Morning Post*, 8 October 1833.
28 *Ibid.*
29 'Death from Starvation', *The Standard*, 10 October 1833, p. 3.
30 *Ibid.*
31 Coroner's Inquest Report into the death of John Bickerton, Muniments Room of Westminster Abbey, 8 October 1833.
32 *Morning Post*, 8 October 1833.
33 *Ibid.*
34 *Ibid.*
35 See W. Tuckwell, *Reminiscences of Oxford* (New York: Dutton, 1908), p. 66.
36 *Morning Post*, 8 October 1833.
37 *Ibid.*
38 *The London Medical Directory* (London: Churchill, 1846), p. 71.
39 Obituary of John Hastings MD, *Medical Times & Gazette* (2 January 1875), p. 23.
40 *Ibid.*
41 *The Times*, 9 May 1862.
42 *Ibid.*
43 *Morning Post*, 8 October 1833.
44 *Ibid.*
45 Mary Beth Emerichs, 'Getting Away with Murder? Homicide and the Coroners in Nineteenth Century London', *Social Science History*, Vol. 25, No. 1, *Special Issue: Bloody Murder* (Spring, 2001), pp. 93–100.
46 Prison Inspector's Report, quoted in Nigel Cross, *The Common Writer: Life in Nineteenth Century Grub Street* (Cambridge: Cambridge University Press, 1985), p. 45.
47 *Morning Post*, 8 October 1833.
48 *The Times*, 10 October 1833.
49 *Morning Post*, 8 October 1833.
50 *Ibid.*
51 Richard Palin Bickerton (1807–68) became a Licentiate of the Society of Apothecaries (LSA) on 5 July 1827 and a Member of the Royal College of Surgeons (MRCS) on 7 March 1828. After a brief spell in Shrewsbury, he practised in London. On 29 April 1834, a new Nonconformist chapel opened in Harmer Hill, Shropshire, built on land given by Bickerton.
52 *Morning Post*, 8 October 1833.
53 *Examiner*, 13 October 1833.

2. Origins

1 Quoted in *The Homoeopathic Record, Medical, Social, and Scientific*, No. 5 (1 March 1856), pp. 66–70.
2 *Ibid.*
3 *Ibid.*

4   *The Times*, 10 October 1833.
5   Coroner's Inquest Report into the death of John Bickerton, Muniments Room of Westminster Abbey, 8 October 1833.
6   See Shropshire Archives, XP241/N/1/1, 'Articles of Agreement'.
7   See, for instance, Samuel Bagshaw, *History, Gazetteer, and Directory of Shropshire* (Sheffield: printed for the author, 1851), pp. 251–52.
8   Middle Temple, London, 'Minutes of Parliament', 10 November 1809.
9   Samuel Garbet, *The History of Wem* (Wem: Franklin, 1818), p. 245.
10 John Bickerton, *A Concise Account of the Fall and Rise of the Family of the Bickertons, of Maiden Castle in Cheshire, to which is annexed, The Gracious Dealings of God in the Life and Conversion of the Rev. John Bickerton, of the Same Family* (London: Trapp, 1777), p. 13.
11 A.T. Gaydon (ed.), *A History of Shropshire* (Oxford: Institute of Historical Research, 1973), pp. 158–59.
12 Shropshire Archives, ED6266/4/1/2/4 – Complaint filed at the Court of Chancery against John Spedding and further later attempts to dismiss him.
13 See A.T. Gaydon (ed.), *A History of Shropshire*, pp. 158–59.
14 John Bickerton, *A Concise Account*, pp. 7–14.
15 *Morning Post*, 8 October 1833.
16 B. Andrews (ed.), *The Torrington Diaries* (London: Eyre and Spottiswoode, 1934–38), Vol. III, pp. 234–35, quoted in *The Victoria County History of Shropshire*, Vol. VI, p. 16.
17 John Bickerton, *A Concise Account*, p. 11.
18 *Ibid.*, p. 13.
19 *Ibid.*, pp. 15–16.
20 *Ibid.*, p. 16.
21 *Ibid.*, p. 18.
22 *Ibid.*, pp. 19–21.
23 *Ibid.*, p. 33.
24 *Ibid.*, pp. 37–38.
25 *Ibid.*, p. 42.
26 H. de B. Gibbins, *A History of the Grammar School of Charles King of England in Kidderminster* (Kidderminster: Printing Office of the Shuttle, 1903), p. 26.
27 John Bickerton, *A Concise Account*, p. 49.
28 *Ibid.*, p. 48.
29 *Ibid.*, p. 33.
30 See John Venn and L.A. Venn, *Alumni Cantabrigienses* (Cambridge: Cambridge University Press, 1940 and 2011), Part II, Vol. I, p. 257.
31 Ronald Hyam, 'Godliness, Hunting and Quite Good Learning: The History of Magdalene College, 1792–1992', *Magdalene College Occasional Papers*, No. 5 (Cambridge, 1992), p. 5.
32 *Ibid.*, p. 6.
33 *Ibid.*, p. 7.
34 Quoted by Peter Cunich, David Hoyle, Eamon Duffy and Ronald Hyam, *A History of Magdalene College Cambridge, 1428–1988* (Cambridge: Magdalene College Publications, 1994), p. 190.

35 Ronald Hyam, 'Godliness, Hunting and Quite Good Learning', p. 7.
36 G.V. Cox, *Recollections of Oxford* (London: Macmillan, 1870), pp. 250–52.
37 See W.N. Hargreaves-Mawdsley, 'Grand Compounders', in 'Notes and Queries', *Oxoniensia*, Vol. XXII, 1957 (Oxford: Oxford Architectural and Historical Society, 1958), pp. 110–11.
38 *The Oxford Herald*, quoted in 'Counsellor Bickerton, Esq.', in *The Gentleman's Magazine* (December 1833), p. 549.
39 John Bickerton, *A Concise Account*, p. 29.
40 Ibid., p. 91.
41 Peter Cunich et al., *A History of Magdalene College Cambridge, 1428–1988*, p. 186. Farrish's role as Bickerton's tutor confirmed in an email to the author from Katy Green, Magdalene College Archivist, 6 April 2023.
42 W. Tuckwell, *Pre-Tractarian Oxford, A Reminiscence of the Oriel 'Noetics'* (London: Smith and Elder, 1909), p. 8.
43 Ibid.
44 For details of St Edmund Hall under Vice Principal Isaac Crouch, I am indebted to J.N.D. Kelly, *St Edmund Hall: Almost Seven Hundred Years* (Oxford: Oxford University Press, 1989), pp. 69–70.
45 John Bickerton, *A Concise Account*, pp. 29–30.
46 Ibid., p. 37.
47 'Counsellor Bickerton, Esq.' in *The Gentleman's Magazine* (December 1833), p. 549.

3. An Incident at St James's Palace

1 W.C. Oulton, *Memoirs of Her Late Majesty Queen Charlotte* (London: Robins and Co., 1819), p. 115.
2 For this account of Fielding's investigation, I am indebted to R. Leslie-Manville, *The Life and Work of Sir John Fielding* (London: Lincoln Williams, 1934), pp. 237–38.
3 W.C. Oulton, *Memoirs of Her Late Majesty Queen Charlotte*, p. 147.
4 Ibid.
5 *The Times*, 4 August 1786.
6 Ibid., 3 August 1786.
7 Ibid., 4 August 1786.
8 Ibid.
9 Ibid.
10 Ibid., 3 August 1786.
11 Ibid., 1 September 1787.
12 Ibid.
13 Ibid.
14 Ibid., 8 September 1787.
15 Ibid.
16 Ibid., 10 September 1787.
17 Ibid., 28 December 1787.

18 *Ibid.*, 3 June 1788.
19 *Ibid.*
20 *Ibid.*
21 *Ibid.*
22 *Ibid.*
23 'The whole proceedings on postponing the trial of John Frith, for High Treason, on Saturday, April 17th 1790 at Justice Hall in the Old Bailey', No. IV, Part I of the Sessions Paper (London: Hodgson, 1790).
24 *The Times*, 26 January 1790.
25 Edgar Sheppard, *Memorials of St James's Palace* (London: Longmans, Green and Co., 1894), Vol. I, p. 330. Although Sheppard quotes from an unnamed contemporary newspaper report, the author has been unable to identify any contemporary accounts of the incident.
26 *The Times*, 2 March 1790.
27 *Ibid.*
28 See Joseph Grego, *A History of Parliamentary Elections and Electioneering in the Old Days* (London: Chatto and Windus, 1886), pp. 202–22.
29 *The Times*, 3 March 1790.
30 *Ibid.*, 2 March 1790.
31 *Ibid.*, 17 May 1800.
32 *Ibid.*, 27 June 1800.
33 *Ibid.*, 17 May 1800.
34 *Ibid.*, 27 June 1800.
35 *Ibid.*
36 *Ibid.*
37 *Ibid.*
38 For this account of Urban Metcalf's attempt on the life of King George, I am indebted to Steve Poole's excellent book *The Politics of Regicide in England, 1760–1850: Troublesome Subjects* (Manchester: Manchester University Press, 2000), pp. 132–34.
39 David V. James, Paul E. Mullen, et al., 'Attacks on the British Royal Family: The Role of Psychotic Illness' in *Journal of the American Academy of Psychiatric Law*, 36 (2008), p. 61.
40 See Steve Poole, *The Politics of Regicide in England*, pp. 128–34.
41 George Augustus Sala, *London Up to Date* (London: Adam and Charles Black, 1894), p. 10.
42 John Brooke, *King George III* (London: Constable, 1972), p. 295.
43 George Augustus Sala, *London Up to Date*, pp. 13–14.
44 *Ibid.*, p. 15.
45 Hannah Greig, 'Faction and Fashion: The Politics of Court Dress in Eighteenth-Century England' in *Se vêtir à la cour en Europe 1400–1815: Cultures matérielles, cultures visuelles du costume dans les cours européennes* (Villeneuve d'Ascq: Publications de l'Institut de recherches historiques du Septentrion, 2011).
46 *The Times*, 15 September 1803.
47 *St James's Chronicle*, 15 September 1803.

48. See Arthur Sherbo, 'A Suggestion for the Original of Thackeray's Rawdon Crawley', *Nineteenth-Century Fiction*, Vol. 10, No. 3 (December 1955), pp. 211–16.
49. *St James's Chronicle*, 15 September 1803.

4. Bow Street

1. *Public Advertiser*, 17 October 1754. Quoted by David Cox, '"A Certain Share of Low Cunning" – The Provincial Use and Activities of Bow Street "Runners" 1792–1839', *Eras Journal* (University of Monash), 5, November 2003.
2. Henry Fielding, *The Journal of a Voyage to Lisbon* (London: Everyman, 1964), p. 192.
3. Anthony Babington, *A House in Bow Street: Crime and the Magistracy, London 1740–1881* (London: Macdonald, 1969), p. 186.
4. John Townsend's evidence in *Report from the Committee on the State of the Police of the Metropolis* (London: Clement, 1816), p. 202.
5. *Ibid.*, p. 201.
6. *Report from the Committee on the State of the Police of the Metropolis*, p. 203.
7. See John Sayer's evidence in *Report from the Committee on the State of the Police of the Metropolis*, p. 315.
8. *Reminiscences of Henry Angelo, with Memoirs of his Late Father and Friends* (London: Henry Colburn, 1828), Vol. II, p. 333.
9. *The Gentleman's Magazine*, Vol. 102 (July 1832), p. 91.
10. *Ibid.*
11. *Ibid.*
12. *The Times*, 2 February 1803.
13. Anthony Babington, *A House in Bow Street*, p. 201.
14. Charles Dickens, *Oliver Twist* (London: Penguin, 1988), pp. 393–94.
15. Anthony Babington, *A House in Bow Street*, p. 32.
16. George Hodder, *Sketches of Life and Character Taken at the Police Court, Bow Street* (London: Sherwood and Bowyer, 1845), p. iv.
17. London Metropolitan Archives, MJ/SP/1803/10/028, R. Ford to J. Stirling, 27 October 1803.
18. John Wight, *Mornings at Bow Street*, p. iv.
19. *Ibid.*, p. 2.
20. *Ibid.*, p. 57.
21. London Metropolitan Archives, MJ/SP/1803/10/028, R. Ford to J. Stirling, 27 October 1803.
22. See Emily Lorraine De Montluzin, 'Worlds Apart from the Turkish Tales: Joseph Moser's "Proposal for a Depository for Infants"', *ANQ: A Quarterly Journal of Short Articles, Notes and Reviews*, 16:4 (2003), pp. 35–41.
23. London Metropolitan Archives, MJ/SP/1803/10/028, R. Ford to J. Stirling, 27 October 1803.
24. *Ibid.*
25. *St James's Chronicle*, 17 September 1803.

26 Percy Fitzgerald, *Chronicles of Bow Street Police-Office. With an Account of the Magistrates, 'Runners', and Police* (London: Chapman & Hall, 1888), Vol. 1, p. 3.
27 Bickerton's committal to Coldbath Fields Prison is confirmed by the *Morning Post* of 16 September 1803.

5. The House of Correction

1 Jerry White, *London in the Eighteenth Century: A Great and Monstrous Thing* (London: The Bodley Head, 2012), p. 446.
2 Act 22 and 23, Charles II. Quoted by John Howard, *The State of the Prisons in England and Wales, with Preliminary Observations, and an Account of Some Foreign Prisons* (Warrington: William Eyres, 1777), p. 46.
3 John Howard, *The State of the Prisons in England and Wales*, p. 488.
4 *Ibid.*, p. 39.
5 *Ibid.*, p. 40.
6 *Ibid.*, p. 43.
7 *Ibid.*, p. 45.
8 Thomas Archer, *The Pauper, The Thief and the Convict: Sketches of Some of their Homes, Haunts, and Habits* (London: Groombridge, 1865), p. 158.
9 John Howard, *The State of the Prisons in England and Wales*, p. 69.
10 *Ibid.*, p. 50.
11 *Ibid.*, p. 65.
12 *Post Boy*, 28 March 1700. Quoted in 'West of Farringdon Road', in *Survey of London: Volume 47, Northern Clerkenwell and Pentonville*, edited by Philip Temple (London, 2008), pp. 22–51 (British History Online: www.british-history.ac.uk/survey-london/vol47/pp.22–51).
13 John Howard, *The State of the Prisons in England and Wales*, p. 187.
14 *Ibid.*, p. 186.
15 Simon Devereaux, 'The Making of the Penitentiary Act, 1775–1779', *The Historical Journal*, 42, 2 (1999), pp. 405–33.
16 *Ibid.*
17 Alexander Pope, *The Dunciad with Notes Variorum, and the Prolegomena of Scriblerus* (London: Lawton Gulliver, 1729), pp. 119–20.
18 James Ewing Ritchie, *Days and Nights in London: Studies in Black and Gray* (London: Tinsley Brothers, 1880), p. 261.
19 John Howard, *The State of the Prisons in England and Wales*, p. 40.
20 The most detailed contemporary description of Coldbath Fields House of Correction is to be found in James Neild, *State of the Prisons in England, Scotland, and Wales* (London: John Nichols, 1812).
21 Leigh Hunt, 'The Prince on St. Patrick's Day', *The Examiner*, 22 March 1812.
22 P.G. Patmore, *My Friends and Acquaintance: Being Memorials, Mind-Portraits, and Personal Recollections of Deceased Celebrities of the Nineteenth Century* (London: Saunders and Otley, 1854), Vol. I, p. 110.

Notes

23 Thomas Archer, *The Pauper, The Thief and the Convict*, pp. 151–52.
24 J.E. Morpurgo (ed.), *The Autobiography of Leigh Hunt* (London: The Cresset Press, 1949), p. 240.
25 George Laval Chesterton, *Revelations of Prison Life; with an enquiry into prison discipline and secondary punishments* (London: Hurst and Blackett, 1856), Vol. I, p. 18.
26 Sir Richard Phillips, *A Letter to the Livery of London, Relative to the Views of the Writer in Executing the Office of Sheriff* (London, 1808), p. 221.
27 George Laval Chesterton, *Revelations of Prison Life*, Vol. I, p. 2.
28 Samuel Taylor Coleridge, 'The Devil's Thoughts' (1812), stanza IX.
29 Thomas Archer, *The Pauper, The Thief and the Convict*, p. 158.
30 Middlesex Sessions: Sessions Papers – Justices' Working Documents, May 1786, London Lives, 1690–1800. London Metropolitan Archives: LMSMPS508100040 (www.londonlives.org).
31 London Metropolitan Archives, MJ/SP/1793/10/215, Middlesex Sessions of the Peace, Court in Session, 25 September–23 October 1793.
32 Middlesex Sessions of the Peace, Court in Session, October 1793. London Metropolitan Archives: LMSMPS508890420.
33 Middlesex Sessions of the Peace, Court in Session, 25 September–23 October 1793. London Metropolitan Archives: MJ/SP/1793/10/215.
34 Middlesex Sessions of the Peace, Court in Session, September 1773, London Lives, 1690–1800. London Metropolitan Archives: MJ/SP/1773/09/016 (www.londonlives.org).
35 Quoted in M.W. Patterson, *Sir Francis Burdett and his Times (1770–1844)* (London: Macmillan, 1931) Vol. I, p. 69.
36 The Duke of Portland to Lord Titchfield, Lord Lieutenant of Middlesex, 2 January 1799, quoted in *The Times*, 7 January 1799.
37 *The Times*, 22 December 1798.
38 [William Mainwaring?], *The Secrets of the Bastille Disclosed* (London: Rivington, 1799), p. 5.
39 Quoted in M.W. Patterson, *Sir Francis Burdett and his Times*, Vol. I, p. 71.
40 *An Impartial Statement of the Inhuman Cruelties Discovered! in the Coldbath-Fields Prison, by the Grand and Traverse Juries for the County of Middlesex, and Reported in the House of Commons on Friday 11th June 1800 by Sir Francis Burdett, Bart.* (London: J. S. Jordan, 1800), p. 6.
41 Ibid., p. 7.
42 Ibid.
43 Orders of the Magistrates, December Sessions, 1799, quoted in Sir Richard Phillips, *A Letter to the Livery of London*, p. 43.
44 'Report of His Majesty's Commissioners appointed to enquire into the management of Coldbath Fields House of Correction', 1 November 1806, p. 39, quoted in Sir Richard Phillips, *A Letter to the Livery of London*, p. 39.
45 Ibid., p. 42.
46 *An Impartial Statement of the Inhuman Cruelties Discovered!*, p. 8.
47 Ibid., p. 9.

48 *Ibid.*
49 Sir Richard Phillips, *A Letter to the Livery of London*, p. 219.
50 *An Impartial Statement of the Inhuman Cruelties Discovered!*, p. 12.
51 M.W. Patterson, *Sir Francis Burdett and his Times (1770–1844)*, Vol. I, p. 71.
52 *Morning Post*, 16 May 1801.
53 *Ibid.*
54 *The Times*, 26 September 1808.
55 Kellow Chesney, *The Victorian Underworld* (London: Penguin, 1979), p. 300.
56 *The Times*, 8 September 1810.
57 *Caledonian Mercury*, 8 September 1810.
58 *Ibid.*
59 *The Times*, 8 September 1810.
60 *Caledonian Mercury*, 8 September 1810.
61 *The Times*, 30 October 1810.
62 Old Bailey Proceedings Online (www.oldbaileyonline.org, version 8.0), April 1813, trial of Sarah Evans (t18130407-23).
63 *Ibid.*
64 *Ibid.*
65 *Ibid.*
66 Sir Richard Phillips, *A Letter to the Livery of London*, p. 221. See also *Journal de Francfort*, Nro. 166, 15 Juin 1807.
67 London, Middlesex sessions: County Administration. London Metropolitan Archives: MA/G/ CBF/005 (23 pages). Report of the Commissioners on the state and management of the House of Correction Cold Bath Fields, quoted by Juliette Reboul, *French Emigration to Great Britain in Response to the French Revolution* (Palgrave Macmillan, 2017), pp. 72–73.
68 'Report of His Majesty's Commissioners appointed to enquire into the management of Coldbath Fields House of Correction' (1 November 1806), p. 39, quoted in Sir Richard Phillips, *A Letter to the Livery of London*, p. 40.
69 George Laval Chesterton, *Revelations of Prison Life*, Vol. I, pp. 2–3.
70 *The Times*, 26 September 1800.
71 George Laval Chesterton, *Revelations of Prison Life*, Vol. I, p. 46.
72 Details of the prisoners' rations are taken from James Neild, *State of the Prisons in England, Scotland, and Wales* (London: John Nichols, 1812), p. 142.

6. Lunatic?

1 Roy Porter, *Mind-Forg'd Manacles: A History of Madness in England from the Restoration to the Regency* (London: The Athlone Press, 1987), pp. 117–18.
2 'An Act for reducing the Laws relating to Rogues, Vagabonds, Sturdy Beggars and Vagrants, into one Act of Parliament; and for the more effectual punishing such Rogues, Vagabonds, Sturdy Beggars and Vagrants, and sending them whither

Notes

      they ought to be sent' [Vagrancy Act], Public Act, 13 Anne, c. 26, Parliamentary Archives: GB-061, Catalogue Ref: HL/PO/PU/1/1713/13An36.
3. *Ibid.*
4. See Roy Porter, *Mind-Forg'd Manacles*, pp. 117–18.
5. 'An Act for the safe Custody of Insane Persons charged with Offences', 39 and 40 Geo. III, c. 94, 28 July 1800. Full text reprinted in Danby P. Fry, *The Lunacy Acts: Containing all the Statutes Relating to Private Lunatics etc.* (London: Knight and Co., 1864), pp. 552–54.
6. Hansard, House of Commons, debate on pauper lunatics, 6 April 1808. The Act became known popularly as 'Mr Wynn's Act'.
7. See Danby P. Fry, *The Lunacy Acts*, pp. 2–3.
8. Roy Porter, *Mind-Forg'd Manacles*, pp. 136–37.
9. *Caledonian Mercury*, 21 February 1801.
10. Attributed to Daniel Defoe, *The Generous Projector, or a Friendly Proposal to Prevent Murder and Other Enormous Abuses, by Erecting an Hospital for Foundlings and Bastard-Children* (London: Dodd and Nutt, 1731), p. 30.
11. Thomas Bakewell, *Letter Addressed to the Chairman of the Select Committee of the House of Commons, Appointed to Enquire into the State of Mad-Houses* (Stafford: Chester, 1815), p. 5.
12. Roy Porter, *Mind-Forg'd Manacles*, p. 141.
13. *Morning Post*, 10 October 1804.
14. *Caledonian Mercury*, 21 February 1801.
15. *The Gentleman's Magazine*, January 1763.
16. Hansard, House of Commons, debate on private mad-houses, 5 April 1814.
17. Edward Wakefield's evidence in *Report, Together with the Minutes of Evidence, and an Appendix of Papers, from the Committee Appointed to Consider of Provision Being Made for the Better Regulation of Madhouses in England* (London: Baldwin, Cradock and Joy, 1815), p. 290.
18. British Museum, Trade card for 'London House Establishment for Insane Persons', in Banks Collection, D, 2.44.
19. Edward Wakefield's evidence in *Report, Together with the Minutes of Evidence*, p. 290.
20. *Ibid.*, p. 296.
21. *Ibid.*, p. 293.
22. John Weir's evidence, *Report, Together with the Minutes of Evidence*, pp. 178–88, and evidence of John Veitch, pp. 179–80.
23. *Ibid.*
24. *Ibid.*, and evidence of John Veitch, p. 190.
25. O.F. Morshead (ed.), *Everybody's Pepys: The Diary of Samuel Pepys, 1660–1669* (London: Bell, 1954), 12 May 1667, p. 394.
26. Edward Wakefield's evidence in *Report, Together with the Minutes of Evidence*, pp. 294–95.
27. Charles C. Langworthy, *A View of the Perkinean Electricity, or an Inquiry into the Influence of Metallic Tractors* (Bristol: Printed for the Author, 1798), title page.

28 *Ibid.*, p. 3.
29 Edward Wakefield's evidence in *Report, Together with the Minutes of Evidence*, p. 297.
30 *Ibid.*
31 Edward O'Donoghue, *The Story of Bethlehem Hospital, From its Foundation in 1247* (New York: Dutton, 1915), p. 69.
32 Sir Thomas More, *The Four Last Things* (London: Art and Book Company, 1903), p. 7.
33 Quoted by Catharine Arnold, *Bedlam: London and its Mad* (London: Pocket Books, 2009), p. 132.
34 Catharine Arnold, *Bedlam*, p. 132.
35 John Haslam, *Medical Jurisprudence as it Relates to Insanity, According to the Law of England* (London: Hunter, Hunter, Taylor and Hessey, 1817), p. 10.
36 Edward Wakefield's evidence in *Report, Together with the Minutes of Evidence*, p. 45.
37 *Ibid.*, p. 46.
38 *Ibid.*
39 *Ibid.*, p. 48.
40 *Ibid.*, p. 94.
41 Catharine Arnold, *Bedlam: London and its Mad*, p. 172.
42 John Haslam's evidence in *Report, Together with the Minutes of Evidence*, p. 84.
43 *Report, Together with the Minutes of Evidence*, p. 2.
44 Hansard, House of Commons, debate on private mad-houses, 5 April 1814.
45 George Man Burrows, *Cursory Remarks on Legislative Regulation of the Insane* (London: Harding, Longman, Hurst, Rees, Orme, Brown and Callow, 1819), p. iii.
46 *The First Annual Report on Madhouses made in the Year 1816* (London: Clement, 1816), title page.
47 George Man Burrows, *Commentaries on the Causes, Forms, Symptoms, and Treatment, Moral and Medical, of Insanity* (London: Thomas and George Underwood, 1828), p. 251.
48 John Haslam, *Observations on Madness and Melancholy: Including Practical Remarks on those Diseases; Together with Cases: and an Account of the Morbid Appearances on Dissection* (London: Callow, 1809), pp. 44–45.
49 *Ibid.*, pp. 46–47.
50 George Man Burrows, *Cursory Remarks*, p. 23.
51 John Haslam, *Medical Jurisprudence*, p. 8.
52 William Blackstone, *Commentaries on the Laws of England*, Vol. I, p. 304.
53 Francis Willis, *A Treatise on Mental Derangement, Containing the Substance of the Gulstonian Lectures, for May, MDCCCXXII* (London: Longman, Hurst, Rees, Orme, and Brown, 1823), p. 223.
54 Matthew Hale, *Historia Placitorum Coronæ: The History of the Pleas of the Crown* (Philadelphia: Small, 1847), Vol. II, p. 30.
55 Thomas Jones Howell, *A Complete Collection of State Trials and Proceedings for High Treason and Other Crimes and Misdemeanors from the Earliest Period to the Year 1783* (London: Longman et al., 1817), Vol. 16, pp. 764–65.
56 Quoted by W. Norwood East, 'Crime and Insanity', *The Post-Graduate Medical Journal*, IV, 48 (September 1929), p. 202.

Notes

57 *The Times*, 27 June 1800.
58 Quoted by W. Norwood East, 'Crime and Insanity', p. 203.
59 Quoted by W. Norwood East, 'Crime and Insanity', pp. 204–05.
60 John Haslam, *Medical Jurisprudence*, p. 11.

7. MIDDLE TEMPLE TO HERTFORD COLLEGE

1 H.A.C. Sturgess, *Register of Admissions to the Honourable Society of the Middle Temple: From the Fifteenth Century to the year 1944*, Vol. II: 1782–1909 (London: Dutterworth, 1949), p. 421.
2 Charles Lamb, 'The Old Benchers of the Inner Temple', *The Essays of Elia* (London: J.M. Dent, 1908), p. 97.
3 W.G. Thorpe, *Middle Temple Table Talk: With Some Talk About the Table Itself* (London: Hutchinson, 1895), p. 2.
4 W.M. Thackeray, *The History of Pendennis: His Fortunes and Misfortunes, His Friends and His Greatest Enemy* (London: Penguin, 1986), p. 311.
5 *Ibid.*, p. 316.
6 *Ibid.*, p. 320.
7 Ben Jonson, *Every Man in his Humour*, dedication to the 1616 folio.
8 William Ballantine, *Some Experiences of a Barrister's Life* (London: Richard Bentley, 1883), pp. 11–12.
9 Thackeray to Mrs Carmichael-Smyth, 14–16 January 1832, in Gordon N. Ray (ed.), *The Letters and Private Papers of William Makepeace Thackeray* (Cambridge, Massachusetts: Harvard University Press, 1946), Vol. I, p. 182.
10 William Ballantine, *Some Experiences of a Barrister's Life*, p. 10.
11 Middle Temple, London, 'Minutes of Parliament', 10 November 1809.
12 *Ibid.*, 22 November 1822.
13 'Counsellor Bickerton, Esq.', in *The Gentleman's Magazine*, December 1833, p. 549.
14 *Ibid.*
15 Mrs Hardcastle (ed.), *Life of John, Lord Campbell, Lord High Chancellor of Great Britain, Consisting of a Selection from his Autobiography, Diary, and Letters*, second edition, Vol. I (London: John Murray, 1881), p. 306.
16 *Remarks and Collections of Thomas Hearne* (Oxford: Oxford Historical Society, 1907), Vol. VIII, pp. 57, 296.
17 Nicholas Amhurst, *Terræ-Filius: or, The Secret History of the University of Oxford; in Several Essays. To which are added, Remarks upon a late Book, entitled, University Education, by R. Newton, DD, Principal of Hart-Hall* (London: Francklin, 1726), p. 304.
18 Jeremiah Finch Smith (ed.), *The Admission Register of the Manchester School*, Vol. II: 1776–1807 (Chetham Society, 1868), pp. 148–49.
19 Quoted in Sidney Graves Hamilton, *Hertford College* (London: Robinson, 1903), p. 94.
20 *Jackson's Oxford Journal*, 9 April 1814.

21 Sidney Graves Hamilton, 'Dr Newton and Hertford College', in Montagu Burrows (ed.), *Collectanea, Third Series* (Oxford: The Oxford Historical Society, 1896), p. 341.
22 Richard Hewitt to the Rector of Exeter College, 19 October 1832. Bodleian Library: MS. Eng. misc. d. 9.
23 G.V. Cox, *Recollections of Oxford* (London: Macmillan, 1870), p. 190.
24 *London Gazette*, 1 October 1803, p. 1338.
25 *Jackson's Oxford Journal*, 12 January 1811.
26 *Ibid.*, 9 February 1811.
27 Richard Hewitt to the Vice Chancellor, Exeter College, 4 April 1832. Bodleian Library: MS. Eng. misc. d. 9.
28 G.V. Cox, *Recollections of Oxford*, p. 190.
29 See 'Obituary of C. Demetriades' by 'J.W.', *The Gentleman's Magazine*, November 1825.
30 *Ibid.*
31 *Ibid.*
32 See Guenter B. Risse, 'Explaining Brunonianism: A Biography of Edinburgh's Master of Conviviality, John Brown MD (1735–1788)', unpublished doctoral thesis (2020).
33 Will of Constantine Demetriades [*sic*], 23 January 1822. National Archives: reference PROB 11/1705/195.
34 J.W., 'Obituary of C. Demetriades', *The Gentleman's Magazine*, November 1825.
35 *The Gentleman's Magazine*, October 1825.
36 'Account of the Greek Demetriades, at Oxford', *The Gentleman's Magazine*, January 1826, pp. 14–16.
37 G.V. Cox, *Recollections of Oxford*, p. 88.
38 See J.E. Smith, *St John the Evangelist, Westminster*, p.277. Smith suggests that the anecdote was originally published in *The Oxford Spy* of 1818, p. 24; however, while Bickerton is described in that work, the editor has found no reference to the unusual stabling of his horse.
39 'Counsellor Bickerton, Esq.', *The Gentleman's Magazine*, December 1833, p. 549.
40 *Ibid.*
41 See Alan Crossley (ed.), *A History of the County of Oxford*, Volume 4: The City of Oxford (London: Victoria County History, 1979), pp. 181–82.
42 James Shergold Boone, *The Oxford Spy in Verse*, Dialogue the Fourth (Oxford: Munday and Slatter, 1818), footnote to pp. 27–29.
43 *Ibid.*, footnote to p. 23.
44 *Ibid.*, footnote to pp. 23–24.
45 Thomas Mozley, *Reminiscences, Chiefly of Oriel College and the Oxford Movement*, Vol. II (London: Longman's, Green and Co., 1882), pp. 200–01.
46 *Ibid.*, p. 201.
47 *Ibid.*, p. 202.
48 *The Gentleman's Magazine*, 26 November 1817.
49 *Ibid.*, October 1825.

50 W. Baxter, *British Phænogamous Botany*, Vol. VI (Oxford: Parker, 1843), pp. 415–16.
51 Gibbes Rigaud, 'Bickerton', in *Notes and Queries*, 5th Series, Vol. 11 (1 March 1879), p. 172.
52 'Account of the Greek Demetriades, at Oxford', *The Gentleman's Magazine*, January 1826, pp. 14–16.
53 G.V. Cox, *Recollections of Oxford*, p. 88.
54 Copies of the first three pamphlets, bound in one volume, are held by the University of California; a copy of the last-named pamphlet is held by the British Library.
55 George Roberson and John Richard Green, *Oxford During the Last Century: Being Two Series of Papers Published in the Oxford Chronicle and Berks and Bucks Gazette* (Oxford: Slatter and Rose, 1859), p. 108.
56 Counsellor Bickerton, *An Address to the Literary Members of the University* (Oxford: Munday and Slatter, 1816), pp. 4–5.
57 A theory first propounded by the publisher John Taylor (1781–1864) in *A Discovery of the Author of the Letters of Junius* (London: Taylor and Hessey, 1813) and subsequently accepted by many scholars, including Rowse.
58 A.L. Rowse, *The English Spirit: Essays in History and Literature* (London: Macmillan, 1966), p. 194.
59 *Notes & Queries*, Series I, Vol. XI, No. 286 (21 April 1855), p. 302.
60 *Ibid.*
61 William Cushing, *Initials and Pseudonyms: A Dictionary of Literary Disguises* (Waltham, Mass: Mark Press, 1885–88 and 1963), p. 146.

8. Place-Seeker

1 *The Oxford Herald*, quoted in 'Counsellor Bickerton, Esq.', *The Gentleman's Magazine*, December 1833, p. 549.
2 Founded in 1814 as the Oxford Society for the Relief of Distressed Travellers and renamed in 1827. For further details, see Richard Dyson, 'Welfare Provision in Oxford During the Latter Stages of the Old Poor Law, 1800–1834', *The Historical Journal*, 52, 4 (Cambridge: Cambridge University Press, 2009), pp. 943–62.
3 'Counsellor Bickerton, Esq.' in *The Gentleman's Magazine*, December 1833, p. 549.
4 Letter from John Bickerton to the Court of Claims regarding his right to Hertford College. National Archives, 23 June 1820: reference C195/1/35.
5 See Richard Hewitt to the Vice Chancellor, Exeter College, 10 April 1832. Bodleian Library: MS. Eng. misc. d. 9.
6 Sidney Graves Hamilton, *Hertford College*, p. 94.
7 Quoted by Stanley Ayling, *Fox: The Life of Charles James Fox* (London: John Murray, 1991), p. 103.
8 *Oxford Dictionary of National Biography*.
9 Richard King, *The Modern London Spy* (London: printed for Alex Hogg, 1781), pp. 106–08. Quoted by Jerry White, *London in the Eighteenth Century*, p. 68.

10 Hesketh Person, *The Fool of Love: A Life of William Hazlitt* (New York: Harper, 1934), pp. 59–60.
11 See P.P. Howe, *The Life of William Hazlitt* (New York: Doran, 1922), p. 148.
12 John Nichols, *Literary anecdotes of the Eighteenth Century*, Vol. V (London: Nichols, 1812), p. 325.
13 Jacob Larwood and John Camden Hotten, *The History of Signboards, From the Earliest Times to the Present Day* (London: Chatto and Windus, 1908), pp. 66–67.
14 *The Atlantic Monthly*, Vol. XIII, June 1864, No. LXXX.
15 *Ibid*.
16 *The Times*, 15 September 1849.
17 John Diprose, *Some Account of the Parish of Saint Clement Danes (Westminster) Past and Present* (London: Diprose and Bateman, 1868), p. 100.
18 *Ibid*.
19 *Morning Chronicle*, 29 April 1822.
20 See evidence of Daniel Friend, *Morning Post*, 10 October 1833.

9. Debtor

1 *Morning Post*, 10 October 1833.
2 Anon., 'Law of Arrest', *The Westminster Review*, Vol. XII (January–April 1830), pp. 358–85.
3 Jerry White, *Mansions of Misery: A Biography of the Marshalsea Debtors' Prison* (London: The Bodley Head, 2016), pp. 1–2.
4 Andy Wood, 'In debt and incarcerated: the tyranny of debtors' prisons', *The Gazette* (https://www.thegazette.co.uk/all-notices/content/100938).
5 Sir Richard Phillips, *A Letter to the Livery of London*, pp. 83–89.
6 Hansard, Vol. 27, Commons Chamber, Tuesday, 7 December 1813, 'Debate on the State of Newgate'.
7 Hansard, Vol. 27, Commons Chamber, 9 May 1814, 'Report from the Committee on the State of the Gaols of the City of London, &c.'.
8 Sir Richard Phillips, *A Letter to the Livery of London*, p. 230.
9 Hansard, Vol. 27, Commons Chamber, 9 May 1814, 'Report from the Committee on the State of the Gaols of the City of London, &c.'.
10 *Ibid*.
11 *Ibid*.
12 *Morning Chronicle*, 8 September 1828. Wade's article on Whitecross Street Prison would later be included in his book *A Treatise on the Police and Crimes of the Metropolis* (London: Longman, Rees, Orme, Brown and Green, 1829).
13 Hansard, Vol. 27, Commons Chamber, 9 May 1814, 'Report from the Committee on the State of the Gaols of the City of London, &c.'.
14 *Ibid*.
15 Hansard, Vol. 37, Commons Chamber, 10 February 1818, 'Debate on London New Prisons'.

Notes

16 Margot Finn, 'Being in Debt in Dickens' London: fact, fictional representation and the nineteenth-century prison', *Journal of Victorian Culture*, Autumn 1996, 1(2), p. 213.
17 Sir Richard Phillips, *A Letter to the Livery of London*, p. 90.
18 *Morning Chronicle*, 8 September 1828.
19 *Morning Chronicle*, 7 October 1824.
20 William Hepworth Dixon, *The London Prisons, with an account of the more distinguished persons who have been confined in them: to which is added a description of the chief provincial prisons* (London: Jackson and Walford, 1850), p. 276.
21 George Augustus Sala, 'What Christmas is in the Company of John Doe', *Household Words: A Weekly Journal, Conducted by Charles Dickens* (Christmas 1851), pp. 11–16.
22 William Hepworth Dixon, *The London Prisons*, pp. 279–80.
23 William Hepworth Dixon, *The London Prisons*, p. 280.
24 *Morning Chronicle*, 28 September 1828.
25 William Hepworth Dixon, *The London Prisons*, p. 278.
26 Charles Dickens, *The Posthumous Papers of the Pickwick Club* (Oxford: Oxford University Press, 2008), p. 507.
27 William Hepworth Dixon, *The London Prisons*, p. 283.
28 *The Times*, 2 October 1828.
29 *The Times*, 20 March 1827.
30 *The Times*, 20 March 1827.
31 *The Times*, 8 June 1827.
32 *Morning Chronicle*, 7 October 1824.
33 Ibid.
34 See Margot Finn, 'Being in Debt in Dickens' London', pp. 203–26.
35 *Morning Chronicle*, 8 September 1828.
36 William Hepworth Dixon, *The London Prisons*, pp. 274–75.
37 *The Times*, 26 June 1823.
38 *London Gazette*, 17 March 1821, p. 645.
39 *The Standard*, 2 October 1828.
40 *The London Medical and Surgical Journal*, 24 November 1832.
41 *The Times*, 26 June 1823.
42 Ibid.
43 Ibid.
44 Ibid., 15 February 1827.
45 Ibid.
46 Ibid.
47 Ibid.
48 Ibid., 2 October 1828.
49 'An Act for Building a New Prison in the City of London', 52 Geo. III, c. 209.
50 Margot Finn, 'Being in Debt in Dickens' London', pp. 203–26.
51 *A Summary View of the Money Annually Expended by the Society for the Discharge and Relief of Persons Imprisoned for Small Debts Throughout England and Wales, from the Institution in March 1772, to the 31st of December, 1831.*
52 Ibid.

53 *Morning Chronicle*, 28 September 1828.
54 *Ibid*.
55 *The Standard*, 28 September 1828.
56 Margot Finn, 'Being in Debt in Dickens' London', p. 212.
57 See William Hutton, *Courts of Requests: Their Nature, Utility, and Powers Described, with a Variety of Cases, Determined in that of Birmingham* (London: Baldwin, 1787), p. 47.
58 Charles Dickens, *The Posthumous Papers of the Pickwick Club*, p. 439.
59 William Hutton, *Courts of Requests*, pp. 66–67.

10. Death and Resurrection

1 *The Standard*, 10 October 1833.
2 *Morning Chronicle*, 10 October 1833.
3 *The Standard*, 10 October 1833.
4 J.E. Smith, *St John the Evangelist, Westminster*, p. 21.
5 Henry Chamberlain, *A New and Compleat History and Survey of the Cities of London and Westminster* (London: Cooke, c. 1771). Quoted by J.E. Smith, *St John the Evangelist, Westminster*, pp. 38–39.
6 Charles Dickens, *Our Mutual Friend* (London: Chapman and Hall, 1865), Vol. 1, p. 166.
7 See Jerry White, *London in the Nineteenth Century*, pp. 451–52
8 Figures from Edwin Chadwick, *A Supplementary Report of the Results of a Special Inquiry into the Practice of Interment in Towns made at the Request of Her Majesty's Principal Secretary of State for the Home Department* (London: HMSO, 1843), p. 133.
9 Quoted by Edwin Chadwick, *A Supplementary Report*, p. 134.
10 A.F.M. Willich, *Domestic Encyclopaedia or a Dictionary of Facts, and Useful Knowledge*, Vol. 2 (London: McMillan, 1802).
11 *The Times*, 12 April 1830.
12 George Alfred Walker, *Gatherings from Graveyards, Particularly those of London* (London: Longman, 1839), p. 1.
13 *Ibid*., p. 150.
14 Churchman (Ecclesiastical Report), April 1842. Quoted in *Provincial Medical Journal*, No. 20, Vol. II (20 August 1842), p. 2.
15 George Alfred Walker, *Gatherings from Graveyards*, p. 103.
16 Edwin Chadwick, *A Supplementary Report*.
17 *Ibid*., p. 27.
18 Quoted in Bertram S. Puckle, *Funeral Customs: Their Origin and Development* (London: Werner Laurie, 1926), p. 72.
19 George Alfred Walker, *Gatherings from Graveyards*, p. 183.
20 See J.E. Smith, *St John the Evangelist*, p. 123.
21 Quoted in *Ibid*., p. 122.
22 Edwin Chadwick, *A Supplementary Report*, p. 27.
23 Henry VIII, xxii, cap. 12, quoted in James Blake Bailey (ed.), *The Diary of a Resurrectionist, 1811–12, to which are added an account of the Resurrection Men in London and a short history of the passing of the Anatomy Act* (London: Swann Sonnenschein, 1896), p. 19.

24 F.C. Waite, 'The Development of Anatomical Laws in the States of New England', *N. Engl. J. Med.*, 233, pp. 716–26 (1945), quoted in Julia Bess Frank, 'Body Snatching: A Grave Medical Problem', *The Yale Journal of Biology and Medicine*, 49 (1976), pp. 399–410.
25 Charles Lett Feltoe (ed.), *Memorials of John Flint South, Twice President of the Royal College of Surgeons and Surgeon to St Thomas's Hospital, 1841–1863* (London: John Murray, 1884), p. 90.
26 *Report from the Select Committee on Anatomy* (London: The House of Commons, 22 July 1828), p. 8.
27 James Blake Bailey (ed.), *The Diary of a Resurrectionist*, p. 147.
28 Figure for 1808 quoted by Jerry White, *London in the Nineteenth Century*, p. 180.
29 See Wendy Moore, *The Knife Man: Blood, Body-Snatching and the Birth of Modern Surgery* (London: Bantam Books, 2005), pp. 424–25.
30 *Report from the Select Committee on Anatomy* (London: The House of Commons, 22 July 1828), p. 83.
31 Ibid., p. 17.
32 Charles A. Cameron, *History of the Royal College of Surgeons in Ireland* (Dublin: Fannin, 1886), p. 183.
33 *The Times*, 1 February 1823.
34 Charles Lett Feltoe (ed.), *Memorials of John Flint South*, p. 100.
35 *The Times*, 20 March 1818.
36 L. Dopson, 'St. Thomas's Parish Vestry Records and a Body-Snatching Incident', *British Medical Journal*, 2, 9 July 1949, p. 69.
37 *The Times*, 1 February 1823, quoting from the *Bristol Gazette*.
38 *The Times*, 2 November 1796.
39 See Jez Reeve and Max Adams, *The Spitalfields Project*, Vol. 1: The Archaeology: Across the Styx (York: Council for British Archaeology, 1993), p. 82.
40 An unnamed Scottish newspaper quoted by James Blake Bailey (ed.), *The Diary of a Resurrectionist*, pp. 79–80.
41 Ibid., pp. 81–82.
42 A contemporary broadsheet, quoted in Ibid., pp. 82–83.
43 Neville M. Goodman, 'The Supply of Bodies for Dissection: A Historical Review', *British Medical Journal*, 23 December 1944, p. 808.
44 Charles A. Cameron, *History of the Royal College of Surgeons in Ireland* (Dublin: Fannin, 1886), p. 183.
45 *Report from the Select Committee on Anatomy*, pp. 7–9.
46 Death announcement in *Berrow's Worcester Journal*, 8 September 1825.
47 See W.M. Childs, *The Town of Reading During the Early Part of the Nineteenth Century* (Reading: University College, 1910), p. 11.
48 P.H. Ditchfield and William Page (ed.), *The Victoria History of the Counties of England: A History of Berkshire*, Vol. 1 (London: Constable, 1906), p. 394.
49 See T.A.B. Corley, *Reading's Nineteenth-Century Industrial Families* (Academia.edu, 2015), p. 3.
50 Will of Constantine Demetriades, 23 January 1822. The National Archives: PROB 11/1705/195.

51 *The Gentleman's Magazine*, October 1825.
52 Will of Constantine Demetriades, 23 January 1822. The National Archives: PROB 11/1705/195.
53 See James Cowles Prichard, *Researches into the Physical History of Mankind*, fourth edition, Vol. I (London: Sherwood, Gilbert and Piper, 1841), p. xvii.
54 James Prior, *Life of Edmond Malone, Editor of Shakespeare, with Selections from his Manuscript Anecdotes* (London: Smith, Elder, 1860), p. 374.
55 Thomas Southwood Smith, *Use of the Dead to the Living* (London: Baldwin and Cradock, 1828), p. 44.
56 *Report from the Select Committee on Anatomy*, p. 3.
57 *Ibid.*, p. 14.
58 *Ibid.*, p. 7.
59 *Ibid.*, p. 8.
60 James Blake Bailey (ed.), *The Diary of a Resurrectionist*, p. 31. Bailey quotes statistics from the appendices of the *Report from the Select Committee on Anatomy*.
61 William Roberts, *Mr Warburton's Anatomy Bill, Thoughts on its Mischievous Tendency; with Suggestions for an Entirely New One, Founded Upon an Available Anti-Septic Process* (London: Ollivier, 1843), p. 8.
62 Sarah Wise, *The Italian Boy: Murder and Grave-Robbery in 1830s London* (London: Pimlico, 2005), p. 248.
63 Indictment of Bishop, May and Williams, London Metropolitan Archives: OB/SR609/10. Quoted by Sarah Wise, *The Italian Boy*, p. 183.
64 James Blake Bailey (ed.), *The Diary of a Resurrectionist*, p. 107.
65 The Act for Regulating Schools of Anatomy: 2 & 3 Will. IV c.75, 1832, clause XIII.
66 Statistics of Subjects and Students, No. 1: National Archives, MH 74/16. Quoted by John Knott, 'Popular Attitudes to Death and Dissection in Nineteenth Century Britain: The Anatomy Act and the Poor', *Labour History*, November 1985, No. 49, pp. 1–18.
67 *The Times*, 8 June 1830. Quoted by John Knott, 'Popular Attitudes to Death and Dissection in Nineteenth Century Britain: The Anatomy Act and the Poor', *Labour History*, November 1985, No. 49, pp. 1–18.
68 *Morning Post*, 8 October 1833.
69 William Roberts, *Mr Warburton's Anatomy Bill*, p. 9.
70 Petition from William Roberts, quoted by Earl Stanhope. Hansard, House of Lords, 25 April 1842.
71 Charles Dickens, *Bleak House* (Oxford: OUP, 1996), Chapter XI, p. 165.
72 See J.E. Smith, *St John the Evangelist*, pp. 128–31.

Bibliography

Manuscript Sources

Bodleian Library, Richard Hewitt to the Vice Chancellor, Exeter College, 10 April 1832 (MS. Eng. misc. d. 9).

British Museum, Trade card for 'London House Establishment for Insane Persons', in Banks Collection (D, 2.44).

London Metropolitan Archives, Middlesex Sessions of the Peace, Court in Session, October 1793 (LMSMPS508890420).

London Metropolitan Archives, Middlesex Sessions of the Peace, Court in Session, September 1773, London Lives, 1690–1800 (MJ/SP/1773/09/016: www.londonlives.org).

London Metropolitan Archives, Middlesex Sessions: Sessions Papers – Justices' Working Documents, May 1786, London Lives, 1690–1800 (LMSMPS508100040: www.londonlives.org).

London Metropolitan Archives, Middlesex Sessions of the Peace, Court in Session, 25 September–23 October 1793 (MJ/SP/1793/10/215).

London Metropolitan Archives, R. Ford to J. Stirling, 27 October 1803 (MJ/SP/1803/10/028).

Middle Temple, London, 'Minutes of Parliament', 10 November 1809.

Middle Temple, London, 'Minutes of Parliament', 22 November 1822.

Muniments Room of Westminster Abbey, Coroner's Inquest Report into the death of John Bickerton, 8 October 1833.

Old Bailey Proceedings Online (www.oldbaileyonline.org, version 8.0) April 1813, trial of Sarah Evans (t18130407-23).

Shropshire Archives - Complaint filed at the Court of Chancery against John Spedding and further later attempts to dismiss him (ED6266/4/1/2/4).

The National Archives, Letter from John Bickerton to the Court of Claims regarding his right to Hertford College, 23 June 1820 (C195/1/35).

The National Archives, Will of Constantine Demetriades, 23 January 1822 (PROB 11/1705/195).

Printed Books

Aitkin, George A. (ed.), *Jonathan Swift, The Journal to Stella* (London: Methuen, 1901).

Amhurst, Nicholas, *Terræ-Filius: or, The Secret History of the University of Oxford; in Several Essays. To which are added, Remarks upon a late Book, entitled, University Education, by R. Newton, DD, Principal of Hart-Hall* (London: Francklin, 1726).

Andrews, B. (ed.), *The Torrington Diaries* (London: Eyre and Spottiswoode, 1934–38).

Angelo, Henry, *Reminiscences of Henry Angelo, with Memoirs of his Late Father and Friends* (London: Henry Colburn, 1828), Volume II, p. 333.

Anon., *The London Medical Directory* (London: Churchill, 1846).

Archer, Thomas, *The Pauper, The Thief and the Convict: Sketches of Some of their Homes, Haunts, and Habits* (London: Groombridge, 1865).

Arnold, Catharine, *Bedlam: London and its Mad* (London: Pocket Books, 2009).

Ayling, Stanley, *Fox: The Life of Charles James Fox* (London: John Murray, 1991).

Babington, Anthony, *A House in Bow Street: Crime and the Magistracy, London 1740–1881* (London: Macdonald, 1969).

Bailey, James Blake (ed.), *The Diary of a Resurrectionist, 1811–12, to which are added an account of the Resurrection Men in London and a short history of the passing of the Anatomy Act* (London: Swann Sonnenschein, 1896).

Bakewell, Thomas, *Letter Addressed to the Chairman of the Select Committee of the House of Commons, Appointed to Enquire into the State of Mad-Houses* (Stafford: Chester, 1815).

Ballantine, William, *Some Experiences of a Barrister's Life* (London: Richard Bentley, 1883).

Barclay, Katie, and Amy Milka (eds), *Cultural Histories of Law, Media and Emotion: Public Justice* (Abingdon: Routledge, 2023).

Bickerton, John, *A Concise Account of the Fall and Rise of the Family of the Bickertons, of Maiden Castle in Cheshire, to which is annexed, The Gracious Dealings of God in the Life and Conversion of the Rev. John Bickerton, of the Same Family* (London: Trapp, 1777).

Bickerton, John, *An Address to the Literary Members of the University* (Oxford: Munday and Slatter, 1816).

Bickerton, John, *The Farrago, or the Lucubrations of Counsellor Bickerton* (Oxford: Munday and Slatter, 1816)

Bickerton, John, *Lamentations for a Bad Use of Good Things* (Oxford: printed for the Author, 1816)

Blackstone, William, *Commentaries on the Laws of England* (Oxford: Clarendon Press, 1768).

Boone, James Shergold, *The Oxford Spy in Verse*, Dialogue the Fourth (Oxford: Munday and Slatter, 1818).

Bibliography

Brooke, John, *King George III* (London: Constable, 1972).
Burrows, George Man, *Cursory Remarks on Legislative Regulation of the Insane* (London: Harding, Longman, Hurst, Rees, Orme, Brown and Callow, 1819).
Cameron, Charles A., *History of the Royal College of Surgeons in Ireland* (Dublin: Fannin, 1886).
Chadwick, Edwin, *A Supplementary Report of the Results of a Special Inquiry into the Practice of Interment in Towns made at the Request of Her Majesty's Principal Secretary of State for the Home Department* (London: HMSO, 1843).
Cheney, C.R., *From Becket to Langton: English Church Government, 1170–1213* (Manchester: Manchester University Press, 1965).
Chesney, Kellow, *The Victorian Underworld* (London: Penguin, 1979).
Chesterton, George Laval, *Revelations of Prison Life; with an enquiry into prison discipline and secondary punishments* (London: Hurst and Blackett, 1856).
Childs, W.M., *The Town of Reading During the Early Part of the Nineteenth Century* (Reading: University College, 1910).
Cox, G.V., *Recollections of Oxford* (London: Macmillan, 1870).
Cross, Nigel, *The Common Writer: Life in Nineteenth-Century Grub Street* (Cambridge: Cambridge University Press, 1985).
Crossley, Alan (ed.), *A History of the County of Oxford: Volume 4, the City of Oxford* (London: Victoria County History, 1979).
Culpeper, Nicholas, *Complete Herbal* (London: Richard Evans, 1814).
Cunich, Peter, Hoyle, David, Duffy, Eamon, and Ronald Hyam, *A History of Magdalene College Cambridge, 1428–1988* (Cambridge: Magdalene College Publications, 1994).
Curzon, Catherine, *The Daughters of George III: Sisters and Princesses* (Barnsley: Pen and Sword, 2020).
Cushing, William, *Initials and Pseudonyms: A Dictionary of Literary Disguises* (Waltham, Mass: Mark Press, 1885–88 and 1963).
Defoe, Daniel, *The History of the Great Plague in London in the Year 1665: containing observations and memorials of the most remarkable occurrences, both public and private, during that dreadful period, by a citizen, who lived the whole time in London* (London: John Offor, 1819).
Defoe, Daniel (attrib.), *The Generous Projector, or a Friendly Proposal to Prevent Murder and Other Enormous Abuses, by Erecting an Hospital for Foundlings and Bastard-Children* (London: Dodd and Nutt).
Dickens, Charles, *Bleak House* (Oxford: OUP, 1996).
Dickens, Charles, *Oliver Twist* (London: Penguin, 1988).
Dickens, Charles, *Our Mutual Friend* (London: Chapman and Hall, 1865).
Dickens, Charles, *The Posthumous Papers of the Pickwick Club* (Oxford: Oxford University Press, 2008).
Diprose, John, *Some Account of the Parish of Saint Clement Danes (Westminster) Past and Present* (London: Diprose and Bateman, 1868).
Ditchfield, P.H., and William Page (eds), *The Victoria History of the Counties of England: A History of Berkshire*, Vol. 1 (London: Constable, 1906).

Dixon, William Hepworth, *The London Prisons, with an account of the more distinguished persons who have been confined in them: to which is added a description of the chief provincial prisons* (London: Jackson and Walford, 1850).

Ewing Ritchie, James, *Days and Nights in London: Studies in Black and Gray* (London: Tinsley Brothers, 1880).

Feltoe, Charles Lett (ed.), *Memorials of John Flint South, Twice President of the Royal College of Surgeons and Surgeon to St Thomas's Hospital, 1841–1863* (London: John Murray, 1884).

Fielding, Henry, *The Journal of a Voyage to Lisbon* (London: Everyman, 1964).

Fitzgerald, Percy, *Chronicles of Bow Street Police-Office. With an Account of the Magistrates, 'Runners', and Police* (London: Chapman & Hall, 1888).

Foster, Joseph, *Alumni Oxonienses: The Members of the University of Oxford, 1715–1886*, Volume I (Oxford: Parker and Co., 1891).

Fry, Danby P., *The Lunacy Acts: Containing all the Statutes Relating to Private Lunatics etc.* (London: Knight and Co., 1864).

Garbet, Samuel, *The History of Wem* (Wem: Franklin, 1818).

Gaydon, A.T. (ed.), *A History of Shropshire* (Oxford: Institute of Historical Research, 1973).

Gibbins, H. de B., *A History of the Grammar School of Charles King of England in Kidderminster* (Kidderminster: Printing Office of the Shuttle, 1903).

Graves Hamilton, Sidney, *Hertford College* (London: Robinson, 1903).

Grego, Joseph, *A History of Parliamentary Elections and Electioneering in the Old Days* (London: Chatto and Windus, 1886).

Hale, Matthew, *Historia Placitorum Coronæ: The History of the Pleas of the Crown* (Philadelphia: Small, 1847).

Hardcastle, Mrs (ed.), *Life of John, Lord Campbell, Lord High Chancellor of Great Britain, Consisting of a Selection from his Autobiography, Diary, and Letters* (London: John Murray, 1881).

Haslam, John, *Medical Jurisprudence as it Relates to Insanity, According to the Law of England* (London: Hunter, Hunter, Taylor and Hessey, 1817).

Haslam, John, *Observations on Madness and Melancholy: Including Practical Remarks on those Diseases; Together with Cases: and an Account of the Morbid Appearances on Dissection* (London: Callow, 1809).

Hearne, Thomas, *Remarks and Collections of Thomas Hearne* (Oxford: Oxford Historical Society, 1907).

Hodder, George, *Sketches of Life and Character Taken at the Police Court, Bow Street* (London: Sherwood and Bowyer, 1845).

Howard, John, *The State of the Prisons in England and Wales, with Preliminary Observations, and an Account of Some Foreign Prisons* (Warrington: William Eyres, 1777).

Howe, P.P., *The Life of William Hazlitt* (New York: Doran, 1922).

Howell, Thomas Jones, *A Complete Collection of State Trials and Proceedings for High Treason and Other Crimes and Misdemeanors from the Earliest Period to the Year 1783* (London: Longman et al., 1817).

Bibliography

Hutton, William, *Courts of Requests: Their Nature, Utility, and Powers Described, with a Variety of Cases, Determined in that of Birmingham* (London: Baldwin, 1787).
Hyam, Ronald, 'Godliness, Hunting and Quite Good Learning: The History of Magdalene College, 1792–1992', *Magdalene College Occasional Papers*, No. 5 (Cambridge, 1992).
Keevil, John, *Hamey the Stranger* (London: Geoffrey Bles, 1952).
Kelly, J.N.D., *St Edmund Hall: Almost Seven Hundred Years* (Oxford: Oxford University Press, 1989).
King, Richard, *The Modern London Spy* (London: printed for Alex Hogg, 1781).
Lamb, Charles, *The Essays of Elia* (London: J.M. Dent, 1908).
Leslie-Manville, R., *The Life and Work of Sir John Fielding* (London: Lincoln Williams, 1934).
Lethbridge Kingsford, Charles (ed.), *Chronicles of London* (Dursley: Alan Sutton, 1977).
[Mainwaring, William], *The Secrets of the Bastille Disclosed* (London: Rivington, 1799).
Moore, Wendy, *The Knife Man: Blood, Body-Snatching and the Birth of Modern Surgery* (London: Bantam Books, 2005).
Morpurgo, J.E. (ed.), *The Autobiography of Leigh Hunt* (London: The Cresset Press, 1949).
Mozley, Thomas, *Reminiscences, Chiefly of Oriel College and the Oxford Movement* (London: Longman's, Green and Co., 1882).
Neild, James, *State of the Prisons in England, Scotland, and Wales* (London: John Nichols, 1812).
Nichols, John, *Literary anecdotes of the Eighteenth Century* (London: Nichols, 1812).
O'Donoghue, Edward, *The Story of Bethlehem Hospital, From its Foundation in 1247* (New York: Dutton, 1915).
Oulton, W.C., *Memoirs of Her Late Majesty Queen Charlotte* (London: Robins and Co., 1819).
Page, William (ed.), *The History of Yorkshire, The Victoria History of the Counties of England* (London: Constable, 1906–1914).
Patmore, P.G., *My Friends and Acquaintance: Being Memorials, Mind-Portraits, and Personal Recollections of Deceased Celebrities of the Nineteenth Century* (London: Saunders and Otley, 1854).
Patterson, M.W., *Sir Francis Burdett and his Times (1770–1844)* (London: Macmillan, 1931).
Person, Hesketh, *The Fool of Love: A Life of William Hazlitt* (New York: Harper, 1934).
Phillips, Richard, *A Letter to the Livery of London, Relative to the Views of the Writer in Executing the Office of Sheriff* (London, 1808).
Poole, Steve, *The Politics of Regicide in England, 1760–1850: Troublesome Subjects* (Manchester: Manchester University Press, 2000).
Pope, Alexander, *The Dunciad with Notes Variorum, and the Prolegomena of Scriblerus* (London: Lawton Gulliver, 1729).
Porter, Roy, *Mind-Forg'd Manacles: A History of Madness in England from the Restoration to the Regency* (London: The Athlone Press, 1987).
Prichard, James Cowles, *Researches into the Physical History of Mankind* (London: Sherwood, Gilbert and Piper, 1841).

Prior, James, *Life of Edmond Malone, Editor of Shakespeare, with Selections from his Manuscript Anecdotes* (London: Smith, Elder, 1860).
Puckle, Bertram S., *Funeral Customs: Their Origin and Development* (London: Werner Laurie, 1926).
Ray, Gordon N. (ed.), *The Letters and Private Papers of William Makepeace Thackeray* (Cambridge, Massachusetts: Harvard University Press, 1946).
Roberson, George, and John Richard Green, *Oxford During the Last Century: Being Two Series of Papers Published in the Oxford Chronicle and Berks and Bucks Gazette* (Oxford: Slatter and Rose, 1859).
Roberts, William, *Mr Warburton's Anatomy Bill, Thoughts on its Mischievous Tendency; with Suggestions for an Entirely New One, Founded Upon an Available Anti-Septic Process* (London: Ollivier, 1843).
Rowse, A.L., *The English Spirit: Essays in History and Literature* (London: Macmillan, 1966).
Sala, George Augustus, *London Up to Date* (London: Adam and Charles Black, 1894).
Salter, H.E., and Mary D. Lobel (eds.), *A History of the County of Oxford: Volume 3, the University of Oxford* (London: OUP, 1954).
Sheppard, Edgar, *Memorials of St James's Palace* (London: Longmans, Green and Co., 1894).
Smith, Gregory (ed.), *Diary of Samuel Pepys*, Globe Edition (London: Macmillan, 1905).
Smith, J.E., *St John the Evangelist, Westminster: Parochial Memorials* (Westminster: Wightman & Co., 1892).
Smith, Thomas Southwood, *Use of the Dead to the Living* (London: Baldwin and Cradock, 1828).
Stow, John, *Survey of London, Written in the Year 1598* (London: Whittacker and Co., 1842).
Stubbs, William (ed.), *Chronica Magistri Rogeri de Houedene* (London: Longman, 1871).
Sturgess, H.A.C., *Register of Admissions to the Honourable Society of the Middle Temple: From the Fifteenth Century to the year 1944* (London: Dutterworth, 1949).
Thackeray, William Makepeace, *The History of Pendennis: His Fortunes and Misfortunes, His Friends and His Greatest Enemy* (London: Penguin, 1986).
Thorpe, W.G., *Middle Temple Table Talk: With Some Talk About the Table Itself* (London: Hutchinson, 1895).
Tuckwell, W., *Reminiscences of Oxford* (New York: Dutton, 1908).
Venn, John, and L.A. Venn, *Alumni Cantabrigienses* (Cambridge: Cambridge University Press, 1940 and 2011).
Wade, John, *A Treatise on the Police and Crimes of the Metropolis* (London: Longman, Rees, Orme, Brown and Green, 1829).
Walford, Edward, *Old & New London: A Narrative of its History, Its People & Its Places – Westminster & The Western Suburbs*, Vol. IV (London: Cassell, no date).
Walker, George Alfred, *Gatherings from Graveyards, Particularly those of London* (London: Longman, 1839).
White, Jerry, *London in the Nineteenth Century: 'A Human Awful Wonder of God'* (London: Jonathan Cape, 2007).
White, Jerry, *London in the Eighteenth Century: A Great and Monstrous Thing* (London: The Bodley Head, 2012).

White, Jerry, *Mansions of Misery: A Biography of the Marshalsea Debtors' Prison* (London: The Bodley Head, 2016).
Wight, John, *Mornings at Bow Street: A Selection of the Most Humorous and Entertaining Reports which have Appeared in the Morning Herald* (London: Charles Baldwyn, 1824).
Willis, Francis, *A Treatise on Mental Derangement, Containing the Substance of the Gulstonian Lectures, for May, MDCCCXXII* (London: Longman, Hurst, Rees, Orme, and Brown, 1823).
Wise, Sarah, *The Italian Boy: Murder and Grave-Robbery in 1830s London* (London: Pimlico, 2005).

Academic Journals and Papers

Blandford, G. Fielding, 'City Life in 1800', *British Medical Journal*, 29 December 1900, pp. 1834–38.
Corley, T.A.B., *Reading's Nineteenth-Century Industrial Families* (Academia.edu, 2015).
Cox, David, '"A Certain Share of Low Cunning" – The Provincial Use and Activities of Bow Street "Runners" 1792–1839', *Eras Journal* (University of Monash), 5 November 2003.
De Montluzin, Emily Lorraine, 'Worlds Apart from the Turkish Tales: Joseph Moser's "Proposal for a Depository for Infants"', *ANQ: A Quarterly Journal of Short Articles, Notes and Reviews*, 16:4 (2003).
Devereaux, Simon, 'The Making of the Penitentiary Act, 1775–1779', *The Historical Journal*, 42, 2 (1999), pp. 405–33.
Dopson, L., 'St. Thomas's Parish Vestry Records and a Body-Snatching Incident', *British Medical Journal*, 2, 9 July 1949.
Dyson, Richard, 'Welfare Provision in Oxford During the Latter Stages of the Old Poor Law, 1800–1834', *The Historical Journal*, 52, 4 (Cambridge: Cambridge University Press, 2009).
Emeljanow, Victor, 'The Theatrical Life and Death of Wych Street', *Nineteenth Century Theatre and Film*, 2019, 45:2, pp. 160–72.
Emerichs, Mary Beth, 'Getting Away with Murder? Homicide and the Coroners in Nineteenth Century London', *Social Science History*, Vol. 25, No. 1, Special Issue: Bloody Murder (Spring 2001), pp. 93–100.
Finn, Margot, 'Being in Debt in Dickens' London: fact, fictional representation and the nineteenth-century prison', *Journal of Victorian Culture*, Autumn 1996, 1(2).
Goodman, Neville M., 'The Supply of Bodies for Dissection: A Historical Review', *British Medical Journal*, 23 December 1944.
Graves Hamilton, Sidney, 'Dr Newton and Hertford College', in Montagu Burrows (ed.), *Collectanea, Third Series* (Oxford: The Oxford Historical Society, 1896).
Greig, Hannah, 'Faction and Fashion: The Politics of Court Dress in Eighteenth-Century England' in *Se vêtir à la cour en Europe 140–1815: Cultures matérielles, cultures visuelles du costume dans les cours européennes* (Villeneuve d'Ascq: Publications de l'Institut de recherches historiques du Septentrion, 2011).

James, David V., Mullen, Paul E., Pathé, Michele T., Meloy, J. Reid, Farnham, Frank R., Preston, Lulu, & Brian Darnley, 'Attacks on the British Royal Family: The Role of Psychotic Illness', *Journal of the American Academy of Psychiatric Law*, 36: pp. 59–67 (2008).

King Fisher, Yvonne, 'Coroners in London and Middlesex, *c.* 1820–1888: A Study of Medicalization and Professionalization'. Unpublished PhD thesis (2019), The Open University, Open Research Online.

Mooney, Jane, 'A Tale of Two Regicides', *European Journal of Criminology*, 2014, Vol. 11 (2), pp. 228–50.

Moran, Richard, 'The Origin of Insanity as a Special Verdict: The Trial for Treason of James Hadfield (1800)', *Law and Society Review*, Vol. 19, No. 3 (1985), pp. 487–519.

Norwood East, W., 'Crime and Insanity', *The Post-Graduate Medical Journal*, IV, 48, September 1929, p. 202.

Reeve, Jez, and Max Adams, *The Spitalfields Project, Volume 1, The Archaeology: Across the Styx* (York: Council for British Archaeology, 1993).

Risse, Guenter B., 'Explaining Brunonianism: A Biography of Edinburgh's Master of Conviviality, John Brown MD (1735–1788)' (unpublished doctoral thesis, 2020).

Waite, F.C., 'The Development of Anatomical Laws in the States of New England', *N. Engl. J. Med.*, 233, pp. 716–26 (1945), quoted in Julia Bess Frank, 'Body Snatching: A Grave Medical Problem', *The Yale Journal of Biology and Medicine*, 49 (1976), pp. 399–410.

Wood, Andy, 'In debt and incarcerated: the tyranny of debtors' prisons', *The Gazette* (https://www.thegazette.co.uk/all-notices/content/100938).

Newspapers and Periodicals

The Atlantic Monthly
Caledonian Mercury
Examiner
The Gentleman's Magazine
Jackson's Oxford Journal
London Gazette
Medical Times and Gazette
The Mirror of Literature, Amusement and Instruction
Morning Chronicle
Morning Post
Notes and Queries
Public Advertiser
St James's Chronicle
The Standard
The Times

Index

Abergavenny Methodist College 40, 42
Act for Regulating Immigration into
    Great Britain (1793) 126
Act for Regulating Schools of Anatomy
    (1832) 202
Act to Amend the Laws Concerning
    the Burial of the Dead in the
    Metropolis (1851) 188
Adams, Sir Thomas 38
Adkin, William 89
Allen, Richard 23
Allen, Sarah 172
Amhurst, Nicholas 122
Amiens, Treaty of 71
Angelo, Henry 66
Archer, Thomas (architect) 184–5
Archer, Thomas (journalist) 79, 81
Aris, Daniel 87, 88
Aris, George 89–91
Aris, Thomas 18, 81–91 *passim*, 93, 174,
    178, 180
Arnold, Catharine 103, 104
Arnold, Edward 110–11
Asgill, General Sir Charles 157
Ashmolean Museum 194
Astley, Philip 158
Aughtie, Gabriel 192, 196

Babington, Anthony 64, 68
Bailey, James Blake 202
Bakewell, Thomas 98
Ballantine, William 117–18
Bannister, Police Inspector 27–9, 32
Baynard, Dr Edward 77
Baynes, Walter 77
Bedlam *see* Bethlem Hospital
Bellingham, John 111
Bennet, Henry Grey 168
Bentham, Jeremy 156
Bentham, John Duncomb 174
Benwell, James 130–2 *passim*
Bethlem Hospital ('Bedlam') 48, 49, 50,
    57, 96, 102–6, 108
Bickerton, John
    abuse at Oxford 132–3
    admission to the Middle Temple 115,
        117
    appearance at Bow Street Magistrates'
        Court 63, 67, 68, 69
    arrest at St James's Palace 60–1
    at Hertford College 120–1
    at Magdalene College, Cambridge
        42–3
    at St Edmund's College, Oxford 43–5
    authorship 61, 133–5
    birth 37

burial 184, 204–5
claims principalship of Hertford College 154–5
corresponds with Duke of Portland 31–2, 119, 153–5
death 26–9
departure from Middle Temple 119
dispute with Mr Dance 31, 32, 161–2, 181
identified as 'Junius' 135–6
imprisonment for debt 161–2
inquest into death 21–2, 26–33, 183–4
kidney disease 30
love of learning 41, 44–5, 117, 118–19
mental illness 45, 69–71 *passim*, 108, 112–13, 120–1, 127, 129, 151–2
parentage 33, 37
portrait by Boone 128–9
portrait by Burt 130–2
purchase of the Five Chimneys 31, 37, 160
relations with Hewitt and Demetriades 127
religious convictions 39–42
runs school on Wych Street 31, 157, 160
schooling 37–9
uncertainty over legal career 118
writes to Court of Claims 152–4
Bickerton, Mary (mother) 37
Bickerton, Admiral Sir Richard Hussey 60–1
Bickerton, Richard Palin (great-nephew) 32–3, 37, 39, 184, 204, 205
Bickerton, Samuel (father) 33, 37, 40–3 *passim*, 45, 153
Bickerton, William (brother) 27, 37
Bishop, John 201
Blackburn, Rev John 185
Blackstone, Sir William 78, 110
Body-snatching 189–94 *passim*, 197–9 *passim*, 201–2
Bone, Henry 69
Boone, James Shergold 128–30

Bow Street Magistrates' Court 63, 67–8, 70–1
Bow Street Runners 64–5
Brasenose College 122
Bridewell Palace 73
Brooke, John 58
Brookes, slave ship 163–4
Burdett, Sir Francis 82–4 *passim*, 86
Burke, Edmund 116
Burke, Police Constable 26–7
Burke, William 201
Burrows, George Man 107, 108
Burt, Albin Roberts 18, 130–3, 197
Bussey, Peter 203
Byrne, Charles 190, 197

Cadell, Thomas 158
Caisley, Elizabeth 180–1
Caldwell, James 205
Campbell, John 121
Cannon, Thomas 53–4
Cass, Christopher 205
Cauch, Robert 175
Chadwick, Edwin 187–9 *passim*, 198
Charles II, King 73
Charlotte, Queen 47, 48, 53, 59
Chesterton, Captain George 80, 92, 93
Cholmondeley, George James, Earl of 60–1
Cline, Henry 56
Club of Owls 158
Coke, Edward 158
Coldbath Fields House of Correction 71, 74, 77–83
Coldbath Fields Prison *see* Coldbath Fields House of Correction
Coleridge, Samuel Taylor 80
Congreve, William 116
Conyngham, Josiah 48
Cooper, Astley 190–1, 199
County Asylums Act (1808) 96
County Asylums Act (1828) 107
Court of Claims 152, 156, 157
Court of Requests 161, 163, 166, 180, 181

Index

Courtney, John 82–3
Covent Garden 63
Cox, George Valentine 124, 125, 127, 133
Cox, Robert Albion 103–4
Craven Street Society 178–9
Creighton, Dr 56
Criminal Lunatics Act (1800) 95–6
Crouch, Isaac 44–5, 155
Crown and Sceptre 21, 26, 183
Cruikshank, George 156
Culpeper, Nicholas 24
Cushing, William *Initials and Pseudonyms: A Dictionary of Literary Disguises* 136

Dance, Mr 31, 32, 161, 181
de Blin, Chevalier Charles 91–2
de Courcy, Rev Richard 39
de Quincey, Thomas 116
de Veil, Sir Thomas 63, 64, 67
Defoe, Daniel 25, 97, 98, 104
Demetriades, Chrysanthus Constantinides 18, 121, 124, 125–8 *passim*, 130–3 *passim*, 194–7
Dering, Sir Cholmley 23
Derrick, Edward 53
Despard, Colonel Edward 82–3, 92
Devereux, Simon 78
Dickens, Charles 67–8, 171, 185, 204
Dickie, William 87
Diprose, John 159
Dixon, William Hepworth 169, 170, 171, 174
Donne, John 121
Dowson, Dr 153

Eden, George 164
Edinburgh 29, 98, 190, 193, 194, 201
Edward III, King 24
Erskine, Thomas 55–6
Evans, Sarah 89–91
Evans, Thomas 158
Evelyn, John 116, 188

Fielding, Henry 64, 116
Fielding, Sir John 47–8, 64, 66, 67
Finn, Professor Margot 169, 178, 180
Fitzgerald, Percy 71
Five Chimneys 21, 25–8 *passim*, 31, 32, 36, 37, 160
Fleet Prison 73, 87, 178
Ford, Sir Richard 61, 63, 67, 68–71 *passim*, 84, 91, 96, 112–13
Fox, Charles James 122
Francis, Sir Philip 135
Friend, Daniel 30–1
Frith, Lieutenant John 52–3

Garbet, Samuel 38
Gentleman's Magazine, The 15, 45, 70, 98, 120, 121, 132, 134, 152
Geoffrey, Archbishop of York 23
George III, King 47–60 *passim*, 69, 96, 109, 131, 135, 136
George, Prince of Wales 54, 79, 158
Giltspur Street Compter 166
Gordon Riots 66, 67
Green, John 134
Gregorie, David 28, 31, 32

Habeas Corpus Suspension Act (1794) 82
Hadfield, James 54–7, 66, 71, 95, 111, 112
Hale, Matthew 55, 110, 111
Hamilton, Emma 131
Hare, William 201
Hart Hall *see* Hertford College
Haslam, Dr John 103, 108–9, 112
Hastings, Dr John 29–30, 36, 184
Hazlitt, William 38–9, 79, 156–7
Hearne, Thomas 121
Heath, James 24
Henry II, King 23, 163
Henry III, King 22, 23
Hertford College 121–5 *passim*, 127, 132, 134, 151–5 *passim*, 160, 194
Hewitt, Rev. Richard 122–5, 127–8, 131, 154, 160

Higgs, Thomas 21, 22, 26, 29, 30, 33, 35, 36, 183, 184
Hodder, George 69, 70
Hodgson, Bernard 122, 123, 154
Hogarth, William 103
Hooke, Robert 103
Hôpital de la Pitié, Paris 199
Horsemonger Lane Prison 79
Howard, John 17, 74–8 *passim*, 81
Hoxton asylum 48, 57, 101
'Humanitas' (pseudonym) 173
Hunt, John 79
Hunt, Leigh 79
Hunter, John 190, 197
Huntingdon, Countess of 40, 41
Hutton, William 181

Inns of Chancery 158
Ireland, John 131

Jackson, Dr Cyril 154, 155
Jackson's Oxford Journal 124, 151, 159, 194
James I, King 77
Johnson, Ben 117

Kelly, Captain William Frederick 175–6
Kent, William 23
Kenyon, Lloyd, First Baron 53, 87, 111
Kidd, John 197
King, Richard, *The Modern London Spy*, 156
King's Bench Prison 73, 89, 90, 175, 178
Kingsdown House Asylum 102
Knowlys, Newman 176–8

l'École de Médecine, Paris 199
Laing, Allen Stewart 68
Lamb, Charles 115, 116, 157
Lamb, Mary 100, 157
Lamb, Musgrave 195–6
Lamb, W. 135–6
Langworthy, Charles Cunningham 102
Laurie, Alderman Sir Peter 172, 176, 178
Lee Brockhurst, Shropshire 37–8, 115
Letters of Junius, The 135–6

Lever, Charles 175
Little Drury Lane Theatre 158
Liverpool, Earl of 31–2
London Corresponding Society 82
Longman, Thomas 158
Ludgate Compter 166
Lush, Charles 70

Magdalene College, Cambridge 42–4 *passim*
Mainwaring, William 83, 84, 88
Mapleston (prisoner) 176–7
Marshalsea Prison 73, 162, 163, 178
Maunsell, Sir John 22
May, May 201
Metcalf, Urban 56–7
Metropolitan Police Act 64
Metropolitan Sanitary Commission 170
Miles, Rev William 41
Miles, Sir Jonathan 48, 101
Mill, James 100, 156
Mill, John Stuart 156
Millbank Prison 78
Mitford, Sir John 55
Monro, Dr John 49
Montague, William 166, 168
Moore, General Sir John 60
Moore, Thomas 116
More, Sir Thomas 158
Moser, Joseph 70
Musson, Valentine 176

Naples, Joseph 190
Neate, Solomon 180
Nelson, Admiral Horatio 61, 82, 131
Newgate Prison 163–4, 166
Newton, Dr Richard 121–3 *passim*
Nichols, John 158
Nicholson, Margaret 49–50, 54, 65, 96
Norris, James 105–6
Notes and Queries 136

O'Hara, Rebecca 48
Old Bailey 53, 63, 89, 91, 117, 201

Onslow, Lord 110–11
Oulton, Walley Chamberlain 47, 48
Oxford Anti-Mendicity Society 152

Palmerston, Lord 205
Patmore, Peter George 79
Pearce, Anne 172
Pearce, Mary 171–2
Peckard, Dr Peter 42–3
Penitentiary Act (1779) 78, 110
Pepys, Samuel 25, 101
Perceval, Spencer 111
Petty France *see* York Street
Phillips, Sir Richard 163–5 *passim*, 169
Phillpotts, Rev. Henry 154
Pickwick, Mr 180–1
Pitt, William 54, 65
Plague 24, 25
Poole, Steve 57
Porter, Professor Roy 95
Portland, Duke of 31, 60, 69, 84, 93, 119, 153–5 *passim*
Poultry Compter 166

Queen of Bohemia Inn, Wych Street 159–60

Raleigh, Sir Walter 116
Reading 194–5
Redmond, Luke 191
Resurrection men *see* body-snatchers
Rice, Charles 27–8, 31, 184
Rich, Mary 84, 92, 93
Richard I, King 23
Ritchie, James Ewing 78
Roberson, George 134
Roberson, Thomas 124–5, 127, 134, 154
Roberts, Robert 87, 88
Roberts, William 200, 203–4
Robson, James 158
Rose, George 99, 107
Rowlandson, Thomas 131
Rowse, A.L. 135

St Edmund Hall, Oxford 43–5 *passim*, 112, 153, 155
St Giles-without-Cripplegate 167
St James's Palace 45, 47, 48, 51–3 *passim*, 57–61 *passim*, 64, 67, 69, 70, 112–13, 115, 133, 157
St John the Evangelist, Church of 184–5
St Margaret's Workhouse, Westminster 28, 152
Sala, George Augustus 59, 169
Sayer, John 61, 64–6 *passim*
Selwyn, George 155
Shakespeare Head Tavern, Wych Street 158
Sheppard, Jack 159
Sheridan, Richard Brinsley 116
Simpson, Mrs 90
Skelton, Joseph 130
Smith, Dr Richard 197
Smith, Thomas Southwood 198
Society for the Discharge and Relief of Persons Imprisoned for Small Debts *see* Craven Street Society
Somerville, Dr James 202
South, John Flint 191
Spang, Henry 51–2
Spang, Michael Henry 51–2
Spedding, John 38
Spencer, James 176–80 *passim*
Sterne, Laurence 197
Stirling, Thomas 69, 71, 113
Stone, Thomas 50–1
Swift, John 121
Swift, Jonathan 23

Talfourd, Thomas Noon 116
Tawney, Mr 134
Thackeray, William Makepeace 61, 116–17
The Oxford Spy 128–30
Thompson, Alderman William 172
Thompson, George 155
Thornhill, Colonel Richard 23
Thorpe, William 115–16

Times, The 31, 36, 49, 50, 51, 54, 58, 70, 91, 159, 171, 180, 186
Tothill Fields 21–5 *passim*
Tothill Fields House of Correction 66
Townsend, John 61, 64–6 *passim*
Townshend, Thomas 99
Tracy, Justice Robert 110–11
Trevecca College 40, 41

United Irishmen, Society of 82

Vagrancy Act (1714) 95, 96, 112
Vagrancy Act (1744) 95, 96, 112
Van Dunn, Cornelius 156
Veitch, John 101
Victoria, Queen 16, 91

Wadd, Thomas Milner 176
Wade, John 167, 169, 170, 173, 174
Waithman, Alderman Robert 176
Wakefield, Edward 99–105 *passim*, 107
Walker, George 'Graveyard' 186–8 *passim*
Warburton, Henry 200–2 *passim*
Ward, John 125, 126

Webster, John 116
Weir, John 101
Wem Grammar School 38
Wem, Shropshire 27, 38, 157
Westminster Abbey 22, 35, 36, 157
Weybridge 56–7
Whessell, John 130–1
White, Professor Jerry 73, 162
Whitecross Street Debtors' Prison 31, 161, 166–81 *passim*
Wigtoft, Ralph of 23–4
Wild, Jonathan 64
Williams, Thomas 201
Williams-Wynn, Charles 96
Willich, Anthony Florian Madinger 185
Willis, Dr Francis 110
Wise, Sarah 200
Wood, Elizabeth 27, 184
Woodfall, Henry Sampson 135
Worcester, Battle of 24
Wren, Sir Christopher 119
Wright, Sir Sampson 51, 53, 54
Wych Street 31, 157–60 *passim*

York Street ('Petty France') 152, 156, 157